# Rockin' Down the Dial

# Rockin' Down the Dial

The Detroit Sound of Radio
From Jack the Bellboy to the Big 8

David Carson

Momentum Books, Ltd.
Troy, Michigan

Printed in the United States of America

01    00    99         3    2    1

Momentum Books , Ltd.
1174 E. Big Beaver Road
Troy, Michigan  48083

ISBN:1-879094-62-6

Library of Congress Cataloging-in-Publication Data

For my wife, Laura, and my daughter Erin,
whose support made the writing of this book possible

# Contents

# Preface

In 1969, as a landmark music documentary was being broadcast over Detroit airwaves, there was time-out for a commercial break. Suddenly, the familiar voice of a disc jockey, popular in the 1950s, jumped out of the speaker:

> Hi, this is Mickey Shorr. I had the pleasure of introducing great artists like Elvis, Chuck Berry, and the Drifters to Detroit radio audiences the first time around and I'm proud to have Mickey Shorr's Tape Shack as a sponsor of the "History of Rock 'n' Roll."

It was hard to believe that rock 'n' roll, had already been around long enough to warrant an "official" history. It seemed like just a short while back when the music and the radio stations that played it didn't exist. Radio was that big box the family gathered around in the living room to listen to their favorite entertainment programs. They tuned in comedy with Burns and Allen, Jack Benny, and Fibber McGee and Molly. There was drama on the "Lux Radio Theater" and adventure with "Captain Midnight" and "Jack Armstrong, the All-American Boy." There were big variety shows,

By the mid-1950s, nearly all of that was gone, lost to television. Across America, radio had survived by reinventing itself and, with few exceptions, had become the land of records, news, and the announcers who personalized their style and became the medium's new stars: the disc jockeys.

By 1960, the listening audience was still tuning to the AM dial for entertainment and out of the dozen or so stations competing for listeners in Detroit, the nation's fifth largest radio market, there were no fewer than five featuring the youth-oriented "Top 40" sound. By 1969, AM was still king but things had already begun to happen on FM.

To follow the rise and popularity of the music and personality disc jockey formats that picked up where old-time radio left off in the Motor City, you have to step into the "way back machine" and head past Mickey Shorr to 1945. There wasn't any rock 'n' roll for kids to listen to, but there were blues, boogie, and "Jack the Bellboy."

# Acknowledgments

I would like to thank the following people for their contibutions to this book: Lee Alan, Marc Avery, Marjorie Binge, Ralph Binge Jr., Marilyn Bond, Sheldon Brown, Eddie Chase, Becky Clague, Herbert Clague, Kim Clague, Jamie Coe, Bob Cordell, Toby J. David, Tom Dean, Dave Dixon, Larry Dixon, Dennis Frawley, Tom Gelardi, Bob Green, Jim Hampton, Bill Hennes, Joe Howard, Dave Hull, Casey Kasem, Dick Kernen, Ron Knowles, Jerry Lubin, Bob Maxwell, Judy McCarthy, Al McCoy, Mike McDowell, Ed McKenzie, Larry Morrow, Charlie O'Brian, Harvey Ovshinsky, Dave Prince, Dick Purtan, Bill Randle, Clark Reid, Dusty Rhodes, Don Schmitzerle, Frances Sebastian, Robin Seymour, Dave Shafer, Tom Shannon, May Shorr, Martha Jean "The Queen" Steinberg, Jack Surrell, Bob Talbert, Rosalie Trombley, Gino Washington, Paul Winter, Emily Wolf, Mike Whorf and Fred Yaffee.

# CHAPTER 1

# The Bellboy and the Bobby-soxers

HE WAS NOT THE FIRST DISC JOCKEY IN DETROIT, but Ed McKenzie's impact was so great that it sometimes seems like he was. Ed was one of those young kids who got caught up in the excitement of radio broadcasting not long after it was invented. The son of a blacksmith, his original attraction had been to the technical side of the business. As a high school student growing up in Flushing, Michigan,[1] he built crystal sets and then a transmitter and became a licensed amateur radio operator. After graduation, Ed found work as an engineer for a couple of little stations in Maryland and Virginia, then, in 1937, he came back to Michigan and was hired as a staff engineer at WJBK, at the time one of Detroit's smaller, low-wattage independent radio stations.

Over the next few years, he added announcing duties,[2] including station breaks and introductions to the foreign language programs that helped pay the station's bills, as they were a weak competitor of the four major network stations that drew the big audiences: WJR/CBS, WWJ/NBC, WXYZ/Blue, and CKLW/Mutual. The only other radio signals of any consequence in the area were independent stations WJLB and WEXL; the latter was licensed in suburban Royal Oak. Both had carved out a niche with local variety programming.

By 1942, Ed McKenzie had risen to become WJBK's chief engineer and chief announcer. Tuning around the dial, he may have picked up on some other local announcers playing records during periods when there wasn't some other type of programming available. But a visiting national advertising rep by the name of Joe Bloom told him about high-profile personalities, such as Martin Block in New York and Arthur Godfrey in Washington, D.C. They were having great success playing records and talking in a more conversational style than the often stilted delivery of the more formal announcers of the day.

The idea of hosting a record show intrigued Ed McKenzie. At least it sounded like more fun than occasionally announcing "Stay tuned for the Italian Hour." As a favor, Bloom recorded Block's show on a sixteen-inch acetate and sent it to McKenzie. After listening, Ed went to station manager Fred Hopkins with a proposition. "I told Fred I'd like to try putting together a little record show myself, just to see what would happen," McKenzie recalls.[3] "He gave me the go-ahead to use some sustaining time we had in the afternoon. We usually just ran some organ music or transcriptions during these unsponsored hours, so we had nothing to lose."

In search of a suitable theme song, Ed auditioned a stack of discs and came across an up-tempo instrumental tune recorded by Nat "King" Cole and Lionel Hampton in 1940.[4] It was a "jumpin' little number." Fearing that he might bomb, McKenzie thought the song's title would serve as a catchy on-air persona, keeping his identity a secret. So, in 1945, a few months after the close of World War II, WJBK introduced its new record show, hosted by "Jack the Bellboy."

McKenzie targeted a young audience and had a knack for choosing the records they wanted to hear. Although plenty of big band music and tunes featuring pop vocalists was available, Ed started to dip more into jazz and "race" music, as they called the records put out by black artists in those days. Charlie Parker, Louis Armstrong, Count Basie, Dinah Washington, and Ella Fitzgerald could be heard along with blues shouters, such as Jimmy Rushing, Roy Brown, and Big Joe Turner. There was boogie-woogie with Louis Jordan and his Tympany Five, who was always on top of *Billboard* magazine's "Harlem Hit Parade." Ed became the first white deejay in town to play an abundance of black music on what was essentially a pop show. "I just picked records I happened to like and we found an audience," recalls McKenzie. "I played a lot of jazz and then I'd slip in a little T-Bone Walker too." Listeners, black and white, would tune their dials to1490 and hear: "Hey youse boys, gals, and kids out there. This is Jack the Bellboy at your service on WJBK. We're coming to you with the sounds from down on the corner of Swoon Boulevard and Jive Alley."[5]

That mythical intersection was inside the old Curtis Publishing Building at Hamilton and West Grand Boulevard. There, WJBK received letters from some in the listening audience complaining that "Jack" played too much music recorded by "Negroes." Ed responded on the air, saying that "music is music and it doesn't matter who makes a good thing,"[6] as he continued to send out the hottest sounds on the dial.

Along with the records on the Bellboy show came a sense of humor sometimes bordering on sarcasm. Teenagers thought it was cool when Ed poked fun at records he didn't like. One of his least favorite singers was Vaughn Monroe, who had a somewhat nasal baritone voice. McKenzie would go on the air and say, "That's Vaughn Monroe with muscles in his tonsils," or "That's old nasal nose."[7] People were not used to hearing an "attitude" like this on the radio, so his verbal assault really got the town talking. Monroe's fans were up in arms, but kept right on listening and the flow of incoming mail continued to grow. The music and comments made Ed, as "Jack the Bellboy," the most talked about air personality in Detroit and definitely, *the* disc jockey of the late 1940s.[7]

When he started the show, McKenzie had been making $75 a week. Toward the end of 1946, the C. E. Hooper Broadcast Audience Measuring Rating System put "Jack the Bellboy" on top in Detroit, beating out larger stations with network programming. In a short time he had become WJBK's biggest moneymaker. It didn't take long for word to get back to Ed that 'JBK was making a killing by selling spots on his show at a much higher rate than the station normally commanded.[8] The admittedly naïve McKenzie got mad and then solicited an offer from WXYZ. WJBK countered with an increase in pay to $15,000 base plus $7.50 for each commercial aired on his show. Within a few short months his yearly income shot to $65,000–and this on a 250-watt station in 1947. "Down the road, 'JBK tried to get me to go on a salary but I told them I was willing to work for my money," says McKenzie. "Of course, I was doing great by then and didn't have any intention of changing our arrangement. I really couldn't believe what was happening because I didn't see myself as an entertainer. I had no background in music or show business. There were other announcers with more experience than I had who were a little upset at how well we were doing. Hell, I was just this country bumpkin, a technical guy and I sort of stumbled into a good thing. I just hoped it would last."[9]

Ed was about the only person in town who didn't quite have a fix on the extent of his own popularity. His show was the hottest thing going. A 1947 review in the show business newspaper *Variety* proclaimed: "To the Bobbysoxers in and around Detroit, 'Jack the Bellboy' has no rival."[10] In a *Billboard* poll, he was voted one of the top disc jockeys in the nation. Originally airing for just an hour, Ed's show could now be heard from 1:00 to 2:00 and 3:30 to 6:30 in the afternoon. The show offered an alternative to the mainstream programming on the network stations that featured soap operas, game shows, and chitchat during the day.

Along with the boogie-woogie, blues, and "jumpin' jive," McKenzie did a little jive talking, although it was a minor affectation to his fairly easygoing "no hype" delivery.[11] In no way was he trying to sound "black" or overly hip. When he would deliver a little slang, it was done in a low-key, friendly kind of way.

It is important to note that, although Ed did play a lot of music by black artists, he also featured pop stars, including Perry Como and Peggy Lee, and swinging white artists, such as Benny Goodman. He didn't play sweet music, such as Sammy Kaye's. Ed played what he thought was quality music and had no qualms about dismissing tunes he felt would insult his listeners. If a record was really bad, he would throw it into a trash can or break it while the microphone was on.

This sort of rebellious behavior was instantly attractive to teenagers who couldn't wait to get out of school so they could get home and listen to "Jay the Bee-Bee," as he was often called. At the same time, disapproving parents accused Ed of corrupting youth with all this "wild boogie-woogie music." In reality, McKenzie was quite responsible when it came to his audience. All spots were done live by Ed in his own inimitable style, which, if not a hard sell, was most definitely a persuasive one, and he refused to do commercials for cigarettes or alcohol.

There was no doubt that the Bellboy ruled with teenagers. On a Saturday afternoon in the spring of 1947, some sixty-five thousand kids blocked traffic on Woodward Avenue attempting to reach Grinnell's downtown music store, where Ed was doing a remote broadcast with singer Frankie Laine, who was enjoying his first chart hit with "That's My Desire."[12] Fans poured into the store, hanging off the pianos and console radios. The Detroit Police Riot Squad had to be called out to restore order. It was the last remote Ed was asked to do at Grinnell's and about the last he was interested in doing.

McKenzie also ran into trouble with the telephone company on two occasions. "I had a contest where I was going to give away five gallons of gas to the first one hundred persons who called in to vote on some singing commercials," he remembers.[13] "It was a promotion for Speedway 79 gasoline. Now, I go on the air with it and eleven phone exchanges go out of service. The phone company was furious, sent me some threatening letters, but I guess it showed there were a lot of people listening out there. This even happened once during the seventh inning of a World Series game," McKenzie recalls with pride.

For personal appearances, Jack the Bellboy did a few dances around town, but most often he could be found on stage at the Paradise theater, on Woodward Avenue in midtown. The Paradise was about the hippest jazz scene in town and drew the top black artists throughout the forties. There, Ed would emcee for greats such as Dizzy Gillespie and Duke Ellington and then check out the action behind the stage. "There were a lot of musicians who were smoking weed down there and doing some real mainline stuff," says McKenzie. "I remember one guy saying to me, 'Hey, man, you wanna fly tonight?' I decided I better stay on the ground."[14]

A photography buff, Ed carried along a camera and took all kinds of pictures of the jazz greats he met there. Louis Armstrong and Stan Kenton became good friends.

"Satchmo" even recorded some show promos for Ed to use on the air: "Hello! This is Louis Armstrong and when I'm in the Motor City I always listen to 'Jack the Bellboy' on station WJBK!" This sort of thing was recorded on disc in the days before tape. A problem was that the discs would wear out after too many spins.

Although McKenzie was a true pioneer in bringing black music to a large audience, race records had been available in small doses on the "Interracial Goodwill Hour," on WJLB, 1400 on the dial. The station went on the air in 1926 as WMBC, and was best known as home to the sensational news commentator Jerry Buckley, who was gunned down in the lobby of the LaSalle Hotel in 1930. It was believed that Buckley had ties to the underworld and was murdered for his participation in the recall of Mayor Charles Bowles, who was supported by Detroit's eastside mob. John Lord Booth bought WMBC in 1939 and, in a tribute to himself, changed the call letters to WJLB.

Bill Randle, a white disc jockey, remembers hosting the "Interracial Goodwill Hour" as early as 1942. "We were playing all kinds of hot jazz by black and white artists.[15] A guy named Ed Baker, who was a black advertising executive and a real hustler, sold the station on the program, so he could sell commercials aimed at the Negro audience. The name of the show made the idea of playing race records more palatable to the Booth family, who owned the station. In spite of our 'goodwill' the race riots broke out in Detroit in 1943, but I kept on with the program."[15] One of the biggest "race" hits that Randle is credited with breaking is the classic "Driftin' Blues" by Charles Brown, when he was still with Johnny Moore's Three Blazers.

According to Detroit musician and broadcaster Jack Surrell, the scene in Randle's studio on the thirty-first floor of the David Broderick Tower, downtown, was often as wild as the music being played. "It was a real party up there," recalls Surrell. "All kinds of musicians liked to hang out and I remember nights when there would be a big tub of cold beer on hand."[16] Randle concurs, "It would really get out of hand, people getting loaded and making a real mess. Detroit was just a wild town."[17]

Bill Randle was surely part of that wild world, filled with characters out of a Damon Runyon novel: "Detroit had more hustlers and con men than you could count, he recalls. "John Roxborough was Joe Louis's manager and also happened to be the "king of the numbers racket" in Detroit, as well as being the owner of Club Sudan, which was one of the hottest spots in town. When he went to jail for a year or so, he gave me the club. Now, authorities had taken away the liquor license so we ran it as a 'blind pig.' Randle proudly remembers being known as the "White Prince of Paradise Valley," which was the black community bordering Hastings Street, on the near east side of downtown.

Randle also owned a popular bookstore near the Wayne University campus, at Second and Warren.

"I think my show was targeted a little more toward the college and intellectual crowd that I was trying to influence, while Ed McKenzie steered his more in the direction of what the audience wanted to hear and he became just the biggest thing with the teenagers," says Randle, who left 'JLB in 1946 to host "Tunes and Topics" at WXYZ. The program turned out to be more stiff and structured than he cared for, so Randle returned to WJLB only to be fired in 1949. However, the reason for his dismissal was not the wild studio parties. "I was canned by 'JLB for playing a song by Nat 'King' Cole on a show during a different time of the day, when you were not allowed to play any records by black artists. Booth was getting his hair cut at the barbershop across the street from the station. Now, the barber, who happened to be black, has the radio on and hears the Nat Cole song and he says to Booth, 'Thanks for playin' my music.' Booth, who didn't even know what he was listening to, jumps out of the chair and races back to the station and tells me I'm through." It wasn't even anything far-out. The name of the song was 'This Would Make You Laugh,' which kinda fit the situation."

THE BEST-KNOWN RECORD SHOW HOST IN DETROIT at the time McKenzie began the Bellboy show was Eddie Chase, who presided over the "Make Believe Ballroom" on WXYZ. Eddie would create the atmosphere of a fine restaurant or ballroom by way of clever descriptions and by blending in the recorded sounds of background conversation and applause between records. His show aired from eight to eight-thirty in the morning and in the afternoon from two to three. During the war years, Eddie hosted the Ballroom's "Victory Swing Shift" late on Saturday night, a program dedicated to the thousands of swing shifters hard at work in Detroit factories.

The "ballroom" concept had been introduced by Al Jarvis at KFWB in Los Angeles in 1932 and made popular on the East Coast by Martin Block of WNEW in New York City. Eddie Chase got his start in broadcasting in southern California in 1933 and brought the "ballroom" sound to the Midwest at WGN in Chicago in 1936.[18]

Right after D day Chase got a call about moving his show to WXYZ in Detroit. "Their station manager was Alan Campbell and he made a great offer, so we began at the start of 1942. They liked my show and preempted some network programs so I could have more air time," remembers Chase.[19]

As early as 1943, Eddie was tabulating the popularity of tunes by polling listener requests, record sales, and jukebox reports from greater Detroit. "I guess it was sometime in late '45 or '46 when ABC bought WXYZ. Well, the network was not very happy that the station was running my show in the afternoon instead of their own programs, so I left and moved over to CKLW. I played the big band sounds and McKenzie was more into rock...well, they didn't call it rock back then. I guess it was more blues and beat music."

On CKLW, Eddie originated his "Make Believe Ballroom" show from the Telenews theater, on Woodward Avenue at Grand Circus Park. "CKLW would send over a sound truck every day and I would tape the show and then the tapes were sent to customs, duty paid, and then on to Windsor for airing in the late afternoon," Chase recalls. When he occasionally did the show live from the Windsor studio, he would always stand to announce, as if he were actually in a ballroom. The show was programmed in segments featuring one artist or band for several selections.[20]

Although Chase attracted a different sort of listener than the Bellboy, his show was very popular and a "must-stop" for famous band leaders visiting the Motor City, including Tommy Dorsey, Bob Crosby, and wild man Spike Jones. Lionel Hampton even recorded a tune on RCA, especially for Eddie. It was a hard driving number titled: "Chasin' with Chase."

"Eddie Chase was a very big personality in Detroit," recalls Bill Randle. "He was quite the dapper gentleman, great dresser and he drove around this big beautiful Buick Roadmaster. I remember thinking, "Man, one of these days, I'm gonna get me one of those babies," Randle laughs.

One night, on a trip to New York, Detroit's two "big Eds" were on the town, and while visiting a popular nightspot, Chase informed McKenzie that none other than Vaughn Monroe was in another area of the club and more than a little miffed about the comments being made about him on Ed's show in Detroit. McKenzie tells the story: "Eddie comes up and tells me that Vaughn Monroe says he's going to punch me in the nose, so I go looking for him. Well, in another part of the club, I tap him on the shoulder and tell him if he punches me, I'm going to punch him right back. He told me 'he had reconsidered,'" Ed laughs. So, that's what happened the night Jack the Bellboy faced down the man with "muscles in his tonsils."[21]

Back on the radio, McKenzie was selling a lot of those newfangled televisions for Muntz Television Company, which was sponsoring about ten hours of the Bellboy show each week. All together, Ed brought on fifty-nine new sponsors at WJBK and made them and the station very successful.[22] In 1948, Storer Broadcasting took notice and bought the station from Fred Hopkins for $750,000, which turned out to be a steal. Storer fired the studio orchestra and dumped the foreign language programming. Dick Jones, the sales manager at CKLW, was hired away to become 'JBK's station manager and he, in turn, lured CK's superstar morning comedy team of "Gentile and Binge" to come over, and added announcers Guy Bowman, Don McLeod, and Bob Murphy, the "tall boy, third row." In January of 1949, WJBK radio, along with its new television station on channel 2, moved into new studios atop the west tower of the Masonic Temple on Cass Avenue.[23]

"Jack the Bellboy" remained the crown jewel in WJBK's lineup. His reputation among musicians was such that several artists and writers submitted new tribute-theme songs, with titles such as "Bellboy Boogie" and "Jack the Bellboy's Last Call." One of the few of these to make any noise in popularity or sales was "Jivin' with Jack the Bellboy" by jazz great Illinois Jacquet.[243] Ed, however, stayed with the original Lionel Hampton recording that had served him so well.

Even though his popularity was sky-high and only a few time slots were open for the new disc jockey–type programs like "Jack the Bellboy," Ed McKenzie was not, however, alone on the Detroit radio dial in the mid-forties.

Besides Bill Randle and Eddie Chase, there was the nutty and very popular team of Joe Gentile and Ralph Binge, broadcasting from a world of sheer lunacy on their "Early Morning Frolic."[25] Billed as "the zaniest comedy team in radio,"[26] this duo kept

Detroit laughing right through the war years on CKLW and later on WJBK as they satirized commercials, performed skits, and created a wild atmosphere in this forerunner of future morning zoos and wake-up crews. Gentile and Binge were like New York's Bob and Ray, who came along some years later, but considerably rowdier and more "in your face."

Joe Gentile had been working as a prop man at WSPD in Toledo in 1931.[27] When a scheduled announcer failed to show up for work one day, the station manager put Joe on the air as a last-minute replacement. Gentile took right to it and soon landed a straight announcing job at a new station in Windsor, across the river from Detroit, that had just a year earlier gone on the air as CKOK, and then changed the call letters to CKLW. His shift included the early morning hours, uninhabited by network programs and included a fifteen-minute record show. To break the boredom, Joe started ad-libbing and clowning on the air. His weekly pay was twenty-five dollars.

By the spring of 1935, CKLW decided to add a second banana to "Happy Joe's Early Morning Frolic," and hired a twenty-one-year-old Chrysler employee named Toby David, discovered as he auditioned for a theatrical group. The son of circus people (his mother was an animal trainer), Toby was almost literally born in a circus trunk.

In the middle of depression Detroit, he quit his steady job at Chrysler to go on the radio. Two weeks into his new "show business" career, David was looking around for the paycheck he assumed he would be receiving. "What pay?" was the response from the office manager. "There is no pay." A stunned Toby David raced to the office of Ted Campeau, the station manager. "Well, I thought you were just interested in getting into radio," he offered meekly.

After coming to terms for a meager salary and picking up some extra work on other CKLW programs, such as chatting on the air with Bob "Oklahoma" Allbright, a singing cowboy, Toby rejoined the "Happy Joe" show in the morning.

Joe Gentile, in a voice that resonated like a cross between Howard Cosell and Archie Bunker, had already started to build a big following in the Detroit-Windsor area, and with Toby adding his talents in comedy, voices, and dialects, CKLW's morning show, now on from six to nine, really took off.

The audience howled when Joe, using a frying pan and a mallet, would simulate the sound of banging Toby on the head during skits where Toby would play lamebrain characters for Joe to needle, such as "Officer O'Houlihan," "Hiram the Farmer," and "Leonard the Dope."

A favorite skit featured a gullible character named Shirley, who would find herself in strange situations, such as being thrown down an elevator shaft, where she would be heard tumbling from side to side. To create this image on the air, an old cymbal filled with bits of metal was thrown down a stairwell with Toby chasing it down the stairs, screaming in a high falsetto voice. This was the sort of "sophisticated" humor that Detroiters began tuning in for each morning. Sponsors, such as Conn's Clothes, a Detroit men's store, found this crazy morning show the perfect vehicle to reach the city's working class.[28]

In no time at all, everyone in town knew the store's slogan: "Wear it, tear it, compare it, don't spare it, and if it isn't the best buy you ever made, bring it back and get your money back!"

Joe's childhood friend from Detroit's east side Ralph Binge came to the studio quite often and watched the performance. Ralph, a guy with a colorful background that included stints as a plumber as well as a boxer, had a great sense of humor and told some pretty funny stories. Soon he was joining in the on-air antics. In 1940, when Toby David accepted a position hosting and producing his own morning show at WMAL in Washington, D.C., Ralph took over full-time and the team of Gentile and Binge seems to have left a lasting impression on Detroit radio listeners. At their peak, the duo was attracting 80 percent of the listening audience each morning.

Forgoing scripts, Gentile and Binge ad-libbed everything and became famous for making fun of sponsors in commercials that were woven into skits that could last up to three minutes.[29] Although they did play some records, the mayhem in between made the show so popular. Joe was the ringleader and looked the part, puffing on a long black cigar. Ralph became whoever he needed to be as the two of them jumped from skit to skit. "We didn't think a lot about what we did," said Joe Gentile in an interview years later. "We just sat down before the program every day, worked out a few ideas, and then went and did it."[30]

Playing to the theater of the mind, they would often appropriate some well-known music, such as a polka or an Irish jig, adding their own wacky lyrics as they sang the virtues of sponsors, such as the McDonald Coal and Coke Company and Jerry McCarthy Chevrolet.

> *O-hhh! McDonald's for coal,*
> *McDonald's for coke!*
> *The men, they shovel away!*
> *McDonald's for coal, McDonald's for coke,*
> *To keep you warm all day!*

> *O-hhh! the hammers they bang,*
> *The wrenches they clang,*
> *The mechanics, they work all day!*
> *McCarthy pumps, the old grease gun*
> *And fixes your Chevrolet![31]*

> *Conn's clothes, Conn's clothes*
> *They're neat and nifty.*
> *Conn's clothes, they're made*
> *For people thrifty.*

For the show's original sponsor, the boys would emphatically guarantee that Conn's durable suits "won't rip, rattle, tear or *bag* at the knees!" On the air, listeners would hear the two of them pulling apart a new box containing a suit from Conn's. A fan with a decidedly Italian accent writes to Joe, asking, "Why you talk so much about this guy Conn? I wear his suits and they feel like paper on wall."

To sell the services of a bank, the duo performed the adventures of the "loan-a-ranger," and then there was a memorable commercial for an auto repair shop in Windsor where thousands of mechanics marched around the huge garage floor, carrying their wrenches at right shoulder arms.

There were no writers, producers, or directors to speak of, only two wild risk-taking performers, improvising some forty commercials as skits each morning. The two would play cops and robbers,

cowboys and Indians, doctors, judges, and other assorted characters as they wreaked havoc with sponsors' products. The audience
couldn't get enough, and soon there was a long list of businesses
begging to have their products given the "G and B" treatment.

In a skit for a laundry product, Joe plays a woman visiting a psychiatrist, who she hopes can cure her of her desire to "strangle"
her husband –to "kill him" with her "bare hands!" Earlier that
morning, while wringing out his shirts, she had been thinking if
only she could wring his neck in the same fashion. Ralph, speaking
in a deep voice, with a Viennese accent, plays the psychiatrist:
"How many shirts do you wring out each day?" The woman
responds, "Eight a week for my husband and all those for my six
sons!" The psychiatrist, feigning outrage, jumps up: "I, too,
would like to wring your husband's neck," he bellows. "You don't
need a psychiatrist–you need Snow White Laundry." Joe, as the
woman now, all excited and happy, exclaims, "I'm cured, doctor.
Now I don't want to kill my husband–I only want to kick him!"[30]

Just before going into a commercial, either Joe or Ralph would
call out the premise, such as "Let's play court." They would then
proceed to ad-lib a trial scene on the air. Judge Joe: "Why were you
going fifty-eight miles an hour on Woodward Avenue?" Ralph as
the defendant: "Judge, please understand, I wasn't driving too
fast–I was running! You can't find me guilty, who wouldn't run to
get Nibbleknuckers Knockwurst?"

For their oldest real estate sponsor, Gentile and Binge developed a recurring character whose voice was always heard in a deep
echo chamber effect. Detroiters got used to hearing this guy pop
up, out of the woodwork, over the telephone, from a deep well,
under the bed or even from a cemetery, with the promise: "I'll get
you *cash* for your property in forty-eight hours!"[32]

If the audience was visualizing Gentile and Binge running,
jumping, and singing around the studio, they were not far off.
Their show on CKLW originated from a big live studio on the tenth
floor of the Guaranty Trust Building in downtown Windsor.
There, the duo worked beneath hanging microphones, standing
on a four-by-four-foot dance platform that doubled as the main
prop for walking, running, stomping, and banging effects, of
which there were many. Besides their loyal radio audience, usually
a small crowd of dedicated fans was pressing up against the studio

window. The door to the studio was always left open during the show. If the studio phone happened to ring while they were on the air, the call would become part of whatever nonsense they were doing at that moment.[33]

Later, at WJBK, they operated from a broadcasting space in the rear of the building near a back entrance elevator. People would walk in each morning on their way to work, say "hi," and stroll right through the program, adding to its hectic and crazy pace.[34]

Besides send-ups of real commercials, Gentile and Binge also created commercials for imaginary products. Again, all of these were created on the spot with no rehearsal. One of these wild skits was for a fictitious reducing pill. It portrayed a fat woman who couldn't squeeze out of a phone booth. In an emergency procedure, she was fed through a straw for three days before the booth could be torn down. "Dr. Quack's Famous Reducing Pills" were then introduced in a trial offer for just one dollar. The station was swamped with letters and money and a clerk had to be hired to return the three thousand dollars weight-conscious listeners had mailed in.[35]

A spot for suspenders told the story of a window washer who forgot his safety belt. No problem; he just hooked his Double A brand suspenders to the thirty-eighth floor window catches. When his foot slipped, he bounced to the pavement and then back, thanks to the "great elasticity of the suspenders." Springy sound effects kept him bouncing back and forth for three days. Finally, Joe and Ralph had to call the sheriff and have the poor guy shot in midair so he wouldn't starve to death!

For bargain seekers who felt they wouldn't live long and yet did not wish to make a bad investment, Gentile and Binge had the solution, advising the purchase of the "combination daybed and casket," available from neighborhood undertakers.

Other make-believe products included the famous "rungless ladder," for people who wish to go only to the basement and the "whipping rather than" machine, for those who would rather take a whipping than do something else. The boys also reminded listeners to be sure to fill up with good "slopo knocko" gasoline. "Remember, it makes your car knock in rumba time!"

After working for peanuts in the early days, Gentile and Binge were earning thirty thousand dollars each by the late forties, bringing in three hundred thousand dollars in annual billing for CKLW. Among the famous celebrities stopping in to sample the madness was Frank Sinatra, who even sang a song for the boys. They, in turn, created the sound effect of the "drooling bib" for Sinatra's female listeners.

In a mid-forties interview, Gentile and Binge offered an assessment of their program. Ralph: "It's hard work to be crazy, even if you are an "artiste." Joe: "Yes, and we are really "artistes," spelled with an *e*. Don't forget that. It says so right here in our contract: not announcers, but artistes, with an *e.*"

For anyone who grew up listening to this wild pair, just the very mention of their names is cause for an instant smile if not a total convulsion of laughter. Radio on any level has seldom been wilder or funnier than "Gentile and Binge."

When Joe Gentile wasn't on the radio, he could be found behind the microphone at Briggs Stadium as announcer for the Detroit Tigers.


AT WJR, Ross Mulholland liked to query his audience: "How ya' gettin' along with your music?"[36] Mulholland had the background of a showman, having made several attempts at organizing college dance bands in the early forties.[37] He also attended the Cincinnati Conservatory of Music and did some radio work that led to a weekly jazz show on CBS called "Matinee at Meadowbrook."

After serving in the Coast Guard, he returned to Detroit in the summer of 1944 and landed a job at WJR, where he launched "Ross Mulholland's Music Hall" mornings at 7:15, a show that, despite the time slot, was aimed at teenagers. Capitalizing on his inability to secure a good pair of shoes during wartime rationing, he elected himself president of the Barefoot Nourishment and Swamp Water Society (Detroit having been built on swampland). Although this was years before rock 'n' roll and the heyday of record hops, Mulholland was hosting "recorded dances" at Detroit area high schools in 1947. He was more of a fast-talking, gag-spouting disc jockey than the Bellboy. Later in the morning, he hosted an audience participation show called "Meet the Missus" and was master of ceremonies on a weekly family quiz show. Ross Mulholland was a hustler and self-promoter who just couldn't get enough.

AFTER SPENDING SEVERAL YEARS IN WASHINGTON, D.C., Toby David and his new sidekick, Larry Marino, had moved on to New York's WJZ, where their seven a.m. variety show went out over NBC's Blue Network, coast to coast. When NBC was forced to sell that network to ABC, the show was canceled. Toby survived, using his skills at voices and dialects to secure acting work on an endless stream of network radio shows.[36] His day was spent running from building to building, studio to studio, where he would rush in, grab a new script, and step up to the microphone to handle different roles on programs including "Bulldog Drummond," Bob Hope, Robert Q. Lewis, "That's My Pop," and "Theater of the Air."

Tiring of the grind, he came back to Detroit at the start of 1946 and went on the air at WJR, hosting various programs, including the afternoon "Music Hall." Late in the evening he starred in "Bedlam Time," a big variety show featuring a full studio orchestra with featured singers. He then ended the day on the "Night Watchman" show, spinning records and talking to listeners until three in the morning.

One of the things talked about quite a bit on that show was food. Listeners would send in everything from snacks to steaks, which Toby and the crew would sample on the air. When the station manager happened to be up late one night and heard this radio smorgasbord, he flipped, thinking that with so many starving people in the world, this sort of thing was definitely in bad taste. A pink dismissal slip was then served to Toby David, who promptly read it on the air before finishing his last show on WJR and heading for the unemployment line.[38]

WJR radio had taken life on May 22, 1922, as WCX, owned by the *Detroit Free Press*. In 1925, Pontiac's Jewett Radio and Phonograph Company took part ownership and the call letters WJR were introduced. C. A. Richards, the president of Pontiac Motors, bought out the *Free Press*'s interest at the end of 1926. Early programs included a variety show in the 1920s called the "Red Apple Club," featuring early crooners, "Whispering Will Collins," and "Little Jack Little." In the 1930s, "Detroit Police Drama" was a big hit. The station also gained early notoriety broadcasting the rabble-rousing political sermons of Father Charles E. Coughlin, pastor of the Shrine of the Little Flower in the Detroit suburb of Royal Oak. Known as the "fighting priest," his power grew after CBS started to air his broadcasts nationally in 1930. He railed against bankers, socialism, and the uneven distribution of wealth, eventually attacking Jews. By the early 1940s, the Catholic Church finally bowed to pressure and forced his removal from the air. It is one of the darker pages from the history of WJR.[39]


BY THE LATE-1940S, Ed McKenzie had become very good friends with Dick Jones, WJBK's vice president and general manager.[40] The two did a lot of bar hopping around town where they discussed the unpleasant side of business at Storer Broadcasting. Jones proved to be too much of an independent thinker for Storer and he wound up quitting the station. Ed followed suit and on January 16, 1952, departed WJBK and was hired that same day by WXYZ, which was owned and operated by ABC.

The station's original call letters were WGHP when it went on the air, October 10, 1925. In 1929, theater executives George W. Trendle and John King bought it, changed the call letters to WXYZ, and moved the studios to the Macabees Building. Originally a CBS affiliate, Trendle bumped heads with that network's management over his desire to do more local programming. After parting ways with CBS, Trendle and King put together their own group of actors. On January 30, 1933, the shouts of "Hi Yo Silver" rang out on the airwaves as "The Lone Ranger" took to the air for the start of a long ride.

WXYZ was also home to the other Trendle dramas broadcast nationally, including "The Green Hornet" and "Sergeant Preston of the Yukon," although by 1952, these two programs were airing on the Mutual network and carried locally by CKLW.

In the morning on WXYZ, Fred Wolf was in his second year with a record show from six to nine that was growing in popularity. Late in the afternoon, Johnny Slagle hosted a local variety program called "Quittin' Time" that featured a live studio band that also performed on another program. When that program's sponsor canceled, WXYZ decided it was too expensive to keep the musicians on staff.[41]

Now Ed McKenzie would be featured with records from 4:00 to 6:15 in the afternoon, coming in with a raise and, as he had at WJBK, a commission paid on every commercial aired on his show.

Ads in newspapers, trade magazines, and in twenty-nine Detroit area high school newspapers promoted the fact that on February 4, 1952, "Jack the Bellboy" could be heard on a new station. In the middle of all the hoopla, George B. Storer announced that he was suing to keep the name "Jack the Bellboy" with his company. He claimed Ed had developed that name while employed at WJBK and therefore the name belonged to that station. Most people assume this was the end of it for Ed as Jack the Bellboy, but this is erroneous. "We got into litigation and it really dragged on," remembers McKenzie. "I continued to use 'Jack the Bellboy' for about six months on WXYZ before the court ruled against me."[42]

The dispute over the name was not, however, the only battle Ed fought. Storer Broadcasting was also suing him for lost business, to the tune of $650,000. "It was a nerve-racking year," Ed recalls. "There were a lot of confusing issues involved in the case, most notably the fact that, besides WJBK, there was something called Jack the Bellboy, Inc., which had been set up by my business partner and former 'JBK owner, Fred Hopkins, possibly with syndication in mind." Hopkins came to the rescue. When Storer bought the station from Fred in 1948, they failed to notice that the lease to the transmitter site was not included. In the meantime, Storer was being charged $150 per month rent. When Hopkins informed Storer of his plans to increase the rent to $5,000 a week, the personal lawsuit against Ed McKenzie was dropped.

WXYZ gave Ed the star treatment and built him a custom studio on the seventeenth floor of the Michigan Mutual Building downtown, where the main offices were, rather than the Mendelssohn Mansion where the rest of the talent was located. "I guess they just wanted me there and I never gave it much thought," Ed comments.

On August 29, 1952, McKenzie received word that the court had ruled in favor of Storer Broadcasting and he no longer had the right to go on the air at WXYZ as Jack the Bellboy. Storer did let McKenzie know that he was welcome to come back and use the name on WJBK; he declined.

By this time, Ed's voice was about the most familiar on Detroit radio and, despite losing his alter ego, his popularity became even greater as he won top ratings in the afternoon on WXYZ.[43] A magazine article written about a year after his switch to 1270 radio credited Ed's "easy, unassuming manner on the air" as a major influence on other announcers in the area who followed his lead rather than the razzle-dazzle style found in many other cities.[44]

Commanding such a large audience gave McKenzie a lot of influence in the music and radio industry, and he developed a reputation as a hit maker. Getting a new record played on the Ed McKenzie Show in Detroit was looked on as an important step to getting a hit, as other stations around the country could soon follow his lead. Tiring of the constant hype from song pluggers, Ed hung a sign on the wall outside his office: [45]

NOTICE: THINGS I DON'T WANT TO HEAR
Don't Tell Me It's Breaking in Cleveland,
Don't Tell Me It's on Top In New York,
Don't Tell Me I'll Be Famous If I Play It.

Ed remembers the day a hotshot record man came flying into his office, going right past the sign. "You wouldn't believe it, he used all three lines on me," says McKenzie.

Along with the music, interviews with visiting celebrities were a regular feature on his radio show each afternoon. Stan Kenton, Ray Anthony, Tommy Dorsey, and George Shearing all stopped by at one time or another. In 1953, Eddie Fisher was about the most popular singer around with adults and teenagers alike. Fisher invited McKenzie along when he traveled to England to do a two-week engagement at the Palladium theater.

Ed McKenzie had been involved in many worthwhile charitable projects over the years, including the Crusade against Cancer and raising money to fight infantile paralysis, and in 1951 he was presented with the Ernie Pyle award for raising $30,000 for hospitalized veterans of World War II. While at WXYZ, he was named Detroit's Man of the Year.[46]

McKenzie and radio were moving in a new direction. Eventually, the path they took would take Ed where he didn't want to go. For now, though, they would comfortably travel the airwaves together, over the more powerful ABC station in Detroit.

## CHAPTER 2

# Sounds and Styles

ED MCKENZIE'S COUNTERPART IN THE MORNING at WXYZ was Fred Wolf, who had joined the station as a part-time "special events guy" in 1946, while holding down a full-time job at Chrysler. Wolf's early assignments had included hosting a radio bowling show called "Tenpin Talker," which gave way to the "Tenth Frame."[1] Fred had lots of experience in the alleys, having been a professional bowler for fourteen years and a member of the World Champion Stroh team of Detroit. After suffering a back injury while defending a world title in 1943, he turned to broadcasting.

Although his interests were focused on sports, Fred was tapped to take over the morning record show in 1950, when Ross Mulholland, who had moved from 'JR to 'XYZ in 1948, left to pursue an opportunity in Hollywood. Not wanting to lose his lucrative show at WXYZ, Mulholland had tried to hire Wolf to fill in for six months.[2] Management balked and told Mulholland he'd better decide where he wanted to work. The "barefoot boy" left for KMPC in Los Angeles, and Fred Wolf became a morning institution in Detroit.

In a warm but somewhat gruff voice, a sort of Walter Matthau with a dash of Leo Gorcey, Wolf would order Detroiters to "Get outta bed!" and refer to the "old per-co-lator" and the "clock on the wall" frequently during his six to nine show. He had a special cadence to his delivery that would keep listeners on their toes. Even with the rough edges, Fred was a tremendous communicator who always sounded as if he were talking to listeners one on one. When Fred Wolf advised his audience to "go see the good folks over at...," they tended to do just that. Advertisers responded and his show was usually sold out.

"When Fred took over the show from Ross Mulholland, he received a similar commission plan, although it was not as high," remembers Fred's wife, Emily. "He was getting five dollars per commercial announcement and after he became so popular, he was making an awful lot of money. Fred certainly earned it because he made WXYZ into the big station it became."

Fred was a lone wolf in that he liked to do things his own way. During a hot spell in the summer of 1951, he decided to escape his windowless studio where the air-conditioning had broken down. "I grabbed a card table, took my chair and microphone and worked from the porch in front of the station," he explained in a 1956 magazine article.[3] At first WXYZ management was incredulous, but Fred convinced them that, with television killing radio, broadcasting from out front would be a good promotional move. In response to the oncoming cold weather, a special broadcast booth with windows on three sides and lights all around was constructed right in front of WXYZ's classic Mendelssohn Mansion, on Jefferson Avenue at Iroquois. "Good morning! How are you! This is Fred Wolf in the Wacky Wigloo."

Soon people were driving by to view Fred Wolf's "poor man's television."[4] On the air he would inquire: "I wonder if anyone's listenin' out there this morning." His answer would be a chorus of honking horns, coming in loud and clear, by way of a special outside microphone that could be activated from inside the Wigloo.

There was an elementary school nearby and Fred would chat on the air with kids stopping by on their way to class, including a little boy named Davey, whose lisp made him an audience favorite. In the background were the sounds of the streetcars zipping up and down Jefferson Avenue. "The conductor would ring the bell when they rode by," recalls Emily Wolf. "When they finally retired the streetcars, they gave Fred a bell taken from one of them, as a memento."[5]

One of Fred's most popular features came late in the show when he would say: "Okay, Mother, the old man is off to work, the kids are gone to school, get the broom and waltz around the kitchen with me."[6] He would then play "Red Roses for a Blue Lady." "This little routine absolutely endeared Fred to the women at home," remembers Emily Wolf. "The station would really pile on the soap commercials around this time of the morning."

Emily says that Fred's great gift was the way he related to the man on the street. "He spoke their language. The first thing he would do was look over any written material and cross off the big words. The other guys would listen and try to fathom his magic," she says.[7]

Wolf, also known as Swampy Joe, a nickname supposedly received from his old lifeguard buddies, struck a chord with listeners in Detroit and became as popular as those streetcars—and he stayed around longer. By the mid-fifties, Fred was capturing a morning audience share as high as 35 percent.

Along with the voice, Fred's face became familiar to early Detroit television viewers as he hosted his own bowling and hot-rod racing shows on WXYZ-TV.

Aside from the record shows with Wolf in the morning and McKenzie in the afternoon, the rest of the broadcast day at the ABC affiliate was filled with old-time-style radio, network, and local programs, including "The Breakfast Club," "Charm Kitchen," "Break the Bank," "Mary Margaret McBride," and the gut-wrenching confessional drama "My True Story," but things were slowly beginning to change.[8]

In 1944–45, 90 percent of all network radio programs had been sponsored. As the popularity of television continued to grow, the individual fifteen- and thirty-minute, single-sponsor programs were starting to disappear one by one as ad budgets shifted to the visual medium. By 1951–52, not more than 45 to 50 percent of all evening hours and still a smaller percent of daytime hours on the networks had national sponsors. WXYZ filled in the gaps with more record shows, and soon the ranks of so-called air personalities at that station grew as Paul Winter and Jack Surrell came on board, although Winter's debut was in the old short-form style.

Paul Winter (real name Saul Wineman) graduated from Detroit's Central High in 1941 and attended Wayne University before switching to the University of Michigan, where he majored in philosophy.[9] He got involved in broadcasting, playing classical music at the university radio station as well as doing a little acting on radio in Detroit. Paul used the money he earned to return to school and receive his master's degree. He then sent an audition record to WXYZ at just the right time, and the station put him on the air in the evening from 6:30 to 7:00, with a show called "Paul Winter and Company," playing records and performing satirical skits that he had written. The show ran for several months in 1952, until the time was bought by Muntz Television, who wanted to sponsor Ed McKenzie.

Although Winter projected a polished, somewhat intellectual delivery on the air, his next assignment found him holding forth over one of the stranger programs to be found on the dial. Each morning from 5:30 to 6:15, preceding Fred Wolf, Paul took on the persona of Lonesome Luke Borgia, who, as he related to his listeners in dialect, "was the long lost descendant of Lucretia Borgia and hailed from down in Bookstrahoota County, Kentucky." Looking back, Winter recalls: "This program was yet another attempt by the station to keep me around in those days until they could figure out what to do with me."[10]

Winter's first meeting with the very personable president of WXYZ, Jimmy Riddell, was memorable. "The station manager took me to the main offices downtown. Riddell greeted me by saying, 'So you're one of those smart college boys. Well, you're our smart college boy!' Somewhat taken aback, I said, 'What does that mean?' He responded, 'It means, do things our way and you'll do all right. Don't do it and you won't do anything at all,'" laughs Winter.[11]

By the spring of 1953, Paul added other specialty programs, such as "Man on the Street" and "Curtain Calls," where he played show tunes. As the station opened up more local airtime in the fall, he found a regular midday home with his "Winter Wonderland" record show, playing the pop standards of the day. The original hours were two to four in the afternoon but were moved around the schedule to accommodate new programming.

Paul Winter on the air:

> That's Tony Bennett with "Just in Time." It's two minutes past two in a wonderland of music on the station that brings you the most popular music in Detroit, WXYZ, AM and FM–ABC Radio in the city, Paul Winter, that's me, mike-side. We'll

have the news and weather complete for you from the WXYZ News Center with Hugh Copeland in exactly twenty-seven minutes. *[Commercial for Carling Black Label Beer, music]* There you have a big hit for Miss Jo Stafford here on Detroit's "Station of the Stars, WXYZ. We have eight minutes past the hour of two and a reminder that Ed McKenzie will be along at three o'clock with the"Record Matinee."[12]

Winter was never really too sure of how well he was doing. "Management never shared any ratings information with me, so I was always operating a little in the dark," he confides. "One day, Phil Brestoff, who was program manager at the time, told me he was putting together a contest for my show where people would have to mail in cards. I was very concerned, frightened if you will, that no one would respond. Fortunately, we received about three thousand cards and I breathed a little easier knowing that there was someone listening out there!"[13]

This has been Paul Winter mike-side, the music recorded, Winter live and I hope lively enough for you. A few million favors if you will: watch where you're going, remember where you've been, be with us in Wonderland tomorrow again. These final favors: McKenzie in just a few, later still, Jack Surrell and tomorrow morning, the morning glory that is your good friend and mine, fearless Freddie Wolf. Till we meet again, don't buy any bad dreams and you never will on the greatest of 'em all, I mean ABC Radio Network, WXYZ.

JACK SURRELL WAS A SEASONED MUSICIAN who became one of the earliest black air personalities in Detroit and the first on one of the major network stations. "I was a big fan of Ed McKenzie when he was on WJBK," remembers Surrell. "Ed did all these live commercials and I told him they would sound better with me playing some piano behind them. He pitched the idea but the station didn't go for it."[14]

Surrell stayed with his regular gig, playing piano, singing, and chatting during the dinner hour at the Chicago Road House, a black-tie restaurant on Michigan Avenue in Dearborn. After Ed joined WXYZ in 1952, Jimmy Riddell, who ran the station, decided he wanted to integrate the air staff, and Ed McKenzie suggested Jack.

A native of Philadelphia, Surrell majored in music at Temple University. He had gained early radio experience in that city on WCAU. On the road, he traveled the world and was piano accompanist for several famous entertainers, including Bill "Bojangles" Robinson, Pearl Baily, and Ethel Waters. He brought a rich background in music and entertainment to Detroit radio.

WXYZ carried ABC network programming in the evening and had been filling the late night hours with local shows, such as "Indian Room Pow Wow Night Club," replaced in 1951 by "Sleepy Head Ted." McKenzie and Riddell thought it would be interesting to have Jack play the piano on his show, much the way he did at the Road House. "I would blend in and out of records using matching chords, recalls Surrell. "Then I would keep playing in the background while I gave the time or read a commercial. I also did a couple of solos and sang a song or two each evening." Jack had a soft-spoken, mild-mannered air persona; along with piano, he would also accompany himself on the celeste.

Detroit's Stroh Brewery Company was interested in expanding their sales in the black community and signed on as Surrell's main sponsor. The WXYZ sales department put together a big in-store merchandising campaign throughout the black community with counter cards featuring Jack's image as well as ads in black newspapers. His show however, was not programmed for any specific group other than those who who were fans of good music.

Surrell pulled his own records, including those he brought from home and the music on his show tended to be somewhat hipper than what was played during the day. Listeners were more apt to hear the likes of Count Basie, Sarah Vaughan, and Earl Bostic, as opposed to Eddie Fisher or Doris Day, on Jack's late evening show, which aired from 10:15 to 1:00. "It was a mix," says Surrell. "I played some rhythm and blues with Bill Doggett, jazz with Stan Kenton, and even some Thelonious Monk, but nothing too far out because I would also work in some pop sounds with Jo Stafford and Kay Star."[15]

Although he picked his own music, there were a few records that were off-limits. "I would receive station memos that would remind me not to program certain songs," recalls Surrell. "A few of these included 'Body and Soul,' 'Strange Fruit' and 'Such a Night.' I guess they were looked on as being a little too suggestive."[16]

The show originated from a studio that was a big living room in the old Mendelssohn Mansion, where WXYZ radio had relocated after leaving the Maccabees Building in 1944. "It was a big old building," says Surrell. "All the actors from the 'Lone Ranger' and the other dramas worked out of a studio on one side of the building. I would be at the piano right in the middle of our studio and my producer was across the room with the turntables and the engineer was in the control booth. We did a lot of hand signaling."

His theme song was "Penthouse Serenade" and the show was called the "Top of the Town," according to Jack, "to give it that penthouse feel."

Jack also became a pioneer on television, hosting "Sunday with Surrell" on WXYZ-TV starting in 1953. The program was billed as "Detroit's Only All Colored TV Show." Motor City jazz guitarist Kenny Burrell and his quartet provided live music.

AT WJBK RADIO, they were carrying on without the services of Jack the Bellboy. After winning the court battle over the rights to the name, WJBK tucked it away. By this time, the station was doing better with the humorous Gentile and Binge in the morning.

Ralph Binge had also added a solo show on 'JBK called the "Headless Horseman" for an hour each day and it really took off with teenagers and college students.[17] Fans would pour into the station's Studio A to watch the goings-on as Binge provided voices for a couple of dubious characters named Sharp Frank and Beautiful Carl, who gave headaches to the mysterious Headless Horseman.

Sharp Frank was a fast-talking, high-pitched voice schemer who had all the angles, and thought of himself as quite the ladies' man. He mangled his pronunciations and misinterpreted his thoughts. When spouting off on science, he would explain that "skeletons is bones with the people scraped off."

Beautiful Carl was known as the Friendly Philosopher and Poet Laureate of Michigan Avenue. As president of "Marriage, the Living Death Society," his main calling in life was to prevent unsuspecting males from falling prey to matrimony. His motto was "better dead than wed." Over some solemn organ music, Beautiful Carl, in his slow gravelly voice, would warn male listeners that "perfume is the mustard gas in the war between the sexes" and advise future grooms to "stay single and your pockets will jingle" and "When she leads you to the alter–halt her!" The slogan "Marriage, the Living Death" became the rage when it was put on promotional buttons imprinted with crossed rolling pins, and thousands were distributed all over the Detroit area.[18]

Although Sharp Frank was a constant on the program, there would be many mornings, invariably Mondays, that Beautiful Carl would fail to show up. Headless Horseman would make it known that the reason was probably Carl was on a drinking spree or sleeping off a bad night

Beer was something held close to the heart of Beautiful Carl, who even had a plan to manufacture "beercicles." One morning, Carl mournfully recounted an accident he had witnessed on the way to the station: "I was drivin' by the Stroh factory when I saw a delivery truck hit a car. All the bottles breaking...it was a painful sight."

Binge ad-libbed the whole show and not to get confused as to who was talking, he would lean to the left when he did Sharp Frank and to the right for Beautiful Carl. Headless Horseman stayed right in the middle. When asked to describe the talents of Ralph Binge, his peers offer several descriptions including "brilliant," "hilarious," and "a genius."

Other record shows on 'JBK featured a former bandleader named Tom George and Don McLeod, who inherited the afternoon hours vacated by the departure of Ed McKenzie. McLeod had been working in the sound effects department of WXYZ in 1946 when he got the bug to be a disc jockey. After a stint on the air in Peoria, Illinois, he returned to Detroit at WJBK in 1948. His afternoon get-together was called "McLeodsville U.S.A." Don also hosted the first dance party-style show on television in the Midwest with "Don McLeod's TV Bandstand" on channel 2.[19]

Joe Gentile's brother Larry was heard on the late-evening "Houseparty" show. WJBK had also been approved for frequency change to 1500 and an increase in power to ten thousand watts daytime and one thousand watts at night.

AT WJR, Marty McNeely was in charge of the records in the "Music Hall" each morning, while the remainder of the day included plenty of CBS network programming and local fare, such as "Mrs. Page," a recipe program, "The Jack Harris Show," and "Guest

House" with humorist Bud Guest. These programs featured live music with Jimmy Clark and the WJR orchestra. There was also some rural humor on a show called "Pie Plant Pete and Bashful Bob." Other WJR personalities included Ron Gamble and Jim DeLand.

Clark Reid was the station's all-night personality beginning in 1952 and recalls the late-night programming policy. "It was just a great experience on WJR because I had complete freedom to do whatever I wanted to do. The station had an extensive record library and I would choose all sorts of music and didn't really worry about playing a particular style. Thursday nights were all request and with 'JR's signal, I'd get mail from all over the country. It was an important show to get a record played on, so I was always being chased by not only record promotion men, but also the song pluggers. These were the guys the music publishers sent out into the field back then."

Reid says that many of his shows resembled a "Tonight Show" on radio. "There were great nightclubs all over Detroit in those days and that meant a steady stream of stars coming to town. Everybody made their way up to our studios after finishing their last show. On any given night we would have people like Sammy Davis Jr., Rosemary Clooney, Nat 'King' Cole, and Frankie Laine on the air with us."[20]


IN 1953, BOB MAXWELL WAS ON IN THE MORNING, hosting the "Fraternity of Early Risers" at WWJ. Back in 1941, he was broadcasting in the wee hours of the night, hosting the "Moonlight Serenade" over WEXL. "I was on all-night with records, eleven to seven, and people would call in and we would put their dedications on the air. Once the war broke out, we were instructed not to accept any more phone calls and to drop the dedications. I was on the air the night the Japanese bombed Pearl Harbor and the owner of the station, old Jacob Sparks, came down to the studios and was pounding on the door but I wouldn't let him in 'cause it was against policy. The next day he wanted the manager to fire me but he had a change of heart and admitted I was only doing what I had been told, so he let me keep my twenty-five cents per hour job," Maxwell chuckles. "We only had an A.M. ASCAP license over there so I would wait till about three A.M. and then I'd play some of my own records, like Glen Miller, who was licensed by BMI. I don't think anyone ever noticed."

Bob also had the opportunity of working in network radio. "My dad was a custodian in the building where George Trendle and John King had their offices for their radio dramas," he recalls. "One day Dad had been taking them up and down the elevator quite a few times and when he found out who they were, he told them that his son really liked radio and had a little experience, and Trendle told him to have me come around. The next thing I know, I'm holding scripts for Brace Beemer on the 'Lone Ranger' when he would get a little tipsy and pretty soon I was doing some acting in not only the 'Ranger' but in the 'Green Hornet' and 'Challenge of the Yukon' [Sergeant Preston of the Yukon]. These were national shows coming right out of Detroit and I would be paid about $38 for my work, which wasn't bad."

Later, while working at WJLB, Bob took a turn at hosting the "Interracial Goodwill Hour," which was targeted at Detroit's black audience. "I was just a staff announcer in the evening when that show became available and Ed Baker, who was the manager and who also happened to be black, thought my accent, which was a little on the southern side, would fit in with the rhythm and blues records, which were called 'race records' back then. So here I was, this white guy, and I'm doing commercials for products being pitched to blacks, like hair straighteners, things like that."

Maxwell left 'JLB for a chance to have his own afternoon record show on a new station in Saginaw, WKNX: "I was pretty wild up there," he recalls. "I'd call myself Luke the Spook and talk kinda crazy. Two people would call in requests for different songs by the same artist and I'd play the two songs at the same time! Sounded horrible, drive 'em crazy. I even accused the mayor of taking graft, anything to get attention. Anyhow, there was a convention of NBC station managers in Saginaw and the local manager was tellin' the guy from Detroit how I was killin' his station in the ratings. A short time later, that guy offered me a job at WWJ. Of course, when I arrived back in Detroit they sort of clipped my wings and I had to adjust to the more conservative style of the station. This is 1947 and the first program I did was a quiz show called 'Dollars for Drivers,' that ran for just a half hour."

Despite its conservative image, WWJ did briefly let Maxwell reprise his "Luke the Spook" routine for a half hour each morning at seven. "They dropped that program pretty quick," says Maxwell. "It just didn't fit their image." WWJ tended to be more conservative in their approach as a result of their ownership by the *Detroit News,* who also owned WWJ-FM and WWJ-TV. Two years later they drew national media attention for banning a song called "I Get Ideas." The ban on radio extended to TV where the song, which was a big seller, was being featured on NBC's "Hit Parade" carried on WWJ-TV, channel 4.

Despite the conservative surroundings, Bob Maxwell began doing a regular show and went on to become one of WWJ's top personalities in the 1950s. Aside from radio, Bob was called on to emcee lots of live performances around the city. "The wildest experience I remember was one night when I was doing a show at the State Fair Coliseum with Carmen McCrae," recalls Maxwell. "Now, she was quite often temperamental and very difficult to deal with but on this occasion she showed up really bombed. After I introduced her, she walked across the stage, reached out and grabbed me by both ears, and gave me a great big kiss! I didn't know what to make of it."[21]

Like a number of other radio personalities, Bob Maxwell was also seen on early Detroit television where he hosted a number of programs on WWJ-TV, including a popular late-night show.

Ross Mulholland returned from California in 1953 and joined WWJ from one to three in the afternoon. His record show was followed by NBC's soap opera lineup, including the long-running "Stella Dallas" and "Pepper Young's Family."

WWJ's claim of being the "world's first radio station" was always challenged by KDKA in Pittsburgh. Although WWJ was first on the air, August 20, 1920, it was under the calls 8MK and therein lies the dispute. The WWJ letters first appeared in 1922 and the station broadcast the first baseball game in 1927. It was announced by Ty Tyson, "the voice of the Tigers."

MULTIVOICED TOBY DAVID and his "cast of thousands" were featured in the morning on CKLW all through the fifties. After his dismissal from WJR, Toby had picked up some work at WWJ as a funny sidekick to Minnie Jo Curtis in the morning. He then heard that his old friends Joe Gentile and Ralph Binge had jumped to WJBK, where they had been offered the chance at fame and fortune in the new medium of television if they would do mornings on radio. Toby contacted Ted Campeau, the same station manager he had worked for eight years earlier, and soon he was back on CKLW with his own morning show. As usual, he carried on the humorous approach, using different voices and dialects, to bring various characters to life. A favorite was "the man under the table," with whom David conferred with but never quite understood.

CKLW's daytime schedule included a woman's program with Mary Morgan and a cooking show with Myrtle Labbitt.

A young Bud Davies hosted the "Good Neighbor Club" and "Your Boy Bud" shows during the midday hours, when he played records and took the votes of fans in his "Battle of the Bands" or "Singers."[22] Born and raised in Windsor, Bud had a classic one-station career. He started working in the mail room at CKLW in 1942, adding duties as a transcription operator and staff announcer. After serving with the Royal Canadian Navy during World War II, he returned to CKLW and started doing early "platter and chatter" shows, as they were sometimes referred to, and began building a base of younger listeners

"Make Believe Ballroom" with Eddie Chase continued to be a moneymaker each day, starting at 3:30 and running until the late afternoon adventure shows, such as "Superman" and "Sky King," aired on the Mutual network.

Bob Cordell was CKLW's all-night disc jockey on the "Dawn Patrol" in 1952, playing the latest hits by Teresa Brewer, Tony Bennett, and Frankie Laine. Cordell (real name Bob Caudill) was born and raised in the Motor City but was living in southern California when he enrolled in the Hollywood School of Broadcasting and took his first job at KXO in El Centro, California. "All I could think of was getting back to Detroit so my parents could hear me. I wanted them to be proud," Cordell remembers.

He took the "Corn till Morn" show at WJBK about 1947 and also worked at WKMH. Cordell recalls that there weren't many stations or disc jockeys back then. "We had a nice little clique, everybody knew everybody." One of the most memorable things about his time at CK' were the show opens that Frank Sinatra had recorded for him on disc. "I had a friend in New York who made that possible. I only wish I had been able to hang on to that recording but it just blew away with a lot of great things over the years while I was moving around a lot."[23]

Owned by Essex Broadcasters of Ontario, CKLW had always had more of an American accent in its programming. In 1949, the station boosted power to fifty thousand watts.

An aspiring young announcer from London, Ontario, named Ron Knowles was working at CFCO in Chatham, Ontario, when he was invited to join the staff of CKLW in 1954. "I came in as a board operator when the station was still located in the Canada Trust Building in downtown Windsor," Knowles recalls. "It was real old-time radio up there. All commercials were on transcriptions, which were acetate discs, there was no tape. You would plan way ahead and make a list that would indicate that a certain commercial was on side two, cut four, that sort of thing. I would get all of this together at night and ready for Toby David in the morning."

According to Knowles, the production of the "Toby David Show" was not an easy task: "The engineer and all the transcriptions were in a separate area of the station, and the announcer and producer-engineer could not see each other and it was difficult to communicate how you wanted each break to go. There were three RCA turntables in the production room to handle all the discs. Toby would call for the order he wanted things, as far as commercials, funny bits, records, and so forth, and you just hoped it came out right."

The evening hours were filled with Mutual Network shows, such as "The Falcon" and "Counterspy." When there was open time they would fill locally with transcribed quarter-hour shows. "These programs were ready to go with script and all. Things like the 'Guy Lombardo Show.' You would announce it like it was happening right that moment," Knowles remembers. Ron also started to take on more announcing duties. "I announced at CFCO in Chatham but it was quite different to be on a station like CKLW. I even took lessons to get up to speed. We had a lot of network programming on back then and we supplied many of their feeds. On several occasions I would get to do the network's identification breaks that went out nationally: 'This is the Mutual Radio Network'."[24]

In late 1954, the station moved to new studios at 425 Riverside

Drive West in Windsor. The building also housed CKLW's new television station operating on channel 9.

THERE WERE EXCEPTIONS, such as WXYZ's Jack Surrell, but the records featured on most radio stations in this pre–rock 'n' roll era included the standard lineup of white pop artists, such as Patti Page, Eddie Fisher, the Ames Brothers, Kay Star, Jo Stafford, Perry Como, and Rosemary Clooney. One of Detroit's first recording acts to break nationally became popular about this time. It was an Italian American trio called the Gaylords and they enjoyed a great chart run during 1953 and 1954.[25]

Ronnie (Vincent) Gaylord, Burt (Bonoldi) Holiday, and Don Rea were attending the University of Detroit when they met. After performing locally, they signed with Mercury Records and scored with hits such as "Tell Me You're Mine," "From the Vine Comes the Grape," "Isle of Capri," and "The Little Shoemaker," the melody of which became even more famous in the Motor City when they adapted a new lyric to it for the Roy O'Brian Ford commercials that ran on radio and TV for years: "Stay on the right track, to Nine Mile and Mack, Roy O'Brian trucks and cars make your money back." The Gaylords were also featured on the early Detroit television programs "Melodies in Money" and "Club Polka."

While the Gaylords were purveyors of mainstream pop, numerous groups of black teenagers were harmonizing on Detroit street corners. Among the best were the Diablos, a foursome that came together at Central High School in 1950.[26] Their lead singer was Nolan Strong, who had a wild, silky falsetto that gave the group a distinctive sound. In 1953, they signed a deal with a small Detroit label called Fortune Records, owned by Jack and Devora Brown.[27]

Formed in 1946, the label originally had specialized in country music, with Roy Hall and the Davis Sisters on their roster (the Davis Sisters, including Skeeter Davis, were featured on a radio program called "Barnyard Frolics" on WJR about the same time). After the death of her husband, Devora Brown continued writing, arranging, and even engineering at the small two-track operation on Linwood Avenue. By the early fifties, Fortune had started to record black artists and signed the Diablos. In 1954, the group had their first local hit, "Adios, My Desert Love," and, later that same year, a spooky-sounding song called "The Wind" was even bigger.

To hear music like the Diablos on Detroit radio in 1954, you had to tune in "Senator" Bristoe Bryant, late at night on WJLB. Where Jack Surrell's "Top of the Town" show on WXYZ featured a lot of music by black artists, it was more refined than Bristoe's, which played the harder sounds from the rhythm and blues (r&b) charts.

Jerry Wexler, working for *Billboard* magazine in 1949, had coined the name "rhythm and blues" to replace the "race music" classification on their record charts.[28] Also vanishing about that same time in Detroit was WJLB's "Interracial Goodwill Hour," where race records had been mixed in with white artists on a show geared to blacks, but hosted by white announcers such as Bill Randle and Bob Maxwell.[28]

The "Goodwill Hour" had been replaced by the real thing, "Rockin' with LeRoy," a show that left no doubt as to content. LeRoy G. White became the first black disc jockey in Detroit to win great popularity. Kids, black and white, tuned in "Rockin' with LeRoy" to find music with a beat and an edge. "Cupid Boogie" by Johnny Otis, "Hard Luck Blues" by Roy Brown and his Mighty Men, "Have Mercy, Baby" by the Dominoes, and "I Got Loaded" by Peppermint Harris were some of the big r&b hits programmed by LeRoy that were never heard on the pop stations.

A graduate of Hamtramck High School and Wayne University (which later became Wayne State University), LeRoy's first interests were in politics. He worked as an inspector on the State Liquor Control Commission in the late 1930s and was a candidate for the state house twice before moving into broadcasting at a time when there were practically no blacks on the air. In fact, during the mid-1940s, out of three thousand disc jockeys broadcasting on some thirteen hundred stations across the country, only sixteen were black. Most of these announcers strived to sound no different from their white counterparts. Bill Randle recalls LeRoy White: "He was the first wild disc jockey on the air in Detroit. He would really lay on the 'shuck and jive' that he thought listeners wanted or expected to hear from a black disc jockey. The guy also had a real testosterone problem." Randle was referring to the fact that aside from gettin'on with the hits, White was known to be gettin'on with the ladies and when he wasn't on the air, and there was a good chance he could be found trying to slip away from a new girlfriend somewhere in the city.

This scenario resulted in his death. He was killed after falling through a railing off a balcony during a lovers spat. This, however, happened sometime after he had left WJLB to run the Wayne Record Distributing Company and an ad agency with his wife, Charlene, who, thanks to LeRoy's political clout, had been elected to to the state house in 1950, serving the 11th Congressional District.[29]

White had been joined at 'JLB by another black announcer, Bristoe Bryant, who also served a term in the state senate as a result of backing from LeRoy. Although not nearly as wild and flamboyant as White, Bristoe carried on, taking over the late evening hours. He was also on hand at the Madison Ballroom in 1954 to award the Diablos a special silver record for "The Wind."


THAT SAME YEAR, Ed McKenzie was asked to develop a variety television show for WXYZ-TV. "Ed McKenzie's Saturday Party" was on for two big hours, noon to two every week on channel 7 starting in September. In a set depicting a corner drugstore, Ed would hang out and discuss the latest records with teenagers. The teens would participate in dance contests, with winners receiving trophies. There were also amateur acts that would be judged by audience applause. Dinah Shore, Patti Page, the Four Aces, and Sammy Davis Jr. were just a few of the major recording stars who appeared with Ed, who did the show with no help from TelePrompTers, cue cards, or scripts of any kind.

The show was a hit from the start. Police protection was provided after an early telecast when seven hundred teenagers stormed the station, broke through lobby doors, overpowered a guard, and almost broke down the studio entrances.[30] Besides teen-oriented recording acts, Ed made sure there was a healthy amount of jazz on the show each week. He had been a champion of jazz and would see that it shared the spotlight with the new wave of popular music.

CHAPTER 3

# "You're Not Planning on Staying in This Business, Are You?"

AT WKMH IN SUBURBAN DEARBORN, Robin Seymour was attracting a youthful audience with his pop music show in the afternoon. Robin joined 'KMH in July of 1947 after serving with Armed Forces Radio. His first taste of the broadcast business, however, had come a few years earlier. "I was just a kid who wanted to get into radio and it was the right time because so many guys were getting called up in the draft," Seymour remembers.[1] "It was Ed McKenzie who gave me my first job doing some announcing and board work at WJBK in 1943 and it was something Ed said to me that gave me the determination to hang in there and be successful. I was working the late shift one Saturday night and Ed [who was the chief announcer in his pre–Jack the Bellboy days] stopped in with one of the gals he was dating. I think Ed would admit that back then he would occasionally have a few too many drinks. Well, this particular night, he was mildly sloshed and he looked straight at me and said: 'You're not planning on staying in this business, are you? You're on the outside looking in.' They were not exactly words of encouragement. It was the kind of situation where you are either crushed or you decide you're going to get better. I do want to say that Ed also did some very nice things for me later on."[2]

WKMH had signed on in mid-1946 as a thousand-watt daytimer at 1540 on the AM dial, before going full-time in 1948 on 1310 with five thousand watts. According to Robin, programming in those days consisted of whatever they could fill the time with. "We had a lot of sports, and Walter Patterson, who later became the manager, would play piano. There was big band music and local Dearborn news and features. I was doing board work, station breaks, that sort of thing. Nothing really started to happen until January of 1948. One day I went on the air with a special program for the March of Dimes, taking requests and playing records, just to see what would happen. Well, we got two to three hundred letters and raised a pretty good sum of money, so the boss came to me and said, 'Why don't you do this every day?' and that's how we got the record show going on a regular basis."[3]

What were those early shows like? According to Robin, it was all by happenstance. "The WKMH studios back then were on the second floor of the Gagnon Furniture store on Michigan Avenue. We were on originally from two to four. The kids from Sacred Heart started to come by the station on the way home from school and they would hang around to do homework and they would start to dance in the lobby on the other side of the glass. I would do interviews with the kids and also record artists who would be plugging their latest release. It was a lot of fun especially because I felt I wasn't that much older than a lot of the kids," says Robin. "It would get pretty wild up there and the people in the store below complained that the ceiling was beginning to sway."

Born and raised in Detroit, Robin went to Central High School and then to Wayne University. He mixed a warm, sincere delivery with some slick deejay patter and ran a fairly fast-paced, structured show. Robin was the first disc jockey in town to do sock hops. " We started going out to the schools to do dances sometime in 1952 and I would get about $15 for my efforts," he remembers.

Seymour was also a talent spotter and is credited with discovering Johnny Ray performing at the Flame Show Bar in 1951 and bringing him to the attention of Columbia Records. Ray went on to great success on records with megahits such as "Cry" and "The Little White Cloud That Cried." Although he was white, these emotionally charged songs were released on Okeh, Columbia's race label, and Johnny Ray became an important link in the development of rock 'n' roll.

Along with fellow deejay Bill Randle, Robin had started to pro-
mote shows at the Broadway-Capitol theater in the late forties.
"We were doing jazz and blues shows back then and we would have
someone like John Lee Hooker come in and we would each get
$35. The crowds were pretty big. The club scene was great around
Detroit and you could go over to Club Sudan and see people like
Illinois Jacquet and Lester Young. It was just great," says Seymour.

As his show progressed, he played mainly records listed on
sales charts printed by the music press.[4] In this, he was ahead of
his time. By 1953 he was named Disc Jockey of the Year by
*Billboard* magazine and again the following year by *Hit Parader*
magazine. He had a spiffy malt shop–era theme song called
"Bobbin' with Robin" that was recorded by the Four Lads:
"Bobbin' with Robin, No more time for sobbin', Go and let the
mob in, Everybody flies–sky high!"

In 1954, Seymour became one of the first white deejays (on a
primarily white pop station) to play an r&b doo-wop-style record
when he broke "Gee" by the Crows and it turned into a big
crossover hit. "The music mix was so weird back then. You would
have Patti Page and then I would throw in the Crows and next you
might hear Mantovani," Seymour laughs.

New records that Robin thought could be hits were previewed
as "Robin's Flyer of the Day." As more rock 'n' roll started to make
its way onto the pop charts, he kept playing the sounds on his radio
show as well as hosting live stage shows billed as Robin Seymour's
Original Rock 'n' Roll Revue. "We put these shows on at the old
Riviera Theater on Grand River at Joy Road and we had headliners
like Chuck Berry, Frankie Lyman and the Teenagers, and a lot of
local talent as well," recalls Seymour.[5]

Frankie Lyman and the Teenagers were back with Robin at the
Fox theater on June 21, 1956, on the strength of their second
smash hit, "I Want You to Be My Girl." Also on the bill were
LaVern Baker, still riding the crest of "Tweedle Dee," Lonnie
Donegan and his Skiffle Group from Scotland, who had a top-ten
hit with "Rock Island Line," and the Rover Boys, featuring Billy
Albert and their version of "Graduation Day." The Royal Jokers,
Bobby Lewis, Eileen Rodgers, the Johnny Burnette Trio, and the
Cleftones filled out the evening. WEXL's Ben Johnson and
CKLW's Bud Davies were co-emcees.

Although licensed to Dearborn, WKMH was programming to the greater Motor City area and maintained additional offices and studios in Detroit to help support their identification as a Detroit station.

Remembering the publicity that Ed McKenzie had generated with his comments on Vaughn Monroe in the forties, Robin decided to do something similar. "You have to remember that it was every man for himself in those days," he says. "There was really not much thought as to station image, it was your show that mattered and whatever you could do to get people to tune in. Just as Elvis was taking off, I got on the air and said I wasn't going to play his records because the way he moved was so 'objectionable.' That's about as strong a language as you were allowed to use back then. I thought he was great but I wanted to get some attention. Well, a couple of hundred kids came over and picketed in front of my house and the *Detroit Times* ran a big story about the whole thing. Then I went back on the air and sort of gave in, saying, 'Okay, if you want to hear him, I will play his records!'" laughs Seymour.

Financially, he was doing great. Like Ed McKenzie and Fred Wolf at WXYZ, Robin was being paid commission on the spots that aired on his show, which was now on from 3:30 P.M. to 7:00 P.M. "I started out making ninety cents an hour and wound up making $90,000 a year," claims Seymour.

"Robin didn't have the greatest voice around, especially in the beginning," recalls Bill Randle, "but he had so much energy and worked really hard to get to the top. His greatest talent, though, was his ability to 'find the money.' I mean, if there was five bucks to be made cutting a ribbon at a supermarket opening, he was gonna be there first."[6]

Other voices on WKMH in the early fifties included Joe Van in the morning and Frank Sims middays. Also very popular with the station's young listeners was Don McKinnon, who hosted the "Scotch Plaid Spotlight" and would sometimes appear in public dressed in a Scottish kilt.

WKMH jingle from 1956:

> *W-K, W-K, W-K-M-H*
> *Is 1310 on Your Dial*

## CHAPTER 4

# "He's a Rockin' Mo-chine"

ON A RAINY SUNDAY AFTERNOON IN THE SPRING OF 1956, police were called to the scene of a disturbance in a usually calm, middle-class neighborhood in northwest Detroit. They arrived to find what looked like a potentially volatile situation, as several thousand teenagers were beginning to overflow the small street. Cars were parked haphazardly and neighbors were cautiously observing the goings-on from the safety of their front porches, while lawns around them were turned into mush. Upon further investigation, it was found that the crowd had gathered by invitation of a local disc jockey who had recently moved into the neighborhood.[1] "They're all my good buddies and good gals" was the only explanation given for the party.[2]

WHO'S THE *HIPPEST* CAT IN TOWN? Gotta be Mickey Shorr, baby, playing that new rock 'n' roll music every night on WJBK's "Party Line." At 6'4" Shorr was as tall as he was hip. Peering out through wide lenses, he viewed a world brimming with opportunities–he just needed the time to take advantage of as many as possible.

On the air, in a medium-pitch voice, Shorr had what could be described as an infectious enthusiasm for the music and was even known to open the mike during a really hot record, such as Little Richard's "Long Tall Sally" or the El Dorados' "At My Front Door" (Crazy Little Mama) and yell "Go, man, go!"[3] He was the epitome of the "hep cat," speaking with a definite swagger in a cool but upbeat delivery: "Oh, man, you're not gonna *believe* how *good* this record is!" he would guarantee his listeners. There were any number of square-sounding white disc jockeys around the country starting to use supposedly hip lingo such as "cool," "man," and "hey, Dad." The difference with Mickey Shorr was that no matter what the words were, he sounded hip, like a "real gone" bass player in a jazz combo.

Rhythm and blues deejay "Joltin' Joe" Howard recalls that he and his fellow announcers, teased Shorr that he sounded more black than they did. "Mickey was very creative in a spontaneous way and he would come up with some pretty wild things right out of the air."[4]

One evening Shorr got a little bored giving the time checks between records and started to refer to the clock as the "time-tellin' mo-chine,"[5] and instead of saying it's six after ten he would say, "It's a half dozen after a sawbuck on 'JBK," or rather than two minutes past the hour he would make it "two hairs past a freckle." This routine really caught on and pretty soon it became his trade-mark and the only way listeners wanted to hear the time.

Mickey Shorr was one of the most colorful and flamboyant characters in Detroit radio history as well as in business. Born Moses Shorr on the west side of the city in 1926, he attended Chadsey High School before dropping out at fifteen to help sup-port his family, his father having died several years earlier. Unpleasant jobs in warehouses and bakeries made him yearn for something better than hauling around two-hundred-pound sacks of salt and flour. He started to hang around CKLW, running errands and doing whatever needed to be done for the popular morning team of Joe Gentile and Ralph Binge. Joe's brother Larry, who handled CK's all-night show, took a liking to Mickey and gave him tips on how to get started in a radio career.[6]

Shorr landed his first radio job at WLEU in Erie, Pennsylvania, where he did station breaks, played a few records, and swept the floor for $22.50 a week.[7] He came back to Michigan to work for WHLS in Port Huron. While employed there, the manager asked him to fill in for the sports director and call a boat race. Shorr did-n't have a clue as to where to begin. "I went out to the middle of the lake in an outboard boat with a shortwave radio and a mike," he recalled in an interview.[8] "There I was with all these powerboats going in circles around me. I not only had to make the drivers' names jive with the boat numbers, but also try to keep my boat from flipping in the backwash! To this day, I don't think listeners know which boat won." It was a typical Shorr adventure.

Like Robin Seymour, Mickey had taken advantage of the scarcity of trained announcers available during the war and was hired by Ed McKenzie for the all night show at WJBK midway through 1944.[9] It was a short stay as he was soon drafted and sent to Fort Lewis, Washington, to begin a two-year stint in the army. On the final day of basic training, he suffered a broken back and spent the next year and a half in the hospital. During this time, the ever resourceful Shorr wrote and produced the first "all-patient" show. After the presentation on the post, he received an offer to stage it at the Palamar theater in Seattle, and he spent his last six months in Special Services, where he continued to produce enter-tainment shows.

After discharge, Shorr wound up in Baltimore working as a bouncer and funnyman in a small burlesque house before return-ing to Detroit in 1947 and setting up a used car business called Joe's Jalopies in the heart of the used car district on Livernois.[10] The business failed but he moved on to start a seat cover company with his brother Jack. Mickey had also returned to radio for a while late at night at WKMH, but with the seat cover business heating up, he let the radio work slide.

Looking for ways to promote their Shorr Seat Cover Store on Grand River,[11] Mickey and his brother put the company name and caricature–"the bright yellow shack by the railroad track"–on a T-shirt as a giveaway in 1949. It may well have been the first promo-tional T-shirt in Detroit and maybe in the country.[12]

Rather than relying on standard ads, Mickey started to buy blocks of time on different stations, where he did his own program and pitched his leopard skin and furry model seat covers. He was so good that a car dealer hired him to do the same for his business. Before long, Harry Lipson, the general manager at WJBK, con-vinced him that he ought to be on the radio full-time. So, in June of 1955, Mickey Shorr left the seat covers behind and took to the air in the evening from seven to twelve-thirty, not exactly sure of what sort of program he would be doing.

After Mickey had spent a few nights playing the same white pop records as everyone else, a tire salesman and part-time song plugger named Nat Tarnapol dropped by the station. Tarnapol was white but he loved r&b music and spent a lot of time hanging around Al Green's Flame Show Bar, a showcase for black entertainment in the Motor City. A hustler, he liked to pass himself off as Green's partner, but was essentially an assistant. In a late-fifties interview, Shorr gave Tarnapol credit for leading him toward rock 'n' roll. "Nat came in and said, 'Mickey, I haven't got a single song that is any good right now, but I want to give you a tip—get with rock 'n' roll music.'"[13] Tarnapol came down to the 'JBK studios every evening for a couple of months and helped pick the records.

Shorr caught on quick and started to program more and more of the early rock 'n' roll, much of which was really rhythm and blues being presented under a new banner. His theme song was a thumping, churning rendition of "Night Train" by the Buddy Morrow big band, and with the horn section pumping in the background, the ON THE AIR sign would light up: "Hi, all you good gals and good buddies! This is Mickey Shorr! Got in my drive mo-chine today and came down to the station, just to talk to you and spin a platter or two!"[14]

He was wailing with Ruth Brown, the Clovers, and the early Drifters, as well as mixing in a little blues from Howlin' Wolf and Muddy Waters. Then, a friend in the talent-booking business, Art Shurigan, called to say he had picked up a good record down South—"some hillbilly singer."[15] Mickey Shorr jumped on the sound and was the first disc jockey in Detroit to play Elvis Presley when he threw the Sun recording of "Mystery Train" on the turntable in September of 1955. "The music made me high and I would sometimes pound on the table to the beat," Shorr recalled years later.[16]

If Robin Seymour had waded into "lake rock 'n' roll," Mickey Shorr jumped in head first and had no reservations about identifying himself with the music. He was even promoted as "WJBK's rock 'n' roll DJ."

He was picking up lots of new fans with gimmicks such as

"Make It or Break It," where he would introduce a new record each night and have the audience vote on it.[17] He was credited with breaking a number of great r&b hits, including "When You Dance" by the Turbans. He was also grabbing attention by letting listeners call in and interview artists on the air.

Rock 'n' roll and Mickey Shorr were proving to be a red-hot combination. More and more kids were tuning to 1500 every evening to hear Detroit's first "fire-breathing rock 'n' roll disc jockey" lay down their kind of music: "Remember good buddy and good gal–if you're in your driving mo-chine: 'Pavolia!'"[18] Pavolia was a special code word that Shorr shared with Detroit teenagers that translated into: be safe, be cool, and you are tuned to the right station.

"Mickey was a great personality and there was no doubt that people tuned in to hear him and not just the records," says pioneer broadcaster Robin Seymour.[19] "When Mickey was on WKMH, he was just too wild and unpredictable for the owners there and they let him go. I don't think they realized how talented he was."

A promoter and entrepreneur at heart, Shorr loved to be in the middle of the action. In September of 1955, he and fellow 'JBK deejay Don McLeod staged a fifty-nine-hour marathon in the front window of Grinnell's downtown music store to raise money for the Torch Drive.[20] In November, he put on his first rock 'n' roll stage show at the Riviera theater. This led to the really big Rock 'n' Rollorama, staged at the Fox theater in January of 1956. There were lines of excited fans jamming the lobby and stagedoor entrances hours before showtime. The three-day engagement featured rhythm and blues acts, such as the Cadillacs, hot on the charts with "Spee-do," the Cleftones, the Chuckles, and a young Detroit songstress named Della Reese, among others. Three rock 'n' roll sextets blasted away and in the middle of it all was the big man himself, cavorting on stage in a wild Hindu headdress, revving the audience into a frenzy as he brought on the acts.

The show was a smash,[21] grossing $57,400 and breaking the house record set by the comedy team of Martin and Lewis five years earlier. More than forty-two thousand rock 'n' rollers attended. Only a few weeks earlier, Alan Freed of WINS in New York, the self-crowned "king of rock 'n' roll," put on his Holiday Jubilee at the New York Academy of Music. His gross was

$150,000, but that figure represented a twelve-day run.[22] Also in New York at the same time, disc jockey Dr. Jive staged his big revue at the Brooklyn Paramount, where he grossed $85,000 over seven days. Mickey's Detroit grosses were earned over three days, making his daily gross about $19,000 compared with daily grosses of about $12,500 for Freed and Dr. Jive in the Big Apple. Mickey's wife, May Shorr, was present at the Fox shows: "The place was packed and everyone was having a great time," she remembers. "There was a lot of clapping and whistling but there was absolutely no trouble or bad behavior by the audience. In fact, I don't recall problems at any of Mickey's shows."[23]

In March, Shorr was back on stage emceeing a big show at the Olympia starring Bill Haley and the Comets, who were then at their peak of popularity.[24]

Shorr was hot! An item in a national trade publication told the story: "Mickey Shorr (WJBK Detroit) building impressively with the teenagers. He has been especially successful in putting over rhythm and blues with a pop audience."[25]

Shorr was *too* hot, it seemed, for WJBK, who had been taking a different kind of heat from conservative listeners concerned with the bad reputation rock 'n' roll was developing through the media, in films such as *Blackboard Jungle* and songs such as "Black Denim Trousers."[26] Also of concern was Shorr's growing influence on teenagers. In a meeting, station management told Mickey that they simply wanted to take a "different direction" in the evening hours and move Gentile and Binge into his spot.

WKMH's Robin Seymour, in a newspaper column at the time, gave his take on the situation, saying that WJBK's reasons for dropping Shorr "sort of remind one of some of the reasons the Citizens Councils down South are giving for their tirades against what they call 'Negro' music." Although he took credit for playing rock 'n' roll first, Seymour added that it was "entrenched by Shorr on that station [WJBK] during the evening hours till midnight." Seymour went on to say that Mickey was "one of the biggest sellers of this brand of music for numerous distributors in Detroit" and that Shorr had "brought more listeners regardless of their ages or colors to WJBK, but it so happens that too many white kids are getting too interested in what Elvis Presley, the Flamingos and Frankie Lyman and the Teenagers are up to. It doesn't make some of the conservative folks happy. It ends up with certain executives cutting off their noses to spite their faces."[27]

So, despite high ratings and advertising revenue, Mickey Shorr was out at WJBK as of April 28, 1956.

He went, but not without a bang. Record distributors had planned a little farewell party to be held at Shorr's new home in northwest Detroit on Sunday. Smelling an opportunity, Mickey got on the air on his final show the night before and invited listeners to "drop by the house tomorrow and say hello."[28] Chaos ensued when thousands descended on his block, parking cars wherever they could find room. Ground zero in this was 20191 Stansbury, where the neighborhood's newest residents resided. "It was unbelievable," remembers his wife, May. "We had only been living in the house for two weeks when Mickey made this announcement. People were arriving by car and cab and on foot."

Disbelieving neighbors looked on from their porches as the kids milled around chanting "We want Mickey!" Police from the Palmer Park station had to be called and they roped off the end of each block to prevent traffic tie-ups. Television and newspaper reporters showed up to see Shorr being mobbed by kids seeking an autograph or just trying to catch a glimpse of Detroit's number one main rock 'n' roller, who they felt had been unfairly dumped by WJBK. The fans, feeding on pop and chips, hung around all afternoon and then stayed on to help clean up. "We had to replace our lawn, as well as some others, then I didn't want to show my face in the neighborhood!" admits May Shorr.[29]

Mickey's big block party only added to his bigger than life reputation and provided a million dollars' worth of publicity. It was probably the last time that WJBK or any other station in town would give a disc jockey advance notice before dismissal.

Shorr was off the air but went ahead with another smash stage show at the Fox theater, taking it on the road to Chicago and throughout Michigan and Ohio. He continued to write a record column for the *Detroit Free Press* and appeared regularly in *Teen Life*, a local paper geared to youth. It was obvious that Mickey Shorr would be a valuable commodity for the station willing to unleash him on its airwaves. There were radio offers from other cities but he wanted to stay in Detroit.

By July 27, 1956, *Teen Life* ran the headline: MICKEY SHORR MAY

BE BACK! The story went on to say that "Shorr was in negotiation with another Detroit station." That station turned out to be WXYZ, the ABC-owned operation that, like other network affiliates, was looking for ways to replace fading network and short local programs. Finally, in August, came the announcement that Mickey would be joining WXYZ starting August 27, for an hour each evening, between seven and eight. There wasn't any more time available, but the station was trying to clear network space.[30]

Now, at the 1270 spot on the dial, where the Lone Ranger had ridden off into a radio sunset, Mickey Shorr arrived with 45 rpms blazing, as WXYZ, a network-owned and operated station, dared to rock 'n' roll. Shorr's impact was immediate and by October 29, 1956, the familiar strains of "Night Train" could be heard opening his show in its new expanded time slot of 7:15 to 10:00 P.M. Monday through Saturday as the last vestiges of ABC network programming dissolved in the evening.

> Okay, you've got Mickey Shorr with a load of big hits on the "Night Train" from the "Station of the Stars." That's WXYZ! *[music begins]* Here's one of the of the most popular records around the Motor City. You just *can't* resist the beat of "The Fool," from Sanford Clark!

As he did on 'JBK, Shorr operated with "no set policy." In a 1956 interview, Mickey explained his programming philosophy, which demonstrates how much new material was getting exposed: "I try to program two current favorites, one new and one standard out of every four records I play. So, out of a hundred new records I get each week, only about four an hour get on the air. You simply have to play the records you feel will do the show the most good. If you play one and the response is good, you keep playing it—if not, you drop it."[31]

Bill Hennes was a high school student who entered a contest to be Mickey's assistant. "I actually came in second, but Mickey liked me, so I got the job," recalls Hennes. "I got to come to the station every night and help him pick the songs. Mickey was just over thirty and I think he wanted to have a younger opinion on the records."[32]

Fellow Wixie deejay Paul Winter remembers that Shorr "was

sensitive to black culture and so was more open than others to the new black artists turning out r&b and early rock 'n' roll."[33] Ed McKenzie felt that Mickey had a good feel for what was happening in the market: "Mickey realized the potential, he was more of a rock 'n' roller than I was."[34]

By early 1957, Shorr had moved into television with a daily half hour show called "Mickey's Record Room," from 4:30 to 5:00 P.M., featuring dancing and conversation with record artists. It stayed on until channel 7 started to carry the nationally televised "American Bandstand" with Dick Clark in the fall.

According to May Shorr, Mickey would wake up at night with new ideas not only for his show, but also for other wild business schemes. "Mickey had this idea that there should be a way to freeze pizza, so he and Larry Gentile started a frozen pizza business. They hustled and got a big order from A & P. They were both still on the radio and probably should have kept a closer eye on things at the plant because there was an electrical malfunction and all these pizzas they had stocked for A & P spoiled and they had to get them hauled off. It was the end of their pizza empire," she laughs.[35]

Fellow deejay Bob Cordell spent a lot of time with Mickey and agrees that there was always something going on: "I was with Mickey and he had this big black hearse back in the late forties. We had it parked in front of the Fisher Building and we were selling electric razors out of it, don't ask me how that came about."[36]

While the pizza went cold, Shorr's rock 'n' roll empire continued to heat up. "Record Stars of '57" was his newest stage show, presented March 15, 16, and 17 at the Michigan theater.[37] Headlining was blind vocalist Al Hibbler, doing his big hits: "Unchained Melody," "He," and "After the Lights Go Down." All three had reached the national top ten. Texas rockabilly artists Buddy Knox and the Rhythm Orchids blasted out the nation's current number one record, "Party Doll," and, with Jimmy Bowen on lead with the same group, did "I'm Sticking with You." Otis Williams and the Charms pounded out their big r&b crossover hit of late 1954, "Hearts of Stone," plus "Ling, Ting, Tong" from 1955 and the more recent "Ivory Tower."

Rhythm and blues diva Ruth Brown was there doing "Lucky Lips." El Boy, Cathy Carr, The Federals, and Dick Jacobs rounded out the bill, with the Sil Austin band on backup. Another impressive gross assured future shows.

"Big Mick" kept up the momentum, pulling off the media coup of the year.[38] Elvis Presley was on tour and being chased by journalists from the largest newspapers and magazines as well as disc jockeys and publicity people. Out of perseverance, and possibly a close friendship with RCA records artists and repertoire (A&R) person Steve Sholes, Shorr scooped them all when he traveled to where Presley was performing in Chicago and taped a 2½-hour exclusive interview with the hottest rock star in the world.

Back in Detroit, Mickey announced that Elvis Presley would be a guest on an upcoming show. In the next few days, more than fourteen thousand people phoned WXYZ, wanting to know where the interview would take place.[39] Callers were told that the show would be "conducted from an unknown spot to prevent riots." Then, on March 29, 1957, Elvis was the featured guest on Mickey's show for the entire three hours. Shorr topped it all off by serving as emcee for Elvis's one-nighter at the Olympia two days later. It was a sell-out, with thirty-two thousand people attending two performances. Tickets were priced at $4.50 top.

In April, Mickey was back with his "Rock 'n' Rollorama," Easter edition, at the Broadway-Capitol theater.[40] Pioneering rhythm and blues performers Amos Milburn and Red Prysock were featured along with Faye Adams, who performed her early r&b hits "Shake a Hand" and "I'll Be True." The Coasters, who were new on the scene and included two members of the former Robins, did "Smokey Joe's Cafe" and their current release, "Youngblood." Also on the bill were Johnny and Joe with "Over the Mountain," the Mello-Tones from Detroit with "Rosie Lee,"and a new rockabilly singer from the Motor City suburb of Hazel Park named Jack Scott, who had recently signed with the ABC-Paramount label and was promoting his first release, called "Baby, She Is Gone."

Mickey was on top of everything, including charity work, donating time to helping polio victims, and arranging for other handicapped kids to be special guests at his concerts. As a member of the Variety Club, he started turning over all duplicate copies of the promotional records he received, and the suitable ones were distributed to children's hospital wards. He urged other area deejays to do the same.[41] Shorr also campaigned for safe driving and was trying to get a drag strip built for use by teenagers.

In mid-August, Mickey presented his "Star Summer Spectacular" at the Shubert theater. "Frantic" Ernie Durham of WJLB was co-emcee for the show. Headlining was Fats Domino, coming off an incredible chart run with "Ain't That a Shame," "I'm in Love Again," "Blueberry Hill," "Blue Monday," and "I'm Walking."[42] He had already sold well over twelve million records. In the summer of 1957, only Elvis was bigger. Billy Williams and his Quartet shared the top of the bill. He had a big record with "I'm Gonna Sit Right Down and Write Myself a Letter," where he calls out "Oh, yeah!"

Also on stage was a new Canadian artist named Paul Anka doing "Diana," the current number one song in the country, and the Bobbettes with their hit "Mr. Lee." JoAnn Campbell, "the Blonde Bombshell" from Alan Freed's New York shows, brought the boys to the edge of their seats as she rocked hard in skin-tight outfits.

Six-foot four-inch, three hundred-pound Shorr wasn't about to be outdone as he dominated the stage, looking like some sort of rock 'n' roll gladiator, dressed in a suit made of what appeared to be metal shingles.

On radio, Mickey Shorr was still operating on a rock 'n' roll island every night on WXYZ, being followed by Jack Surrell, who played his piano in between records that leaned toward jazz, and preceded by an hour of news and information on "Assignment: The World." Ed McKenzie had a mostly contemporary show in the afternoon, but Mickey was the one shaking the studio walls as he spun rock 'n' roll discs on his "beeootiful record playin' mo-chine."

Shorr seemed to be everywhere in 1957–radio, TV, stage, record hops, and charity events. He was a rockin' mo-chine that never missed a beat. His high-powered oratory on the music kept him high in the ratings and on the list of stops for independent record promoters, including the Chess brothers from Chicago, who viewed him as one of the key disc jockeys in the Midwest when it came to influencing hit records.[43] They were all there to pitch new releases to the guy who could make 'em or break 'em.

WHILE MICKEY SHORR WAS ROCKING at night at WXYZ, Fred Wolf was another story in the morning. Because of his strong ratings, he saw no reason to play music that he neither liked nor understood.[44] Although Shorr and McKenzie were playing more rock 'n' roll, there would be no "Hound Dog" or "Tutti Frutti" on the "Fred Wolf Show."

Two years earlier, in 1955, all live music and dramatic programs had ceased production at WXYZ and only the ghosts of "The Lone Ranger" and "The Green Hornet" were occupying the large wood-paneled studios where the Trendle actors had performed live each evening for so many years. In a cost-cutting move, station president Jimmy Ridell had made plans to sell the great Mendelssohn Mansion and move radio operations to the caretaker's cottage at the transmitter site at Joy Road and Greenfield.

Fred Wolf had panicked at the thought of losing his famous Wigloo and getting trapped inside again. So he arranged for one of his sponsors, the McDonald trailer company, to customize a thirty-foot trailer, installing three sides of glass at the back end just like he had in his permanent booth.[45] Now Wolf's Wacky Wigloo became the Wandering Wigloo.

To communicate with his producer, who would be playing records and commercials back at the station, Fred had a second off-the-air microphone installed. Wearing a headset, Fred would hear the programming in one ear and his producer in the other.

Instead of the sales department just selling a remote for a flat fee, Fred used the Wandering Wigloo as an enticement for sponsors to sign longer contracts. A local Desoto dealer was happy to provide a white convertible with Fred's name on it, to haul the trailer around town. By reacting in a swift, timely fashion, Fred had gone mobile and his Wandering Wigloo was a huge commercial success.

Soon, he and the other Wixie deejays, including Mickey Shorr, would be broadcasting from car lots, paint stores, shopping centers, and anywhere else a salesperson could sell a remote in the Detroit area. Fred Wolf may not have done much to promote rock 'n' roll, but he was a major innovator and, as a highly rated morning man, contributed (like it or not) to the success of one of the stations that would become synonymous with playing rock 'n' roll.

A new record fails to make the grade with "Jack the Bellboy" (Ed McKenzie). 1948. *Courtesy of Marilyn Bond Legends in Music Collection*

WJBK promo targets advertisers. *Courtesy Ed McKenzie*

**59 ADVERTISERS**

Reaping greatest results ever with

**Jack The Bellboy**

the nation's greatest Salesman

*DAILY ON WJBK*

Capture 25.4% of Detroit's Listening Audience*

Let

**America's Favorite Disc-Jockey**

Sell Merchandise For You

*According to C. E. Hooper - October, 1950

REPRESENTATIVE

1490 kc
Same Programs
on WJBK-FM
Channel 226
93.1 Megacycles

TOM HARKER - NATIONAL SALES MANAGER
NATIONAL SALES OFFICE OF THE FORT INDUSTRY COMPANY
488 Madison Ave., New York
Eldorado 5-2455

Sec. 34.66 P. L. & R.

WJBK's "Jack the Bellboy" swamped by fan mail again. *Courtesy Ed McKenzie*

Eddie Chase enjoys a joke backstage with band leader Kay Kyser and vocalists Ginny Simms and Harry Babbit. 1943. *Courtesy Eddie Chase*

Eddie Chase, host of Detroit's "Make Believe Ballroom," at WXYZ in 1942. *Courtesy Eddie Chase*

Eddie (below left) strikes a more than similar pose with Tommy Dorsey. Photo taken after "Make Believe Ballroom" moved to CKLW in the late 1940s. *Courtesy Eddie Chase*

"Kings of the morning," Gentile and Binge go at it to the delight of fans at a Sears store appearance in 1943. *Courtesy Ralph J. Binge Jr.*

"Happy Joe's Early Morning Frolic." Left to right: Ralph Binge, Joe Gentile and Toby David. 1938. *Courtesy Ralph J. Binge Jr.*

Along with big ratings, Gentile and Binge drew big mail. *Courtesy Ralph J. Binge Jr.*

Toby David at the WJR mike in 1946. After returning to Detroit, his first assignment was to read the comics from the newspapers on Sunday morning as "Uncle Toby." He referred to this photo as "Nasty Toby." *Courtesy Toby J. David*

WJBK promo from 1948. At 6'7" Bob Murphy was the "Tall Boy." On his early evening show he occasionally sang along with the records he played.

*At Grinnell's*

WJBK's
**TALL BOY**
IN THE 3rd ROW
**Bob Murphy**
will broadcast at 2 p.m.
Saturday .. during
*Grinnell's*
ANNUAL
**RADIO AND TELEVISION**
**EXPOSITION**
Get Your Co...

Bill Randle played hot jazz throughout the 1940s on WJLB's "Interracial Goodwill Hour."

Now on

WXYZ

every weekday from

4 to 6 $^{\underline{15}}$ PM

"JACK the BELLBOY"

BEGINNING **TOMORROW**, MONDAY, FEBRUARY 4TH at a different spot on your dial! Yes, the one, the only **JACK THE BELLBOY** will be spinning your favorite records over **WXYZ**! Don't forget the time, 4 to 6:15 p.m.! And don't forget the station, **WXYZ**!

W X Y Z

A large newspaper ad announces that "Jack the Bellboy" (Ed McKenzie) is switching stations. February 4, 1952. *Courtesy Ed McKenzie*

Ed McKenzie and Louis Armstrong share a good time around 1954. *Courtesy Ed McKenzie*

Frontal view of the "Wacky Wigloo" at Jefferson and Iroquois. *Courtesy Emily Wolf*

Fred Wolf broadcasting from inside the "Wacky Wigloo," facing Jefferson Avenue, about 1953. *Courtesy Emily Wolf*

Fred Wolf of WXYZ–Detroit's legendary morning radio personality. *Courtesy Emily Wolf*

Publicity photo for WXYZ's Jack Surrell who broke the color barrier in 1952 with his "Top of the Town" show. *Courtesy Jack Surrell*

Caricature shows Jack at the "Top of the Town."

Ad for Jack Surrell's television show, "Sunday With Surrell," which ran on Channel 7 from 1953 to 1959.

Detroit's Most
*Sensational*
DISC JOCKEY

HEADLESS
HORSEMAN

...he's running away
with the town!

Another Terrific Selling
WJBK
Feature 6:30 to 7:30 P.M. Daily
Take it from Hooper!
More Listeners than 5 other
Detroit Stations at the Same Time

Headless Horseman has been making
headlines in Detroit for 2 years! And,
he really gets results for participating
advertisers . . . a few spots available
at quickly.

Ralph Binge as
"Beautiful Carl" on the
"Headless Horseman"
show at WJBK in 1953.
Carl was president of
"Marriage, the Living
Death Society." *Courtesy
Ralph J. Binge Jr.*

In the Detroit
Area it's

CKLW

50,000
WATTS
800 KC.

This powerful radio voice is hitting
a 17,000,000 population area in
5 important states and is open to
advertisers at the lowest rate of
any major station in this region.
A tremendous buy for action and
sales that is establishing new records daily. Get the facts now.

CKLW
Guardian Bldg., Detroit 26
J. E. Campeau, President
Adam J. Young, Jr., Inc., Nat'l Rep.
Mutual Broadcasting System

CKLW promoted its vast
coverage area to poten-
tial advertisers in 1954.

WJBK's popular afternoon
disc jockey, Don McLeod, in
1955. His show originated
from "McLeodsville U.S.A."

Toby David hams it up with Tony
Bennett at the CKLW studios in
1955. *Courtesy Toby David*

Bob Maxwell on a WWJ remote broadcast.
*Courtesy Bob Maxwell*

Sammy Davis Jr. drops in on "Ed McKenzie's
Saturday Party" on WXYZ-TV in 1955.
*Courtesy Ed McKenzie*

(Above) WXYZ's Ed McKenzie chats with
band leader Harry James at a social function in 1956. Seated at left is Mrs. Harry
James, Betty Grable. At right, WWJ's Bob
Maxwell. *Courtesy Bob Maxwell*

Dinah Shore greets WJR's Clark Reid and WWJ's Bob
Maxwell at an RCA party around 1954. Shore's husband,
George Montgomery looks on. *Courtesy Bob Maxwell*

## Robin Predicts

### By Robin Seymour WKMH

1. Yes, Tonight Josephine .................................... Johnnie Ray
2. Mule Skinner Blues ........................................ Joe D. Gibson
3. True Love Gone ............................................ Betty Madigan
4. My Faith, My Hope, My Love .............................. Roy Hamilton
5. A Little Lonliness ......................................... Kay St...
6. We Can't Sing Rythm and Blues ...... Patience and Prude...
7. Harem Dance ................................... Armenian Jazz Se...
8. I Love My Girl .......................... Cozy Morley, Hilltop...
9. Mama Guitar ..................... Don Cornell, Julius La...
10. Honey Man _____ Sammy Hayw...

Weekly feature of "Teen Life" magazine,
from April 1957.

WKMH promo from 1954.

**Everybody Likes**

# WKMH
### because
**Everybody Likes**

## NEWS
## MUSIC
## SPORTS

...and in Michigan, where
everybody drives, and 85%
of the cars have radios

### WKMH IS YOUR BEST BUY
### FOR OUT-OF-HOME LISTENERS!

| Look at these figures on | |
| --- | --- |
| **SHARE OF AUDIENCE** | |
| WKMH | 19 |
| Station B | 17 |
| Station C | 11 |
| Station D | 11 |
| Station E | 9 |
| Station F | 8 |

Pulse, July 1954, 12 noon to 6 p.m.
Monday through Friday.

Tell your story where
77% of Michigan's
buying power is
concentrated. Buy
the package
...WKMH,
Dearborn-
Detroit,
WKHM,
Jackson,
WKMF,
Flint.

SAVE **10%**
BUY MICHIGAN'S
GOLDEN
TRIANGLE!
WKMH Dearborn-Detroit

WKHM - Jackson    WKMF - Flint

**Everybody LIKES**

# WKMH

Frederick A. Knorr, Pres.
George Millar, Mg. Director
**Represented by HEADLEY-REED**

Ed McKenzie shakes hands with competitor Robin Seymour, around 1953. The two were on against each other for over a decade in Detroit. *Courtesy of Marilyn Bond Legends in Music Collection*

Robin Seymour of WKMH takes his popular "Bobbin' with Robin" show on remote in 1957. Seymour was the first disc jockey to play rock 'n' roll in Detroit. *Courtesy of Marilyn Bond Legends in Music Collection*

Mickey Shorr signs autographs in the lobby of Detroit's Fox Theater, January 1956.
*Courtesy May Shorr*

Newspaper ad for Mickey Shorr's Rock 'n' Rollorama at the Fox Theater, held January 21-23, 1956.
*Courtesy May Shorr*

"Welcome to the '50s." Mickey Shorr peers out from a crowd of fans in the lobby of the Fox Theater, January 1956.
*Courtesy May Shorr*

Mickey and friend backstage.
*Courtesy May Shorr*

WXYZ promos from 1957.
*Courtesy May Shorr*

Mickey Shorr on stage
at the Fox Theater for
Rock 'n' Rollorama.
January, 1956.
*Courtesy May Shorr*

WJLB's "Frantic" Ernie Durham, on stage at a 1956 record hop. *Courtesy of Marilyn Bond Legends in Music Collection*

Promo for Ernie Durham's nightime show. April, 1957.

Larry Dixon was known as the "Velvet Voice" on WCHB each afternoon. *Courtesy Larry Dixon*

"We're mobile!" WXYZ's Fred Wolf in front of the "Wandering Wigloo" in 1955.
*Courtesy Emily Wolf*

Front cover of WJBK's "Top Tunes Survey." Pictured on top are Clark Reid and Tom George and below, Don McLeod and Casy Kasem.

Inside WJBK's "Top Tunes Survey." June 3, 1957.

## W-J-B-K Hit Tunes
SURVEYED DAILY—PUBLISHED WEEKLY

BIG FOUR

1500 KC

### WAX WINNERS
FOR THE WEEK OF JUNE 3, 1957

# W ✶ J ✶ B ✶ K

| | TITLE | ARTIST | LABEL | LAST WEEK | | | TITLE | | |
|---|---|---|---|---|---|---|---|---|---|
| 1 | Love Letters In Sand | Pat Boone | Dot | 1 | 21 | Wonde | | | |
| 2 | Bye Bye Love | Everly Bros | Cadence | 3 | 22 | Don't C | | | Turabia |
| 3 | Start Movin' | Sal Mineo | Epic | | 23 | My B. | | | Mercury |
| 4 | Gonna Sit Rite Down, etc | Billy Williams | C | 21 | 24 | Ringo L | | | Gee |
| 5 | I Like Your Kind Of Love | Andy Williams | Cadence | | 25 | Fabulous | Charlie Gracie | Cameo | |
| 6 | Freight Train | Wisley/Draper | Chic Mer | | 26 | Crepadin | Harry Belafonte | Victor | |
| 7 | I'm Walkin | Ricky Nelson | Ve | | 2 | Rock Ballo | McGuire Sisters | Coral | |
| 8 | Rang Tang Ding Dong | The Cellos | Apol | 32 | 2 | Rockin No 4 | Ames Bros | Victor | |
| 9 | Shangri La | Four Coins | Epic | 2 | 2 | Valley O. Tears | Fats Domino | Imperial | |
| 10 | Four Walls | Jim Reeves | Victo | | 30 | Searching | Coasting | Atco | |
| 11 | Dark Moon | Gale Storm | | | 3 | ZOZA | Pitch Pipes | Mercury | |
| 12 | Girl With Golden Braids | Perry Como | Vic | | 32 | It's N I F . M T Say | Johnny Mathis | Columbia | |
| 13 | A Fallen Star | Newm /Noble | D /Mer | 25 | 33 | I Just Don't Know | Four Lads | Columbia | |
| 14 | A White Sport Coat | Marty Robbins | C lu, uia | 9 | 3 | Next Stop Paradise | Teddy Raadazzo | Vik | |
| 15 | Baby, She's Gone | Jay Scott | ABC | 1 | 35 | I'll Be T | J. Stafford | Columbia | |
| 16 | With All My Heart | Sandy Scott | Carlton | 20 | 3 | Little Wl.t Lies | Betty Chor o | I | |
| 17 | So Rare | Jimmy Dorsey | Fraternity | | 37 | D Y Em T OI M. Stev Allen | | | |
| 18 | Young Blood | | Al | | 3 | Rock Y Litt Baby B M, K | | Brell | |
| 19 | Teenage Romeo | R y Nelson | Verv | | 3 | Sugar C dy | Gogi Grant Gibbs | Victor | |
| 20 | Over The Mountain | J unie & Joe | Chess | 1 | 4 | Shepard I R | Sarah Leigh | Roulen | |

ALBUM OF THE WEEK
— ALONE —
by JUDY GARLAND
on Capitol

WINNER THIS WEEK'S
"LONLOH 10"
Contest
Betty Wetzel

Everyone is eligible to win
Listen To The BIG FOUR F

# W ✶ J ✶ B ✶ K 1500 ON YOUR DIAL

CLARK REID   TOM GEORGE   DON McLEOD   CASEY KASEM
## YOUR BIG FOUR

A STORER STATION

CKLW morning personality, Toby David, moves into television as Captain Jolly on Channel 9 in 1958. *Courtesy Toby David*

Ron Knowles, powered by 50,000 watts on CKLW's "Platter Express" in 1957. *Courtesy Ron Knowles*

Rock 'n' roll on television. Ed McKenzie with Chuck Berry on a 1956 broadcast of Ed's "Saturday Party" on Channel 7. *Courtesy Ed McKenzie*

A group of teenagers try to convince Bob Maxwell to play rock 'n' roll. *Courtesy Bob Maxwell*

WXYZ brass visit Fred Wolf on remote. Left to right: Jimmy Riddell, president; Hal Neal, who pushed the station toward Top 40; Fred Wolf, and program director Bob Baker. *Courtesy Emily Wolf*

Detroit radio personalities participate in a promotion at Doner Advertising in 1957. Left to right: Bob Maxwell of WWJ, Fred Wolf and Mickey Shorr of WXYZ and Casey Kasem of WJBK. *Courtesy Bob Maxwell*

"Let's rock!" CKLW's Bud Davies on "Detroit's Top Ten Dance Party," April 1956. The show was on from 5 to 6pm, Monday through Friday on Channel 9. *Courtesy of Marilyn Bond Legends in Music Collection*

CHAPTER 5

# "Frantically Yours"

EVERY EVENING, after foreign language programming in Polish and Greek, an audience craving some hot and heavy music would tune to 1400 on the dial and hear Detroit's top rhythm and blues disc jockey as he cranked up his theme song, an instrumental that started out with a repetitive guitar riff, followed by a wailing saxophone over a loping beat. Once the music had established itself, he would sail over the top:

> Ooo Wee! It's Ernie D on W-J-L-B! The host that loves your swingin' musical entertainment most! We're gonna play the best–later for the rest! I know you can't wait, so let's not hesitate! Time to call on Little Willie John! He's not gonna *leave* her, cause he's got the "Fever!"[1]

Ernie Durham, like Mickey Shorr, exploded on the Detroit airwaves in 1955. At the time, he was working for station WBBC, to the north in Flint, and for a while he tried to juggle both jobs. It was a daily exercise that made him "frantic." "I'd leave Flint with the theme for my show still playing because every minute counted and get to Detroit with my opening theme already playing. That's how close the time was," Ernie recalled in a later interview.[2] As in

Flint, Durham was one of the first deejays in Detroit (along with Robin Seymour) to do record hops.

While everyone knew him as Frantic Ernie and the station promoted him that way, it wouldn't have been cool to refer to himself like that, so he would say, "This is the Frantic One" or "Ernie D." When he wasn't spinning great rhythm and blues, he would be talking in rhymes and telling outrageous stories about a group of wild characters who inhabited his frantic world. Adapting different "Amos 'n' Andy"–style street voices, he would narrate and play the different parts:

> The otha' day, Hezekiah and Nicodemus were standin' on the corner, waitin' for the bus, when Oogie Coo came by and told 'em 'bout a party he went to over at Poppa Stoppa's. Oogie Coo said [*very high voice*], "Blah, blah, blah," and then Nicodemus said [*low voice*], "Blah, blah, blah."

And so on. This dizzying exchange was ad-libbed on the spot and could go on for two to three minutes, or as long as needed.

During his show, Durham would heartily recommend a locally produced wine: "You'll jump for *joy* when you meet Nature *Boy!*" and remind listeners to "reach for Dixie Peach," the hair straightener popular with blacks in those days, and in the most extreme case of mangling of the English language, Ernie would exclaim: "Be sure and ask for Colt 45 Jet Malt Liquor –it'll get ya' lit much more quicker!"[3]

On many nights, the show was broadcast from the Twenty Grand Night Club on John R., one of the top black entertainment venues in the Motor City. After burning down, the place had been spectacularly rebuilt, with a bowling alley downstairs and two big showrooms on the second floor. Tuning in WJLB, listeners would hear: "This is Ernie D for thee, live from the Gold Room of the Twenty Grand. Come on down, but don't goof, bring your proof, one lean green will get'cha on the scene!"

There would always be some hard-core r&b artist like a Walter Jackson on stage and lots of conversation and clinking glasses in the background. It all sounded quite exotic. Saying you listened to "Frantic Ernie" carried a certain amount of status for white kids who wanted to be ultracool. This wasn't "Jumping Gene" or

"Rocking Ray." It wasn't even "Frantic Freddie." "Frantic Ernie" just sounded so out of sync that he had to be for real. What Durham may have lacked in a big, deep voice he made up for with red hot energy. He had a unique cadence and sounded like no other as he rhymed the night away. He described his image as "happy, care-free and most frantic."[4] "Great googa mooga, shooga wooga! Welcome to another inning of spinning with Ernie Durham, your ace from inner space, on the swinging-est show on the ra-d-io! Let's cut the chatter an' roll another platter! It's 'Treasure of Love' from Mr. Clyde McPhatter!'"

It was a surprise to most people to find out that behind the wild on-air persona was a man with a master's degree in journalism from New York University, who had begun his broadcast career as a newsman. He was born Ernest Lamar Durham in Bronx, New York City, in 1919, the son of a banker and a nurse. Ernie put himself through school, selling pots and pans door to door in Harlem. By his mid-twenties, he was working for the famous black newspaper the *Pittsburgh Courier.* From there, he took a radio news position in New York.[5]

According to Ernie, the move from news to music came about when he had to fill in for a deejay in New York who got sick at the last minute. "I dug it very much, just from the first go-round," said Durham some time later. "I found it more exciting and more interesting." From then on it was good-bye news and hello rhythm and blues.[6]

In Flint, Ernie would wait to meet the bus that would deliver the latest stack of hot r&b records. Back at the station he would quickly give a listen and then put the ones he liked right on the air. His reputation grew and soon Booth Broadcasting wanted him on their Detroit station.[6]

According to "Joltin' Joe" Howard, Ernie was frantic only on the air. "Ernie was a seasoned businessman and he did not party or drink. At the end of his hops, he would wrap things up, move the kids out, and disappear. He didn't hang around the clubs and party like the rest of us," Howard laughs.[7] Other disc jockeys did like to hang around Ernie, and announcers, black and white, would make the pilgrimage to the Twenty Grand to say hi and catch the show. It is next to impossible to find anyone without something good to say about Ernie Durham.

Although he moved around the schedule over the years, Frantic Ernie was at his peak of popularity in the late fifties and early sixties with a four to six "Hubcap Caravan" show in the afternoon and a nightime show that got under way at 9:30. Jesse Belvin's recording of "Goodnight My Love" became Durham's closing theme. Ernie, along with Bristoe Bryant, who had shifted to mornings, gave many early Detroit hits their first spin. In his autobiography, *Smokey, Inside My Life,* Smokey Robinson recalls trying to study at night in his bedroom, a transistor radio plugged into his ear, waiting and hoping for Ernie to play his first release: "Please, Frantic Ernie, please play my song!"[8] Then, after "Rockin' Robin" and "Sweet Little Sixteen," the "Frantic One" lays on that new local sound "Gotta Job" and Smokey starts bouncing off the walls.

If Ernie Durham had been broadcasting on a fifty thousand-watter, he would have been a national cult figure. As it was, he remains a Motor City legend.

ELSEWHERE ON THE DETROIT RADIO DIAL, WJLB picked up some direct competition when WCHB, licensed to suburban Inkster, signed on the air November 7, 1956, as the first radio station in the country to be built from ground up by black owners. The station was owned by Dr. Haley Bell and Dr. Wendell Cox. The first voice heard on the 1440 frequency was that of "Joltin' Joe" Howard, coming in from WERD in Atlanta. Earlier, he had hosted the "Beehive" rhythm and blues show at KNUZ in Houston.[9] Also featured on the new station were "Long Lean Lanky" Larry Dean and the "Velvet Voice" Larry Dixon.

While WJLB's airtime was split between black programming and foreign language shows, WCHB was programmed 100 percent for the black community from 5:00 A.M. to sundown. "We literally put the whole station together, towers and all," says Joe Howard. "We were a little slow off the launch pad, but after a couple of months we really took off and grabbed a lot of audience away from 'JLB. The station had a little bit of everything on back then. We had a gospel show early in the morning and a little kids' show called 'Teeney Time' and there was a jazz show with George White. The rest of the time we played r&b. We were making a profit after only eight months, in spite of the fact that we came on the air too late to get all kinds of political money that would have fallen into our lap because it was an election year, but we did okay."[10]

Berry Gordy was an aspiring songwriter and he and his sister would come out to the station and ask "Joltin' Joe" and the guys to play their latest effort. "I broke a lot of records in those days, including the songs Berry wrote for Jackie Wilson, like "Reet Petite" and especially "Lonely Teardrops," which was a monster," says Howard.

In his autobiography, *To Be Loved*, Gordy recalls how "thrilled" he was the day he heard "Joltin' Joe" Howard from WCHB say, "And now folks, the hottest new record in the land 'Reet Petite' by Jackie Wilson!"[11]

Arriving a few months after "Joltin' Joe" was Larry Dixon. Originally from Denver, Colorado, Dixon worked on stations in Springfield, Massachusetts, and Hartford, Connecticut, before signing on with WCHB. Larry's friend Steve Allen advised him to be himself on the air, rather than sound like a lot of other deejays. So, in a world of fast-talking "daddios on the rad-dio," Dixon became the soft and seductive "Velvet Voice," floating out of Detroit speakers, never seeming to be in too much of a hurry.[12] The mellow, laid-back as well as articulate sound became his trademark, which was especially popular with the ladies.

From 3:30 P.M. to 5:30 P.M., he did his regular hit record show, competing with WJLB's Ernie Durham. At 5:30, Dixon sequed into an early evening program called "Sundown," where he played romantic jazz and shared philosophies.

Why was WCHB so successful? Larry Dixon: "WCHB served the community. What we tried to get across was that 'this is your station, this is your show,' and I think that's the way people related to it."

Larry Dixon was an innovator in a number of ways. He sold commercial time on his own show, which was normally not allowed at stations in markets the size of Detroit. Larry remembers telling the owners of the station that the "black buck is beautiful to the white man." In other words, instead of just going after local mom and pop business in the black community, he was going to bring in some major clients. "I went to agencies like BBD&O and accounts like Pepsi, Michigan Milk Producers Association, and Liggett and

Myers with ideas rather than just a rate card," says Dixon. "I sold Pepsi on sponsoring a chain of Youth Teen Clubs. I figured if the kids didn't have a club to go to, they would probably find a gang to join. The clubs were very successful and it was a way to bring someone like Pepsi onto a relatively new, untried station like WCHB."

For Liggett and Myers, Dixon sold the company on an idea in which each disc jockey on the station would have a nickname, like "Mr. Chesterfield" or "Mr. L&M." "For a while I was constantly on the go, but it paid off when all the agencies in town were buying us on a regular basis."

Larry also remembers the early days of Berry Gordy. "Berry was handling Marv Johnson and the two had written a record Marv recorded called "Come to Me," which we were laying on pretty heavy, and it became a big local hit."

Berry Gordy had used his last cent recording that song, pressing it and getting airplay.[13] He had no more resources to take the record to the next level. He then found out that United Artists Records in New York was interested in a deal in which they would distribute the record nationally.[13] Larry Dixon: "I had a relationship with Norm Ruben at United Artists and I contacted him on behalf of Berry and was able to arrange for them to pay for his airline ticket to New York. They really liked Marv and the song and instead of just agreeing to distribute the record, they bought Marv's contract and Berry Gordy came back to Detroit with twenty-five thousand dollars. Berry has never mentioned it," says Dixon, sounding a bit disappointed but without any bitterness.[14]

Besides his other activities, which included many record hops at the Graystone Ballroom, Larry found time to answer mail sent in from a huge fan club.

HE WASN'T A DISC JOCKEY, but Prophet Jones was well listened to on black radio in the mid-fifties. As leader of the Church of the Universal Triumph, the Dominion of God, Inc., he offered "love prayers" for cash and supposedly had a secret code for the numbers racket in Detroit.[15] Dressed all in white, he could be seen around town, driving a white Cadillac. Jones would show up at public appearances strutting his stuff, flanked by two bodyguards.[15]

A preacher who garnered a lot more respect was the Reverend

C. L. Franklin of the New Bethel Baptist Church, at Linwood and West Pennsylvania. His services were so popular and his sermons so powerful that WJLB persuaded him to have them carried on the air every Sunday night. There were forty-five hundred seats in the church, and the congregation included lots of aspiring talent from the surrounding neighborhood, including Mary Wilson and William "Smokey" Robinson. Also inspired by the church's great choir and guest singers such as Clara Ward were the pastor's two daughters, Erma and Aretha Franklin.[16]

## CHAPTER 6

# The Beat of the Top 40

WHEN MICKEY SHORR WAS FIRED FROM WJBK in late April of 1956, the station, for some reason, had moved the famous morning team of Gentile and Binge to evenings and put together a new morning program hosted by Clark Reid, who had been doing all-nights at WJR during the preceding four years.[1]

Midway through the year, Kemal (Casey) Kasem, who had been working as an all-purpose announcer and board operator at WJLB, was hired by WJBK as a newsman. It didn't last long. One day he was asked to fill in for the vacationing Gentile and Binge team. While away, the famous duo decided to call it quits, most likely because of their unhappiness at being moved from mornings to evenings and Joe's conflicting schedule announcing the Detroit Tigers. Casey was kept on as a deejay and when the ratings went up, 'JBK made it a permanent move.[2]

The son of Lebanese Druse parents, Kemal Amin Kasem graduated from Northwestern High School, and had got his first taste of broadcasting as an intern at city station WDTR in the summer of 1950. In the fall he started his first paying job, earning $5, as the usher on a Saturday morning program called "Quizdown," broadcast from the Detroit Institute of Arts with host Tom Waber, and carried over WXYZ.

61

At the same time he was attending Wayne University, Kasem was starring as "Scoop Ryan, Cub Reporter" in a Wayne Radio Guild–produced drama heard over WJR. Aimed at kids, the program followed the adventures of Scoop as he traveled the world covering big stories.

An engineer with whom he had worked on "Quizdown" told him that the producers of the nationally broadcast "The Lone Ranger," which originated from the studios of WXYZ, were looking for a new actor to play the role of Dan Reid, the Lone Ranger's nephew. "I auditioned but the part never became available," recalls Kasem. "I was lucky enough to be called upon to play various other roles on the show and I portrayed characters ranging in age from twelve to twenty."[3]

In 1952, he was drafted into the army and while stationed at Armed Forces Radio Headquarters in Taegu, Korea, Kemal set up a little production studio in a Quonset hut and learned the basics of being a disc jockey. Remembering back to 1949, he had been impressed when he heard CKLW's Eddie Chase count down the top hits on "Make Believe Ballroom." Now, in 1953, Kasem was doing his first countdown show on "Radio Kilroy" in Korea. "When I got to the number one song, which was 'Vaya con Dios' by Les Paul and Mary Ford, I mistakenly called it 'Go Buy a Dose,'" Kasem recalls, looking back to that first show.[4]

After getting out of the service in 1954, he returned home to Detroit and resumed studies at Wayne University as well as rejoining the cast of the "The Lone Ranger" and "Sergeant Preston of the Yukon." A WXYZ announcer gave him a tip that led to his job at WJLB, which helped augment his income, especially after the cancellation of the "Ranger."

Now, on WJBK in 1956, there were no scripts; it was just "Casey at the Mike" from seven to twelve-thirty every evening and, as Kasem remembers, it took a while to get it right. "When I first went on the air at WJBK, I guess I was looking around for a style. I had mainly been an actor on radio. Don McLeod, who did afternoons and was acting program director at the time, became my mentor, if you will. It was Don, who recommended I change my air name to Casey, which came from 'Case,' an off-the-air nickname friends had called me since high school. One day, after I had been there a couple of months, he called me over and in a very nice way told me that when he would be listening to me on his drive home, I was sounding an awful lot like him! I give Don credit for breaking this to me in a way that did not destroy my confidence. Anyway, I started to find myself on the air."

Casey never did think of himself as such a hot deejay in Detroit and he didn't do a lot of ad-libbing. "I decided I would concentrate my efforts at doing a great job on the commercials," he recalls. "Ed McKenzie had a wonderful way with the spots and there were a number of businesses in Detroit that owed their success to him. He just had great credibility and that's what I strived for."

While Casey was playing the hits, he had to stop every evening at ten to do "Sound Off," a half hour talk program built around community issues. "I went to management and said, 'You guys have to dump this program, it's throwing a wrench right in the middle of my show!' They told me that it was a public-service commitment and it was a popular feature on the station. I left that meeting feeling like these people didn't know what they were doing. When the Hooper ratings came out, guess which half hour of my show ranked the highest? That's right, 'Sound Off,'" he laughs.[5]

Casey Kasem hit at WJBK, just as the station was moving toward the new Top 40 sound. The often-told story describing the origin of Top 40 surfaced in 1954. Todd Storz, the president of Storz Broadcasting, and programmer Bill Stewart were in a tavern one evening and noticed how patrons kept playing the same songs over and over in the jukebox, and even at closing time, the waitress went back and played the same songs again. It became obvious that people might have a hard time tuning away from a station that was playing the top hits as they did on a jukebox. It worked for KOWH, the Storz station in Omaha, Nebraska, starting in 1955. That company then went on to buy stations and go Top 40 in markets such as New Orleans, Kansas City, Minneapolis, and Miami. At about the same time, broadcaster Gordon McLendon was doing a similar format at his station in Dallas, Texas, KLIF.

Clark Reid remembers when Top 40 came to WJBK. "I was hired by Harry Lipson, the general manager of WJBK, and it was a combined effort on the part of myself, along with Don McLeod and our record librarian, Rosemary McCann, that resulted in our 'Top Tunes Survey.' As far as I know, this was the first printed Top 40 style survey in town and you could pick it up at the record shops. Sometime in 1957, we had a new program director come in, by the name of Bob Martin. He changed the name of the record list to 'Formula 45,' which became the catch phrase for the station. We used to have Tuesday meetings to pick the records each week and the deejays could make suggestions and then Martin would go over store sales reports and the trade papers to come up with the list."[6]

Despite the station playlist, Clark says the disc jockeys still had quite a bit of freedom: "We could play a song five or six times during our show if we liked it and we could even add one or two on our own."

There was a countdown of the new "Formula 45" every Saturday morning, but Casey Kasem would have to wait a few years before he hosted this type of show. At WJBK Clark Reid did the honors. Program director Bob Martin also introduced singing jingles performed by a Hi-Los/Four Freshman-type group:[7]

*"At 1500 on your sound dial,*
*twenty-four hours a day.*
*It's the sound of music with the built-in smile,*
*on WJBK."*

The jingles, deejays, contests, and more consistent music policy really made 'JBK stand out, although the contests were far from spectacular. "Storer Broadcasting was a tightfisted organization and we hardly ever gave anything away," says Clark Reid. "To give you an idea of what I'm talking about, I remember one contest we had that was like a spelling bee. The winner got fifteen dimes! That was about it for our big money giveaways."[8]

Before coming to work in Detroit at WJR, Clark Reid broadcast on WAKR in Akron, Ohio, where he had the distinction of replacing the legendary Alan Freed when he moved up to WJW in Cleveland and started the "Moondog" show. They remained friendly over the years. Clark's nickname was "the Reid Keed," which came from a character in the *Terry and the Pirates* comic strip. His main theme song at 'JBK in the fifties was something called "Cornball No. 1" by the Commanders.

Although others have claimed to be first, it was, in fact, WJBK that broke through with the Top 40 sound full-time in Detroit in late 1956, making it (along with sister station WIBG in Philadelphia) one of the very first major-market Top 40 stations. Top 40, however, did not necessarily mean rock 'n' roll. These changes were being made just several months after the departure of Mickey Shorr, who the station felt had been rocking too hard. Most of the songs on the Top 40 list were not the hard r&b style that Shorr had featured.[9] Yes, there was Elvis and Little Richard, but also "Hot Diggity" by Perry Como, "No, Not Much" by the Four Lads, "Moonglow–Theme from Picnic" by Morris Stoloff, "The Wayward Wind" by Gogi Grant, and "Friendly Persuasion" by Pat Boone. More important was that there was more consistency in the music played throughout the day on WJBK, and a listener tuning in at 9:30 in the morning, 4:00 in the afternoon, or 8:00 at night would find basically the same music–hit records. It just so happened that rock 'n' roll records started appearing more frequently on the Top 40 charts, so the Top 40 stations attracted the youthful audience looking for rock 'n' roll. These stations projected a fresh, exciting presentation that also appealed to kids. Instead of having just a favorite deejay, kids could now have a favorite station, one that they could depend on to sound pretty much the same throughout the day.

Meanwhile, Mickey Shorr continued to program his own show at WXYZ, which was unique from what was on during the other times of the day at that station. In other words, people tuning in to hear show tunes with Paul Winter at lunchtime were not likely to be listening in the evening when Shorr was laying on Bill Haley and the Comets and Fats Domino.

How did some stations come to play rock and not others? "I don't recall that it was ever even considered at WWJ," remembers Bob Maxwell. "None of the announcers on 'J were in favor of programming any rock 'n' roll and the station was quite conservative, so it just wasn't an issue."

BY 1957, ROCK 'N' ROLL HAD STARTED TO SHOW UP on Radio 80 but they did not have the consistency of Top 40-formatted WJBK. "We really got more into the record show programming as the network shows dropped off," remembers Ron Knowles. "We were rocking pretty good by '57."[10]

Ron was heading up the "Platter Express" every evening from nine to midnight, playing mainly from listener requests, but not always. "For a while, a portion of my show was sponsored by 'Jerry's Record Mart,' which was really a front for Cadet Distributing, and I would be forced to play some pretty bad stuff, if that's what they were pushing," he confides.[11]

As a result of CKLW's fifty thousand-watt signal, Ron received mail from all over the eastern United States and Canada. "We used to get letters from ships at sea and one time someone sent us a recording they made of CKLW from Norway; it was pretty amazing," he recalls.[11]

In 1957, aside from "Hound Dog" Lorenz booming out from WKBW in Buffalo and John R and the crew on powerful WLAC from Nashville serving up rhythm and blues, the big clear-channel stations, including the powerful New York outlets, were featuring adult, old-line programming or live country music shows, such as the WLS "Barn Dance,"out of Chicago. So, for many of the kids growing up in small towns, throughout twenty-eight states and four Canadian provinces, scanning the dial, unable to pick up regional big-city stations, Ron Knowles was the messenger in the night, delivering fifty thousand watts of rock 'n' roll, from CKLW. Barely out of his teens and probably unaware of the influence he wielded, Knowles displayed a youthful enthusiasm for the music. On Thursday nights, he would play back a half hour of Elvis Presley's most requested hits

Very much a first-generation rock disc jockey, Ron could be heard to enthusiastically exclaim: "This is R. K., your swing and swaydeejay on CK',"[12] as he opened his nightly "Platter Express" with a driving big band version of "Take the 'A' Train."

Toby David was established in the morning at CKLW, where, in his warm but authoritative voice, he was serving up gimmicks such as his "Crazy Cash Contest,"offering listeners from one to fifty dollars for unusual items such as old dog tags and "Dewey for President" buttons.[12] By 1958, he was also appearing as kids' favorite"Captain Jolly" with Popeye cartoons on CKLW-TV in the early evening.

Although David, like other announcers, had made an embarrassing goof on the radio at one time or another, on television he really blew it. During one broadcast, some children who had been in the audience found their way out to the hall of the studio and were creating a lot of noise. Unaware that his mike was still open, Captain Jolly yelled: "Get those goddamned kids out of here!" This was not the typical reaction of Toby David, who really loved the kids and took his role seriously. After he sat down to talk with the *Detroit Free Press*, the paper ran a story attributing the comment to some technicians who were at work nearby, thus saving the broken hearts of kids all over the Detroit area.[13]

Back on CK' radio, Joe Van had moved over from WKMH to do middays, and Eddie Chase was still on in the late afternoon. As the big bands faded, Eddie started using a new custom theme song called "Magic Carpet," on his "Make Believe Ballroom." Vaughn Monroe and a chorus would invite listeners to take a trip: "There's nowhere we can't go–Eddie Chase will make it so." According to Ron Knowles, "Eddie was playing more hit records but stayed away from rock 'n' roll."

The personality with a huge following among teens at CK' was Bud Davies, who was doing a split shift, 1:30 to 3:30 in the afternoon and 7:30 to 9:00 in the evening. In between, Bud hosted "Top Ten Dance Party" on channel 9 where he flashed a great smile and a set of French cuff links across the screen each day. Bud had introduced Elvis Presley on stage to Detroit for the first time, at the Fox theater in July of 1956.


ED MCKENZIE'S TV SHOW WAS BEGINNING to reflect the growing influence of rock 'n' roll. When the show started, there was a lot of jazz mixed in with the more youthful acts. Louis Armstrong, Jimmy Rushing, and Joe Williams had been guests along with rockers such as Bill Haley and the Comets and LaVern Baker. Now the scales were tipping in favor of more teen-oriented acts. Smokey Robinson and his friends from Northern High, calling themselves the Five Chimes, won the talent show competition in 1957.[14]

After a period where he was off the show for medical reasons, Ed decided he didn't want to do it any longer.[15] Mickey Shorr, who had subbed for him during the summer, was chosen to carry on and the show was revamped as "Mickey's Saturday Dance Party" and ran until the end of 1958.[15]

ON THE LOCAL MUSIC SCENE IN 1957, Fortune Records, coming off a national No. 12 r&b hit with the Diablos' "The Way You Dog Me Around," had another smash on the r&b charts in the Midwest with Andre Williams's recording of "Bacon Fat."[16]

Detroiter Jackie Wilson, who had left his spot with Billy Ward and the Dominoes, started a national solo career, recording songs written by a pre-Motown Berry Gordy.

"Reet Petite" was the first, followed by "To Be Loved" and the 1958 top-ten smash "Lonely Teardrops."

On most Thursday evenings, record promotion men, along with songwriters such as Berry Gordy and deejays such as Clark Reid, Bud Davies, and "Frantic Ernie" Durham, could be found at the Flame Show Bar at 4664 John R, the corner of Canfield, for "Music Business Night."[17]

The Flame was a "black and tan" club owned by the Wassermans and managed by Al Green, a white man. Although the audience was primarily black, whites were welcome and on hand to see performances by the top black record and night club stars. Dinah Washington, Billy Eckstine, Sarah Vaughan, Billy Holiday, Carmen McRae, and Roy Hamilton were the caliber of top-notch entertainers appearing on the Flame's unique stage, which had been constructed as part of the bar.

Berry Gordy's sisters, Anna and Gwen, operated the photo concession downstairs. Aside from the club, Al Green also managed the careers of Johnny Ray, LaVern Baker, and Jackie Wilson.

Upon Green's sudden death, Nat Tarnapol assumed the position of Jackie Wilson's manager, as well as taking control of his label, Brunswick Records.[18] Tarnapol became known for keeping Wilson in a state of servitude, having the artist sign contracts that, despite substantial record sales, left him always owing money to the label. Tarnapol's son, Paul, was given writing credit for Wilson's "Doggin' Around," although he wasn't yet born when the song was recorded.

"He really was 'Nat the Rat,'" says Marilyn Bond, who was involved with the record business in Detroit during the formative years of rock. "It was true about Jackie Wilson except to say that Jackie was one of those people who was always happy as long as he had money in his pocket and he was making a lot from personal appearances. He just didn't pay attention to details, and that's how

Nat got such control."[19] Marilyn was close to many of the popular disc jockeys and record artists of the fifties, snapping photos for *Teen Life* magazine and doing independent record promotion.

MORE LOCAL TALENT MADE GOOD on the record charts in 1958. After local success with "Baby, She Is Gone" on ABC-Paramount, singer Jack Scott broke through with "My True Love," a national top-five smash on Carlton Records. A rockabilly tune called "LeRoy," featured on the flip side, also did well. Born Jack Scafone in Windsor in 1936, his family moved across the river when he was ten and he grew up in Hazel Park. Hank Williams was a major influence as Jack started to play guitar and write songs, including just about all his hits. Scott finished off 1958 with another top-ten winner called "Goodbye Baby."

Also in 1958, a four-man instrumental group from Dearborn called the Royaltones, hit No. 17 on the national charts with "Poor Boy."[20]

In 1957, Robin Seymour hit the big screen...well, sort of. He was featured with Dick Clark and several other prominent deejays in the Clark-produced quickie rock 'n' roll flick *Jamboree*, a vehicle to showcase Jerry Lee Lewis and other rockabilly artists.[21]

Seymour also maintained a high industry profile at the 1958 disc jockey convention held in Kansas City.[21] It was organized by Top 40 pioneer Todd Storz. Columbia Records' Mitch Miller spoke to the crowd of deejays, criticizing them for programming to the "pre-shave crowd." Meanwhile, Robin participated on a panel discussion titled "Is Rock 'n' Roll a Bad Influence on Today's Teenagers?" After being on the forefront of rock music in Detroit, his answer to no one's surprise was "no."

OVER THE YEARS, WXYZ's vice president in charge of radio, Hal Neal, had done just about everything there was to do around Wixie, from announcing to promotion and sales. Although Bob Baker held the title of program director, it was largely an administrative position in those days, and Neal was directly influencing what went over the air.

By the mid-fifties, WXYZ was admired by all the other ABC-owned stations, because it was the only one in the chain making money.[22] This was because WXYZ had been the most successful of the group in making the transition from old network programming and local chitchat and homemaker shows to a more modern sound. At the end of 1957, Neal had impressed the ABC brass in New York with a presentation tape demonstrating how the station sounded throughout the day with highlights of the various disc jockey shows, newscasts, and early station jingles.[23] Although WXYZ was not yet consistent musically, it was developing an impressive sound. The station's first singing jingle aired in 1956 and was played on an electrical transcription: "This is the station of the stars, WXYZ." However, while the other ABC-owned stations (WABC New York, KABC Los Angeles, and KGO San Francisco) were looking toward Hal Neal as a visionary, the ABC radio network was about to take several steps backward, taking Neal and WXYZ with it.

Network radio programming had been rapidly dying off, the victim of the popularity of television.[24] The radio networks had cut their rates to compete, and in 1955, experienced a $19 million loss in revenue from the previous year. NBC radio had met the challenge by creating "Monitor," a weekend programming service of recorded music, personalities such as Gene Rayburn, and lots of fast informative and entertaining features designed for people on the move, as the new radio audiences were being perceived. It was programming that NBC affiliates could easily work into their schedules.

Now, in the fall of 1957, ABC was bringing on board one Robert Eastman, president of the Eastman Company, a radio rep group. ABC had been sold on a new programming strategy created by Eastman that was supposedly going to save the network. His concept was something called Live and Lively, which would consist of five daily hour-long entertainment shows hosted by well-known personalities. It would all commence with the long-running "Breakfast Club" every day.[25] All the shows were to feature full orchestras, male and female vocalists, and guests performing pop music favorites. Unlike NBC's experience with "Monitor," there were few ABC affiliates interested in giving up so much airtime to such a chancy concept. WXYZ, as an ABC-owned station, was once again saddled with the very type of programming Hal Neal had been clearing off locally as he axed "Lady of Charm" and other such fare that got in the way of his new disc jockey shows. There was nothing he could do about "The Breakfast Club," which had been on for years but at least had a loyal audience and commercials could be sold locally.

Now the WXYZ schedule would again be a mishmash. As usual, Fred Wolf would be on from six to nine, followed by "The Breakfast Club." At ten they would carry New York personality Herb Oscar Anderson's new "Live and Lively" variety show and then squeeze in a couple of local hours with Paul Winter. At one it was back to the network for a country-style variety program hosted by singer Jim Reeves. Television actor Jim Backus was featured for an hour at two o'clock. Ed McKenzie was untouched from three to six-fifteen but rock 'n' rollin' Mickey Shorr's show time was pushed back to eight to eleven to accommodate the network's "Merv Griffin Show," airing at seven-fifteen.

According to former ABC executive James Duffy in his book *Stay Tuned: My Life and the Business of Running the ABC Television Network*, ABC invested five million dollars in this fiasco. The sales staff as well as knowledgeable programmers such as Hal Neal knew that "Live and Lively" was dead on arrival. The concept lasted a few months and then mercifully was pulled from the air.

Hal Neal wasted no time, now that the WXYZ schedule was once again open. After "The Breakfast Club" it was Paul Winter from ten to twelve and then Mickey Shorr was shifted to a noon to three slot leading into Ed McKenzie. Staff announcer Fred Weiss was selected to handle the seven-fifteen to ten evening show, although why remains a bit of a mystery. Where Mickey Shorr had cooked at night, Weiss was reluctant. He did not see himself as a disc jockey, having been happiest announcing Cheerios commercials on the Lone Ranger broadcasts...but those days were long gone. Now management wanted him to deliver snappy patter in between rock 'n' roll records he could in no way relate to. Weiss, it turned out, was an opera buff and had little tolerance for the Coasters or Ricky Nelson, but it was a case of rock 'n' roll or go, so Fred Weiss did his best to fit into the sound, a sound that was still evolving.

Speaking of opera, Paul Winter remembers that, although the station was becoming more contemporary, there were still anachronisms on the air, such as weekly network broadcasts of the

New York Metropolitan Opera as late as 1958. Winter, who says he always felt like "an odd duck" at the station, had added yet another peculiar program to his plate: a one-hour classical show sponsored by Discount Records that aired just before the opera broadcast. At the close of his hour, Winter would jokingly say, "Stay tuned for Milton Cross and play-by-play of the New York Metropolitan Opera." Texaco, the program's sponsor, got wind of the comments, and soon Winter was receiving memos from ABC reminding him "not to mess with the Met."[26]

Now that he had his lineup in place, Hal Neal summoned his six disc jockeys into a meeting and informed them that from now on they would be playing the same one hundred records on all shows on WXYZ. Neal had been impressed with the success of broadcasters Todd Storz and Gordon McClendon in their respective markets, and, locally, it was hard to ignore the excitement being created with the format at WJBK, based on playing only hits from the best-seller charts in a fairly repetitive fashion for the entire broadcast day.[27]

The Top 40 format was taking hold in a number of major markets by 1958,[28] most notably KFWB Los Angeles, WINS New York, and, of course, in Detroit, WJBK, which was ahead of the curve, having been into it since late 1956. In these markets, rock 'n' roll had been available on the radio, but usually it was featured on a particular program and did not represent the music or content of the station at all times of the day. In Los Angeles, for example, Art Laboe played early rock and r&b in the afternoon on KPOP, a smaller daytime-only station. KFWB, a major full-time station, shifted its entire programming when it launched its "Color Radio, Channel 98" Top 40 format twenty-four hours a day and swept the ratings. WINS in New York, already had pioneering rock disc jockey Alan Freed on the air in the evening since 1954, although the rest of the day was filled with talk shows or other types of music. In 1957, the station kept Freed, who continued to program his own show while the station went with the Top 40 sound the rest of the day. By May of 1958, Freed was gone, replaced by Bruce Morrow and Top 40 along with deejays such as Jack Lacy and "A Smith Named Irv." WINS also went to the top of the ratings.

In Detroit, Robin Seymour had staked an early claim to rock 'n' roll on his "Bobbin' with Robin" show over WKMH and Mickey

Shorr had put together his own rock 'n' roll show in the evening at WJBK that sounded quite different from the rest of the station. After Shorr's dismissal, management came along and instituted their Top 40 format and played the same sounds throughout the day.

Deejays on WXYZ were still basically picking the music for their own shows, so that, on one station, you would have a program of show music, on another one jazz, and on still another more rock 'n' roll. These were the days when a disc jockey could flip on the mike and say, "Here's a brand-new record I think you'll like" and play something he may have just received earlier that day. Mickey Shorr played a number of new records that never made the charts, as well as r&b hits such as "Ruby Baby" by the Drifters and "Oh, What a Night" by the Dells that never dented the pop list. If a jockey really dug the sound, he might do something radical such as playing it twice in a row!

Unlike WXYZ, the stations that had gone Top 40 were mostly independent, nonnetwork stations with no programming conflicts, who overnight introduced a completely new sound of music, jingles, and deejays. Stations who made this radical move to Top 40 were usually low-rated in their markets and thought nothing about dumping their current programming and personalities to take on a new identity. What made Wixie different was its ABC ownership and the fact that the station was already making money with Fred Wolf's top-rated morning show and Ed McKenzie in the afternoon. Also, it continued to carry network programming as well as keeping its entire versatile air staff as it made the final transition.

The freewheeling days of the early fifties had been an exciting time, but now Hal Neal was obsessed with WXYZ having a more consistent sound throughout the day and though it never developed a hard-driving manic pace like the Storz and McClendon rockers, Wixie did tighten up. As Fred Wolf, Paul Winter, Mickey Shorr, Ed McKenzie, Fred Weiss, and Jack Surrell listened, Hal Neal laid down the law. From now on, he and Bob Baker would choose the records, and air personalities were required to cut down on talk and give station call letters and slogans more often. "WXYZ sounds good like a radio station should"[29] would be dropped in at regular intervals. "Oh, yes, play the number one song once each hour," ordered Neal.

Hal Neal's announcement was not greeted with enthusiasm by any of the Wixie deejays, who didn't think Top 40 would fly at their station.[30] Fred Wolf would resist the changes, including playing Elvis Presley records, while Mickey Shorr, who had expected this day to arrive, was already rocking. He would just have to get used to working under a more restrictive format, where, for the first time, he would not have complete control of the music. Paul Winter had survived at WXYZ by adapting. He had played show tunes, pop, classical and "Lonesome Luke Borgia." Now Paul would find his greatest challenge as a rock 'n' roll Top 40 disc jockey.

Jack Surrell recalls the big move to Top 40: "It was exasperating. Hal Neal had gone over to Cleveland to hear a pretty hot rock station that had a deejay who stood and jumped around during his show. Well, when Hal came back he decided we should all be standing when we were talking to create more excitement. They also took away the piano segues that I had always done."

For six years Jack Surrell had chosen the music for his show. Overnight that privilege was taken away. "I came into the studio and there was a box of records waiting for me. I wasn't even able to choose the order of play. It was just singles, jingles, slogans, and keep it moving. It just stopped being fun," Surrell lamented, adding: "Because Fred Wolf was the big breadwinner, he was given a little more freedom as far as music and comments, but it was pretty tough on everyone."[31]

Ed McKenzie's response to the changes was a sour one to say the least. McKenzie had never been as happy at WXYZ as he had been during those early days at WJBK. To him, ABC was all business and the atmosphere could get downright frosty. "I never really felt at home at WXYZ," remembers Ed. "It kept getting worse, but I was making too much money to quit."

Now with the big push to conformity, Ed battled with Hal Neal constantly about breaking format and questioned why he had to be forced to play records he considered junk. It wasn't so much that Ed was opposed to rock 'n' roll, but it was his desire to do what had made him successful in the first place: choose the records he thought were worthy and screw the rest. Example: Clyde McPhatter–yes; Frankie Avalon–no. "I just couldn't deal with it anymore, all the nonsense. We did these remotes in the trailers and the station wanted me to wear this damned red jacket with the ABC logo on the pocket and I didn't like it. Then there were those goofy slogans they wanted you to say over and over. I had enough," says McKenzie.[32]

It all finally came to a head in March of 1959. Neal said he fired the outspoken disc jockey while McKenzie claims to have quit after telling Neal to "shove it."[33] When Ed McKenzie left WXYZ, it made headlines as far away as London, England, where *Melody Maker* magazine reported the story. It was the end of an era.

Mickey Shorr moved into McKenzie's afternoon slot and although he wasn't thrilled about the changes any more than Ed, he continued to adapt his personality to Hal Neal's Top 40 formula. "You're on the Shorr line at channel 1270,"[34] he would say each day between three and six-fifteen as he sent forth the hit sounds from the Wixie Tunedex. Those sounds included Detroiter Marv Johnson's "You've Got What It Takes," another hit from songwriter Berry Gordy. WXYZ proved it had what it takes in 1959 as the Hooper ratings showed them moving up.

ACROSS THE RIVER IN WINDSOR, CKLW officially went Top 40 in March of 1959 and that brought down the curtain on the "Make Believe Ballroom." In a newspaper interview, Eddie Chase announced his break from CK': "I have always insisted on playing music, not numbers and the new policy calls for the playing of sixty records selected by the station. I like to say I play the top ten thousand."[35] Eddie also thought that format radio "makes the radio entertainer a robot, not a personality."

Chase's resignation came just eight days after Ed McKenzie separated from WXYZ. That station's lineup now included Fred Wolf, 6 to 9; Lou Sherman, 10 to 12; Paul Winter, 12 to 3; Mickey Shorr, 3 to 6:15; Fred Weiss, 7:15 to 10; Jack Surrell, 10 to 1; and Chuck Dougherty, 1 to 6 in the morning.[36]

CHAPTER 7

# "Words and Music"

In October of 1957, Casey Kasem had made plans to leave WJBK to help out with his family's grocery business in Fenton, Michigan.[1] His replacement was Tom Clay, from WSAI in Cincinnati, where he hosted a late-evening show called "Last Date."[2]

Thomas Clague grew up in Binghampton, New York, where he worked with his two brothers in the family window-cleaning business. One of their clients was the local radio station, WKOP. One afternoon, Tom put down his squeegee and asked the station manager if he could audition to be an announcer. Impressed with what he heard, the manager gave Tom his first job in radio in 1951 as "Mr. Moon-Beam."[3] From WKOP it was on to Buffalo, where he worked under the name Guy King at station WWOL, introducing rock 'n' roll to upstate New York on his afternoon show called "Words and Music."[4]

On the Fourth of July weekend of 1955, Clay, stoked on the power of rock and radio, had broadcast his show standing on top of the WWOL billboard, which sat high above the Palace Burlesque building at Sheldon Square in downtown Buffalo. As crowds of screaming teenagers stood below with their car radios blaring, Tom played "Rock Around the Clock" over and over. "Honk your horns if you want to hear that one again,"* he teased, as he worked the crowd for more than two hours.[5]

A short time later, he was hired away by another station in the Buffalo area that was putting together an impressive deejay lineup that included Lucky Pierre and Al McCoy. As the name Guy King was the legal property of WWOL, Clague became Tom Clay at WHLD. To make the transition, he would open his show every afternoon by saying, "This is a guy...a guy by the name of Clay."

"Tom was always coming up with something catchy," recalls McCoy, looking way back to those days in Buffalo. "I remember him doing stunts like broadcasting his show, hanging off the side of a building. He liked to attract attention."[6] Tom's older brother, Herbert Clague, says that Tom used his experience washing windows to pull off the stunts in high places: "He was a fearless window washer, fast and good."[7]

Al McCoy recalls another Clay stunt. "In 1956, Tom went on the air and told his audience that Elvis was in Buffalo and gave a phone number of where he was staying. He said, 'Why don't you make him feel welcome by giving him a call!' Well, when kids started dialing they found the voice on the other end of the line was not that of Presley but, in fact, Buffalo's chief of police!"[8]

Attracting attention was nothing new for Tom Clay. At sixteen, he had enlisted in the Marines, where it was not uncommon for a young recruit to get a tattoo. Anxious to prove his manliness to the older guys, young Tom went out and got seven tattoos...in one evening. After recovering from a life-threatening case of blood poisoning, Private Clague received an early discharge and returned home, where he found employment as a short-order cook before joining the family business.[9]

Casey Kasem recalls the changing of the guard in Detroit. "I had done my last show on 'JBK on a Friday night. The following Monday evening I was sitting in my car waiting to meet a friend of mine, WWJ's Les Martens, outside of the old Hedges Wigwam restaurant on Woodward Avenue in Royal Oak–we were going over to play the horses at Hazel Park Raceway. Anyhow, it was around

---

*Three biographies on the life of rock star Buddy Holly erroneously claim that Tom Clay as "Guy King" played Holly's recording of "That'll Be the Day" for twenty minutes straight on WWOL in Buffalo. By August of 1957, when the record was released, Clay was already working in Cincinnati. The story probably grew out of confusion with the Bill Haley story.

seven and I had the radio on and tuned to WJBK. When I heard the first few minutes of Tom Clay's first show, I thought to myself, Casey, no one in this town is gonna remember you, after they hear this guy. Tom Clay was just so good. He was fast at the controls and just had a way with his voice."[10]

On WJBK, it was "Tom Clay, on the 'Jack the Bellboy Show,'" from seven to midnight, as the station decided to dust off the famous nickname they had retired after wresting it away from Ed McKenzie five years earlier. Clay brought a new style to Detroit radio, redefining what it meant for a radio personality to communicate. Clay painted pictures with words, such as the mouthwatering, live commercials for the soft drink Squirt. In his superconfidential tone of voice, he would advise the audience to "tip it, sip it...see the real bits of fruit, floating inside...aah."[11]

"Tom Clay always sounded like he was talking to only one person," recalls Lee Alan, who, for a time, followed Tom on the air at 'JBK.[12] "Tom could create things on radio that you could see, much the way they did on the old shows like 'Fibber McGee and Molly' or 'The Lone Ranger.' He knew how to generate excitement, how to get people to get up and come out to an event, like the big dances he put on at the Light Guard Armory. He was creative and controversial and that's why he was so popular."[12]

Tom rocked hard in the early evening and, as he had done in Buffalo, generated a lot of excitement, broadcasting his show from the top of the three-story-high sign above Jax Automatic Car Wash and dancing to "Willie and the Hand Jive" as thousands of fans looked on.

Casey Kasem was right about Clay's on-air production skills. Detroit broadcaster Dave Dixon remembers visiting Clay in the studio at WJBK: "Clay would open each hour by promoting some of the big hits he would be playing. He would say, 'This hour we'll hear from the Coasters!' and play a little bit of 'Charlie Brown' and then, 'We'll also hear from the Crests!' and he would have the title line cued up and then, 'Let's kick it off with the sound of Lloyd Price!' He was doing all this live, talking on the air and cueing up a certain line from a record in his headphones. He was the best board operator I'd ever seen."[13] Clark Reid agrees that Clay was something to watch in the studio, his hands shuffling through record stacks, fingers twirling the discs like six-shooters as he slipped 'em on the turntables, never losing track of what he was saying.[14]

Most fans, however, remember how, around records such as "It's All in the Game," "One Summer's Night," and "All I Have to Do Is Dream," not to mention the early hits of Johnny Mathis, Tom Clay created a romantic and moody atmosphere. He was the first "make-out" disc jockey, number one on Lovers Lane.

He related to the music like no one before him, speaking in a soft, sometimes whisper-like voice, as he recited lyrics as poetry. Weaving tales of lost loves and broken dreams in the dark of night, he evoked a dramatic interpretation of his own image: a loner, a guy who had been around and who surely, after his midnight sign-off, left the studios, passed under a dim lightbulb, and drove off alone into the night. The image was also of a guy who understood his audience. He could say, "Hey, I know what you're going through" and not sound like a phony trying to cater to teenagers.

One night, as a record played, Tom took a call from an obviously troubled girl who was contemplating suicide. "He told her, 'No, you just can't do that,' and continued to comfort her," relates one of Tom's three daughters, who says that, although her dad never met the girl, "they stayed in touch."[15] Sometime later, this same girl, whose name was Kimberly, found herself flying on a private plane, where she took time to write a letter to Tom, again saying, "Thanks, you saved my life." The letter was never mailed, because that same afternoon she was killed when the plane developed engine trouble and crashed.

Her father came across the letter while going through the wreckage and sent it on to Tom Clay. It had been written on black paper with white ink.

Over the years, fans writing to Tom Clay would always receive a letter back...a letter written on black paper with white ink. This according to Kimberly Clague Tally, born several years later and named for the girl who had dialed up Kimberly's father out of desperation one evening.

"He was a helpless romantic," says daughter Kim, referring to Tom Clay's intimate and sometimes dreamy style. "He never felt like he was on the air. He used to tell me that he didn't see the microphone. It was like he was just sitting across from another person, having a conversation. That's the kind of magic he created on radio."[16] Aspiring disc jockeys were listening, and hoping to catch some of that magic.

As Mickey Shorr had moved to a midday shift at WXYZ, Detroit nights now belonged to Tom Clay on WJBK. By the summer of 1958, he was number one in ratings and held Detroit's teenagers in the palm of his hand.

Berry Gordy, in his autobiography, *To Be Loved,* gives Clay credit for being one of the first white deejays to play some of his early efforts and for introducing him to record promo man Barney Ales, who became the chief architect of Motown's powerhouse sales and marketing department.[17]

Still on the air at WJBK were Tom George in the morning, Clark Reid, now in middays, and Don McCleod, afternoons. Dan Baxter followed Clay on the all-night show, replaced in 1959 by Lee Alan.

After helping out his family, Casey Kasem went to New York to "try his hand at acting." Six months later he was back on the radio at WJW, the Storer station in Cleveland.[18]

IN SEPTEMBER OF 1959, WXYZ radio and TV combined all their operations and moved into new studios at Broadcast House in Southfield. Unfortunately, all the planning had focused on television, so radio wound up in a couple of cement rooms on the second floor.[19]

WXYZ's Fred Wolf, who by 1954 had moved into first place in the morning ratings race, picked up a new competitor when WJR named staff announcer J. P. McCarthy host of the "Music Hall" midway through 1958. Also, WJR severed ties with CBS in a dispute over the amount of network programming they were being required to carry. Unlike the other networks, CBS was still providing a full slate of programming at a time when the audience for the soaps and other network fare had been dwindling and 'JR wanted more local airtime.[20]

In an odd pairing and ignoring the current trends, WKMH became the new CBS affiliate. Marty McNeely moved over to do the 'KMH morning show, after which came a three-hour block of CBS variety and soap operas, including Arthur Godfrey, "Young Dr. Malone," and "The Romance of Helen Trent." Then, it was back to rock 'n' roll with "Bobbin with Robin." "Amos 'n' Andy" (still on but revamped as a disc jockey show), "Houseparty" with Art Linkletter, and "The Gary Moore Show" were on in the early evening, then back to rock with Harvey Kaye.[20] It was very weird. The station wanted the credibility that the CBS affiliation gave it, but at the same time that affiliation conflicted with the station's music programming. It was a lose-lose situation as WKMH continued to flounder.

Elsewhere on the radio dial in 1959, late-night listeners could tune into "Pat's Place" with Conrad Patrick playing "music for night people," midnight to 6:00 A.M. on "Radiant Radio 80," CKLW. Toby David, Joe Van, Bud Davies, and Ron Knowles played the sounds of the Top 40 the rest of the day.

Ben Johnson was hosting a popular late-night jazz show from 10:30 to 2:00 over WEXL. His studio was a favorite hangout for record promo men around the Motor City.[21]

WWJ called their sound "Melody Parade"; announcers included Hugh Roberts, Bob Maxwell, and Dick French.

The most popular station with teenagers continued to be WJBK, with Tom Clay and the hits from the "Formula 45" survey, twenty-four hours a day.

## CHAPTER 8

# Put Another Nickel in the Jukebox

AFTER SITTING OUT A FEW MONTHS, Ed McKenzie went back on the air in the afternoon at a new station that had been purchased by his old friend Dick Jones along with Ross Mulholland and the Brink family. WMIC was licensed to Monroe but the owners had their sights set on the Detroit market. New studios were installed in the Brink Building behind Hudson's in downtown Detroit, and the call letters were changed to WQTE. Joining Ed were Detroit radio veterans Ralph Binge (along with pals Sharp Frank and Beautiful Carl) in the morning and Eddie Chase from CKLW from noon to three. Joe Bacarella, going by the air name Danny Murphy, continued on from the old staff, handling nine to noon. Although a daytime-only station, WQTE had a pretty strong signal at 560 and, with top personalities, hoped to do great things with a pop format that shied away from hard rock.

On November 18, 1959, the Detroit radio industry was caught off guard when the *Detroit Free Press* ran a story headlined MCKENZIE PUTS NEEDLE ON PAYOLA. The story featured excerpts from an article that Ed McKenzie was going to have published in the November 23 edition of *Life* magazine.

"A reporter from *Time* was looking into this whole payola thing and had been told that I would be a person to talk to about it," recalls McKenzie. "Out of that contact came the piece I wrote for *Life* magazine."[1]

So, as opposed to what many people think, Ed McKenzie did not wake up one morning and decide to write an exposé, but when asked he did give his opinions.

If McKenzie was bitter about his experiences at WXYZ and the direction radio was taking, he had found an opportunity to vent some hostility. In the article, he came out against what he called "formula radio," talking about its "bad music, its incessant commercials in bad taste, its subservience to ratings and its pressures of payola." He went on to describe in detail how payola got started and how it worked–the money, gifts, parties, and girls that could be provided to a disc jockey if he promised to "ride" a record a certain number of times. According to Ed, several local deejays were on the take and one had even had his home landscaped as a favor from a record distributor.[2] Ed claimed that he too had been approached but had turned down all offers because he thought it was "completely dishonest."

McKenzie talked about detesting the commercials he had to do on his show even though the commercials are what keep radio stations on the air and, in his case at WXYZ, had paid him quite handsomely, to the tune of sixty thousand dollars per year–huge money in any market during the 1950s. Wrapping up the article, Ed summarized his reasons for quitting what he called "big-time radio," again listing "all the payola, ratings, bad music and bad commercials," as if those things were exclusive to his former station. Perhaps Ed was under the impression that the management at WQTE would not be so interested in high ratings and commercial revenue. Whatever, if he had wanted to create waves with his article, he succeeded to a certain degree.

"Payola" was certainly nothing new.[3] In the 1920s and 1930s, music publishing companies made payments to singers for performing a particular song and influencing the sale of sheet music. These payments were even made to store salespeople for recommending the music customers could buy for their home piano.

The current scandal brewing over payola had grown out of an ongoing battle for market dominance in the world of recorded music between the older, more staid music-licensing company, American Society of Composers, Authors, and Publishers

(ASCAP), and its feisty competitor, Broadcast Music, Inc. (BMI).

BMI had come to life in 1939 after ASCAP had attempted to raise the fees it charged radio stations to play the music it controlled. ASCAP saw itself as a sort of exclusive club representing the publishers of esteemed and established composers such as Cole Porter, George Gershwin, and Rogers and Hart. BMI, meanwhile, opened its doors to folk, country, blues, and other forms of fringe music. The postwar boom in independent record production and the birth of rock 'n' roll really built BMI into a powerhouse, posing a financial challenge to ASCAP.

As a strategy for attacking BMI, ASCAP contended that all rock 'n' roll was junk and the only possible way it could be successful was by paying disc jockeys to play it. Rigged quiz shows on TV, most notably "Twenty-one" and "Dotto," had been big news recently. When it was found out that the two producers of these programs, Jack Berry and Bill Enright, also owned some Top 40 radio stations,[4] ASCAP found the link it needed and pushed the government to open an investigation. So, radio was already in trouble by the time Ed McKenzie's article hit; he just turned up the heat.

The press was on a feeding frenzy searching out Detroit disc jockeys for their reaction to Ed's story. At McKenzie's former station, WXYZ, only Fred Wolf could be found. The *Detroit Free Press* reported that Wolf "exploded" after hearing McKenzie's story. "I told Ed, 'If you can't get with radio as radio is going, then get out,'" claimed Fred in pure "Wolf-ese," going on to say, "Everything he says I've heard but I must be nobody in this business because I never had offers come to me."[5]

Walter Patterson, manager at WKMH, announced that his disc jockeys "wouldn't be talking to anyone on the subject of payola."[6]

A reporter dialed up CKLW in the evening where Ron Knowles was on the air and he answered the phone. "I didn't know what the heck was going on," remembers Ron. "The reporter asked me if I knew anything about a deejay getting his house landscaped and I said, 'No, but gee, I wish someone would do that for me.'[7] Well, the next day there it is in the papers, 'Ron Knowles says this,' and the management at CK' was more than a little upset. I really got called on the carpet. They said, 'We have people to handle this sort of thing, don't comment on it again!' I didn't," says Ron, still wincing. CKLW's public-relations man, Art Gloster, stated officially: "CKLW has no policy on payola because it hasn't come up before."

WCAR distanced itself from the controversy by saying its good-music policy took away any opportunity to get the kind of records on the air that payola usually supported, namely, rock 'n' roll.[8]

On his November 19, 1959, broadcast, Jac LeGoff, Detroit's top-rated television news anchor, went on the air at WJBK-TV and attempted to end the witch-hunt, citing that "payola in one form or another is a part of American business...let him who is without sin cast the first stone."[9] LeGoff was then cast out of a job as a result of his comments. Channel 2 stated that LeGoff was fired not for his beliefs but because he broke the station's policy of not editorializing on the air.

Events continued to unfold at a dizzying pace when, two days later, Tom Clay was dismissed from WJBK radio. Clay's photo was on the front pages of all three Detroit daily papers. The large bold headline in the *Detroit News* read WHY I TOOK $5,000 PAYOLA, DISC JOCKEY TOM CLAY FIRED FROM WJBK.

Clay called a news conference for Sunday afternoon where he humbly offered his side of the story: "During my first six months in town, I accepted nothing. Then, after I went to number one in the ratings the offers started to come," he explained. "At first I thought, no, don't. But I'm human and wanted to give my family security, so I did." Clay, who was married with two kids and lived in Mt. Clemens, also said, "Out of the seventy-five records I play each night, maybe one or two a month are payola plugs."

Clay likened the record pluggers to a "little boy who takes an apple to the teacher." He wondered if the record company executives "were wrong in condoning payola or were they just good businessmen?"[10]

Tom Clay's downfall came about when he refused to cooperate with a character named Harry "the Nightshade" Nivins, a record producer and manager of a singer with the dubious name of Melrose Baggy. On 'JBK, Clay was undisputed pied piper to Detroit teenagers every night from seven to midnight and Harry wanted Clay to play Baggy's record real bad. In August, Clay had turned down Nivins's offer of $200, because he thought it was a lousy record. "I told him I wouldn't play that record for $200,

$300 or $500," said Clay.

Nivins was hanging around WJBK, complaining about the poor treatment, and a couple of employees who were not fond of Tom, notably, sports director Barney Lee, pitched in some money so that Nivins could buy a midget tape recorder. The next time Nivins met with Clay, they were riding in Tom's nice shiny new Lincoln and Nivins offered him $100 to play the Baggy record. Clay was still not interested in the record but his ego got the best of him. "What happened to the $200 we were talking about last time?" he inquired.

Nivins played the tape for WJBK general manager Harry Lipson, who at first didn't seem to think it was such a big deal and gave Clay a minor reprimand.

Dissatisfied, Nivins then sent a letter detailing his charges to Storer Broadcasting's headquarters in Miami on August 24 but received no response. Finally, in mid-November, he sent a telegram directly to company president George B. Storer, who then ordered an in-house investigation of all his stations.[11]

On November 23, with the threat of an inquisition at hand, Dale Young, the host of "Detroit Bandstand" on WJBK-TV, resigned as did 'JBK radio's longtime afternoon disc jockey Don McLeod. Young refused any comment while McLeod stated that his departure from WJBK was over "programming differences." As far as payola was concerned, McLeod said, "I'm not clear as to what payola is." In a case of not knowing when to stop, Don offered this memorable understatement: "I realize I chose a most inopportune time to resign, but it was strictly my decision."[12]

"Don McLeod was a great talent, very smooth and believable," recalls Lee Alan, who was doing all-nights at WJBK when the firestorm over payola broke.[13] "Don had been on in Detroit for a long time and was one of the top personalities. The record companies would approach people like Don and say, 'We'd like to send you a pack of records each week, set up a conference call, and have you give us your opinion.' They would do this with a top guy in Chicago, Philadelphia, and so forth. Don tried to explain to management that he didn't take payola, he was a 'consultant,' and was paid a fee for that service. They didn't buy that explanation and he was forced to resign."

As for Tom Clay, like everything else, his firing became a cause célèbre, even attracting national attention. Rather than running from the bad publicity, Clay embraced it and made himself one of the very few deejays willing to talk to the press. The *New York Times* ran a story headlined DETROIT RADIO STAR CONFESSES PAYOLA and *Time* magazine did a piece on him titled "Wages of Spin." Clay went on to say that, while "he had never forced anyone to give him money to play a record, several record companies and distributors wanted him to take it—and he did."[14]

George Goldner, who owned the End and Gone record labels in New York, said he paid Clay approximately $100 per month for a year to play his releases. Lorrie Marks, a showgirl, came forward to say that Clay took $200 to push "Lazy Bonnie," a release by the Imperials on Goldner's label. Tom denied that he had ever been approached by Mrs. Marks, but admitted that he had taken the money from her husband.[15]

In the early fifties, independent record labels, such as Goldner's, felt payola was the only way they could break the stranglehold that the major labels such as Columbia, RCA, and Decca had on radio station playlists. Ed McKenzie had even alluded to this in his article if only in a critical way, as if these independent labels had no business existing. In 1959, the Federal Trade Commission had gone after several independent record labels, charging them with unfair competition, as a result of paying deejays to play their product. When the record companies, including Goldner's and Chicago's Chess, said, "Sorry, we won't do it again," the attention turned to the disc jockeys.

Admitting that, although paying for play did seem unsavory, Clay said there was, in fact, no real law against it on the books. According to Tom, "Nobody was wrong, it's just business." Being a business, he kept an accurate record of the payola he received so he could pay income tax on it. He also stated that he took money only to promote records he thought were good and never accepted percentage deals offered by many aspiring artists.

Fellow 'JBK deejay Clark Reid stayed the course through the whole mess and recently commented on it: "Tom Clay was the only guy around who would openly talk about payola. Believe me, there were other people in town, some big names, who had accepted gifts from artists, but didn't see any conflict."[16] One of the people Reid was referring to was Ed McKenzie, who had accepted a gift of a diamond ring from singer Eddie Fisher. Ed felt that Fisher was already an established artist and he didn't view the gift as having any effect on whether his records were played. Others would disagree with his view.

If WJBK had a record survey, how was Tom Clay able to plug records for payola? Clark Reid: "While WJBK was a Top 40 station and we did have the printed survey, it was not an official playlist. We worked from that list but we still had the leeway to play a few new records if we thought they had potential. That policy came to an end very quickly after the payola troubles."

Tom Clay said his only regret was that "some of the guys and gals might think I had tried to fool them. I haven't. I have only tried to entertain them." He went on to say: "I could play a record twenty times a night for two weeks and if the guys and gals didn't like it, believe me, they wouldn't buy it."

In a strange about-face, Harry Nivins, in an exclusive interview with the *Detroit Times*, had praise for the discharged Clay. "He is a great disc jockey, he sold records. He was entertaining. He was a good technician and he could spot a hit. I don't think any amount of money would have got him to play a bad record."[17]

Nivins didn't like the role of a snitch but said he felt he was "fighting for his livelihood and the career of Melrose Baggy," who he claimed was a "talented singer." In other words, he had carried out a personal vendetta against the WJBK disc jockey because Tom had turned down a payoff for a record he didn't think was any good.


ROBIN SEYMOUR REMEMBERS being asked if he was taking any payola: "I told my bosses that I had so many things going in the way of promotions, appearances, and the commission structure I was on that I didn't need to get involved with hundred-dollar payoffs. I was, however, forced to sell my interests in a company I co-owned, called Arc Distributing. [Arc controlled record distribution for many record labels in Detroit.] The station did not want the slightest suspicion to cast a shadow," says Seymour.[18]

In a case of the kettle calling the pot black, both WKMH and WJBK had questionable activities in the play-for-pay area. WKMH featured an "Album of the Week," where one song on the album could be played 114 times a week, with a commercial aired before and after. The cost was $350 per week for a minimum of six weeks.[19]

WJBK had something called the "Sound Special,"[20] which, according to Clark Reid, was clearly a radio commercial–bought and paid for by the individual record distributor or record company. "Everytime the Sound Special was played, it was announced that the seventy-nine-cent record could be bought for fifty cents on that day," Reid recalls. When questioned whether this practice constitutes payola, WJBK general manager Harry Lipson commented that this view was "distorted."[21] Clark Reid remembers that the station was so guilty about it that they went back and erased any mention of it from past commercial logs.

WXYZ stated that the very music policies Ed McKenzie had complained about, whereby the management picked the records, not the deejay, had removed the threat of payola.[22] On November 18, Harold Neal Jr. had issued the following statement: "Information available to WXYZ affirms that no disc jockey, now performing on this station, no person who participates in the selection of music for broadcast over WXYZ, nor I, this WXYZ station manager, has either solicited or accepted any personal consideration, money or otherwise, to have any record played on WXYZ."

However, on November 26, 1959, a few days after the Clay firing, Mickey Shorr was let go. SHORR FIRED BY WXYZ; DENIES HE TOOK PAYOLA screamed the headline on the front page of the *Detroit Free Press*. In a newspaper interview at the time, Mickey gave the blow-by-blow. "Hal Neal called me at home and told me to come down to the station. When I arrived, he said he had a very unpleasant duty to perform. I told him it was much less unpleasant for him than it was for me," he chuckled at the time.[23]

Mickey's wife, May Shorr, believes there were already problems developing between Mickey and WXYZ and they wanted him out: "Perhaps he was making too much money or had too many outside interests," she comments.[24] WXYZ was, in fact, concerned about Shorr being part owner of a company called Aussie Records. Leave it to Mickey Shorr to get involved with an Australian record company. "It's payola in reverse," he explained. "We pay record companies for the Australian rights to their records."[25] Shorr also claimed that WXYZ was aware of his involvement and that Hal Neal had even given him permission to form the company with partner Art Shurigan, almost two years previously.

It appeared that Shorr himself was aware that WXYZ wanted him out but he didn't want to leave at a time when it might appear linked to payola. "I told him [Neal] previously that I would gladly resign when these payola troubles were over, but I wouldn't do it now," Shorr stated. Supposedly, he was given the choice of resigning or being fired. Shorr went on to say, "The station gave me no reason for asking for my resignation and I had none of my own. I didn't feel I wanted to quit, but if he didn't want me on his station it was his prerogative to fire me."

Shorr more than denied taking any money to play records: "I swear on my father's grave that I have never taken any payola."[26] Mickey stated that he had even returned numerous checks that he had received in previous years. He did admit to receiving a few gifts from record makers, promoters, and artists, usually at Christmas, but nothing of great value. Despite this, he found himself vulnerable when his name came up in a court case one week earlier. A local recording group called the Royaltones was after their former manager, Stuart Gorelick, for money owed them. Gorelick testified that 10 percent of the money had gone to "pay off a loan from Mickey Shorr." It didn't sound very good but there was, in fact, not much to it.

In February of 1958, Mickey had loaned Gorelick $2,000. Gorelick said some of the money was used to "promote the group and some used for personnel expenses." He went on to testify that a $1500 check sent to Shorr in January of 1959 was partial repayment for the loan. Another $280 payment was made on the loan in October. That's all there was, no payola, just repayment of a real loan from Mickey Shorr.[27]

There were no other people pointing fingers at or accusing Mickey of doing anything wrong. There was no evidence of his ever taking cash to play records. The loan had been one made between friends. It was never shown that he had even a small interest in the group. If that had been the case, it would have been a conflict of miniscule proportions compared with the dealings of Alan Freed in New York, who was collecting bags of cash from a number of record companies and distributors on a monthly basis and was regularly given percentages of songs he would play on his WABC radio show.[28]

ABC was surely hypocritical in all of this, as just a year earlier, they had been putting pressure on Freed to play more records released on their ABC-Paramount label as well as records handled by their Am-Par Distribution company.[29] WXYZ, as an ABC-owned station, had played their share of company product. It didn't matter. They didn't want or need any more details—the "big man" was out.

Shorr was quoted as saying, "I refuse to be glum about it. Things always turn out for the best. I said that in 1956 when WJBK made a shift and dropped me and I'm saying it now."[30] He went on to say that he doubted that he would return to the air. "The business today isn't what it was when I started at WXYZ. There is no creativity on the part of air personalities." This was obviously in response to Hal Neal's format restrictions that had even resulted in Mickey dropping much of the crazy style that had made him so popular with teenagers. "I've been brainwashed," claimed Shorr.

"Mickey never took a red cent from anyone," says May Shorr.[31] Paul Winter agrees that Mickey never took any money to play records and believes he "should have never been fired."[32] After what had just gone down at WJBK, it seems that WXYZ was in a state of paranoia and was very worried about license renewal. Although it appears that there was no fire around Mickey Shorr, the station did not want even a wisp of smoke to float over Broadcast House. That, combined with the station's apparent displeasure with his other outside interests, sealed Mickey's fate. When pressed, station manager Hal Neal issued a terse statement: "WXYZ today exercised its right to terminate the employment of Mr. Mickey Shorr."[33]

IN NEW YORK, Alan Freed, the godfather of rock 'n' roll disc jockeys, had been ousted from his evening show on WXYZ's sister station, WABC, when he refused to sign an affidavit saying he had never accepted any form of payola for playing records.[34] Two weeks later, he lost his television show on WNEW-TV. For Freed, who championed rock 'n' roll by refusing to play white-cover versions of r&b hits, this was the next step down the career ladder. A year earlier he had been let go by New York's WINS because of riots breaking out at his live stage shows that were promoted on his radio program. The station owner, concerned about his upcoming license renewal, viewed Freed as a liability. With the ABC firing, Alan Freed never recovered; charges of income tax evasion added to an already sullied reputation.

On February 8, 1960, the U.S. House Subcommittee on Legislative Oversight, led by Rep. Oren Harris of Arkansas, opened an investigation of payola in the record industry. Soon the heads of deejays across the country were rolling, or were at least on the block. Congressional investigators found that 207 disc jockeys in forty-two states had accepted close to $300,000 in payola. Dave Maynard and Alan Dary of WBZ in Boston confirmed what Ed McKenzie had alluded to in his *Life* magazine article. They told of receiving cars, carpet, liquor, and a hi-fi system along with cash from various record distributors.[35]

In May of 1959, more than two thousand industry people had attended a second disc jockey convention, organized by Storz Broadcasting and held in Miami, Florida. A headline in the *Miami News* at the time described the scene: FOR DEEJAYS: BABES, BOOZE AND BRIBES. The story gave details of how eight major labels, including RCA, Capitol, and Columbia, had wined and dined the deejays.

Back at the hearings, Joe Finen of KYW in Cleveland admitted to receiving money from the local RCA distributor because, aside from Elvis Presley, RCA was having problems getting airplay for its more traditional record acts, such as the Ames Brothers and Dinah Shore. Finen had even had an RCA color television delivered to his home, unsolicited. It was becoming apparent that it was not only the little upstart independent labels and rock 'n' roll that were involved with payola.

The main event of the hearings came when Dick Clark was called to testify. Although no one was handing him hundred-dollar bills to play records, Clark was positioned to make much more, because when he played a Duane Eddy or Freddie Cannon record, he was in for a piece of the action, having owned stock in their record labels, Jamie and Swan. Clark also owned the publishing rights to 160 songs, many that he played heavily on his TV show, including "At the Hop" by Danny and the Juniors and "Sixteen Candles" by the Crests. Many of these copyrights had been gifts.

Before he owned the copyright on "Sixteen Candles," it was

shown that Clark had played the record four times in ten weeks. Once the song was his, he played it twenty-seven times in roughly the same amount of time. He even had interests in record-pressing plants. A songwriter named Orville Lunsford said that his record of "All-American Boy" by Bill Parsons (Bobby Bare) shot quickly to number two in record sales—but only, he said, after placing an order with Clark-owned Mallard Pressing Corp. to print fifty thousand copies. "Almost immediately," said Lunsford, "I heard my song played almost every day on Clark's show."[36]

To be fair, Dick Clark hadn't set out to break any laws; he was just a very savvy guy with a great business sense who saw how to make the system work to his advantage. Clark testified that he had "never agreed to play a record or have an artist perform on a radio or television program in return for a payment in cash or any other consideration." He did, however, go on to say that although his record interests were "set up to operate in a normal competitive manner," he realized that some of the copyrights received by his publishing firms and some of the records owned, distributed, or pressed by the companies in which he had an interest were "given to my firms at least in part because of the fact that I was a network television personality."[37]

Unlike Alan Freed, Clark's bosses at ABC went out of their way to protect him. Special language had been drafted for the affidavit Clark had been asked to sign regarding whether or not he had ever taken payola. Unlike the affidavits other ABC personnel were required to sign, including the WXYZ air staff, only cash payments were defined as payola in Clark's, not interests in record and publishing companies, and so forth. He was then given the opportunity of divesting himself of those so-called questionable interests and remaining as host of "American Bandstand." Of course, it didn't hurt that "Bandstand" was pulling in $12,000,000 in annual billing for the struggling ABC network.[38] Appearing well scrubbed and wholesome and with Leonard Goldenson, the president of ABC, speaking on his behalf, Clark came out of the hearings unscathed, although he had taken quite a beating.[39]

In his autobiography, *Rock, Roll, and Remember*, Clark summed up his experience with payola and the government hearings: "I learned not just to make money but how to protect my ass at all times."[40]

The same could not be said for Detroit broadcasters Jac LeGoff, Tom Clay, Don McLeod, Dale Young, and Mickey Shorr–all cut down in the wildest week in Motor City broadcasting history.

## CHAPTER 9

# Radio Rebounds

BY THE SPRING OF 1960, it was becoming apparent to management at WQTE that their programming with Ed McKenzie and company was not drawing a significant audience and at the same time was costing a fortune in salaries. As a result, the station decided to change direction and go with a full-blown Top 40 rock format, and in an ironic twist of fate, they hired none other than Tom Clay for afternoons, replacing the man who blew the whistle on payola in the first place: "This is Tom Clay with something old, something new, something borrowed, and something blue–especially for a 'cutie' like you!"[1]

Harv Morgan was hired for mornings and Danny Murphy (Joe Bacarella) for nine to noon. A disc jockey from WONE in Dayton, Ohio, named Dave Hull, came on at noon. In Dayton, Hull picked up the memorable nickname "the Hullabalooer." A woman had written in, saying "she couldn't stand all that hullabaloo" on his show. After looking up the word in a dictionary and seeing it defined as "a tumultuous outroar," Hull decided it would make the perfect nickname.

Because WQTE was licensed to Monroe, some forty-five miles away, the FCC required that 51 percent of the broadcast day originate from there, so deejays Harv Morgan and Danny Murphy did their shows from Monroe, while Hull and Clay held forth from the downtown Detroit studios, in the Brink Building, on Library Street behind Hudson's Department Store.

The station had professional production and jingles promoting "Fabulous 56" and their record survey was called the "Cutie Music Meter." Dave Hull remembers that, although the station sounded good, there was a problem with the dial location. "All the radio action in town was from 760 on up and the other rock stations were way up the dial, so people were not used to going all the way down to 560. We did, however, start to build an audience when the kids discovered us down there and the low position made it kinda cool to listen."

WQTE could also measure its impact by the crowds lining up for the big dances Tom Clay was hosting at Cobo Hall. "They started with monthly dances and grew every week," recalls Hull. "You would look out there and see three, four, or six thousand kids lined up to get in. They [the dances] were very successful, mainly records, but we did have recording artists too. I think it was very exciting because Cobo Hall was brand-new and just the sheer size of it and the crowd made it special."[2]

Tom Clay was signing off his show with a version of "That's All" by Johnny Mathis.

The programming on "Cutie Radio" brought the number of stations competing for Detroit's Top 40 audience to five.


WHILE TOM CLAY MADE A QUICK RECOVERY, Mickey Shorr wound up exiting his beloved hometown. After a brief radio job in Florida, he headed for California, where he got into business with his brother.[3]

Meanwhile, WXYZ shifted Paul Winter to Mickey's slot. Possibly a bit professorial sounding for the afternoon crowd, Winter pulled good ratings and did his best to rock 'n' roll, signing off his show each evening with "Goodnight, Detroit Baby."[4]

When the dust had settled at WJBK, there were new voices on the air. Harvey Kaye from WKMH replaced Tom Clay on the "Jack the Bellboy Show" from seven to midnight.

A deejay with the historically famous name of Robert E. Lee was brought in for afternoon drive. Originally from Detroit, Lee graduated from Cooley High School in 1950. He claimed to be an actual descendant of Gen. Robert E. Lee. He was working for a station in Muskegon, Michigan, when he was hired at WJBK. One of the wilder disc jockeys on the air in Detroit, he opened his show each afternoon with the "rebel yell," a screaming "Yee-hah!" Then over some rousing Dixieland music he would announce: "Welcome into the Robert E. Lee spree on 'JBK! From now till seven, we'll have all the hits from the 'Radio 15 Record Review' and a few 'Flashbacks' too."

WJBK was the first station in Detroit to creatively program oldies with specially produced introductions, made over the instrumental opening of a song: "Here's another WJBK flash-back...flash-back...flash-back."

There were some deejays who liked to arrive early and do lots of preparation for their shows, laying everything out in advance. Robert E. Lee did some of his best show prep at a favorite pub down the street, called MoMo's, where he earned the nickname "Last Call Lee."

There were days when two o'clock rolled around and the rebel was nowhere to be found. Someone would race out to the parking lot where they would find him taking a post-lunch siesta. After an abrupt wake-up call, Lee would race into the building, up the stairs, hit the air, and carry on for the next five hours, clowning and singing along with records.

His memorable close each evening included the advice: "Be sure and save your confederate bread, your Dixie cups, and, of course, always walk tall. Till tomorrow, long about 2:05, this is your boy, Robert E. Lee, the rebel with a cause, saying, farewell, *cool* world."

It probably seems incongruous that in Detroit, a city with a large African-American population, someone would go on the air with this sort of thing, but at the time no one read any racial over-tones into it. It was just looked on as "cool" to be a rebel, period. As it was, no one seemed to be rating what was politically correct, and Robert E. Lee became an afternoon fixture on 'JBK.[5]

Middays at radio 15 featured Clark Reid, "On the Sunny Side," from ten to two. Reid, having survived the purge of 1959, opened his show each day with "I Wanna Be Happy" by the Four Freshmen.

Bob Larimer did the "Morning Express" from five-thirty to ten.

In 1960, "Joltin'" Joe Howard moved from soul station WCHB to WJLB, which had been trying to lure him for some time. Tom Warner was the general manager, but on this occasion, the grand old man himself, John Lord Booth, was on hand at contract-signing time. "I thought I made a good deal, but later found out I could have done a lot better, recalls Howard. "Like a lot of guys back then, I was inexperienced when it came to business dealings and probably could have used some help. Whatever, it was more money than I had been making."

The WJLB studios were downtown on the thirty-first floor of the David Broderick Tower and, unlike WCHB, it was a union operation. "I had a mike and a kill switch and that was it," says Joe. "On the other side of the glass was an engineer who would play the records and commercials. I had my own exclusive engineer and we worked real well together."

Joe would sign on with his theme song, a funky little number by Big Jay McNalley called "The Goof." About ten bars into it, the music would abruptly stop for a few seconds and he would jump in with: "Who you expectin', the Lone Ranger?" Or he would say: "Who you expectin', Little Red Riding Hood?" People would tune in to hear what he was going to say next.

"Joltin' Joe" would take to the air from noon to four, and although the rock stations in town were already abiding by approved playlists, Joe says he had complete control of the music on his show the whole time he was with 'JLB: "Frantic Ernie paid a little more attention to the charts and the teen hits," says Howard. "I played it real bluesy, layin' down some Muddy Waters, Howlin' Wolf, and Jimmy Reed every day." Larry Dixon, who worked with Joe for years, says that "Joe Howard knows blues music better than anybody."

If Joe was really stuck on a certain song, he might play it two or three times back to back and then come on the air pretending that he was just getting off the phone with an irate listener: "All right, all right, I *won't* play it again!" He then would proceed to crank up the same record one more time!

Although he did hops and club appearances, "Joltin' Joe" could usually be found heading things up at the Phelps Lounge on Wednesday nights. At the corner of Oakland and Owens, the place would seat four hundred but there were many nights when the walls were bending and the crowd looked more like six hundred. Joe would emcee and record companies would be "beggin'" to get their acts on stage: "We had all the early Motown acts like the Contours and the Temptations before and after they got big. The

Temps would come over and sing a cappella! We also had folks like Chuck Jackson and the Dells out of Chicago. Some artists would lip-synch but most went on live with our house band," recalls Howard. That very hot house band happened to be the same group of guys who cooked by day in the Motown studios: Earl Van Dyke, James Jammerson, and the crew.

Joe also remembers having to really hustle to get some of his performers to the club: "I had an arrangement with the people at the Twenty Grand, whereby I could have their headliner also appear at my Phelps Lounge gig on Wednesday, as long as I got them back in time to hit the stage over there. I would take off, pick up the artist, transport them to the Phelps for a show, and then get them back to the Twenty Grand. I don't remember ever blowin' it."

The worst memory Howard retains from his days at 'JLB stems from that November day in 1963 when news director George White came into the studio and informed him that President Kennedy had been shot. "At first I thought he was joking but after a few minutes I found out the bad news. I went down to the general manager's office and said, 'Don't you think I should wind down this music and get into something a little more suitable?' The manager says: 'Naw, just keep going.' People were calling in, telling me how terrible I was for continuing on with the regular records," Howard painfully recalls.[6] Despite it, "Joltin' Joe" recovered and did just fine over the years at WJLB.


ROBIN SEYMOUR, WHO USUALLY WENT BY HIS FIRST NAME only, was moved to mornings at WKMH in 1960. The station had dropped its CBS affiliation and was trying to recover. The new deejay attracting a lot of attention in the evening was Lee Alan. On the air it was "Lee Alan on the Horn" and the records he played were referred to as "round ones."

Alan had departed WJBK in the aftermath of the payola scandal. "I was doing the all-night show one night and at about two-thirty, I started to talk about the whole payola mess that had gone down," he remembers. "I was commenting about how it had all begun with the rigged quiz shows. This went back years and years and was so prevalent because the worst thing you could have happen on one of those question-and-answer programs was have contestants who didn't know any answers. So, the shows would find clever ways of tipping people. I said that I had been on one of these shows myself, which was true. When I was a kid, I went to New York with a group from school and we appeared on 'Break the Bank' and sure enough, they made sure we were able to come up with the right answers. Well, when I got off the air at six in the morning, there's a photographer waiting outside the door and he snaps a picture. I thought, Gee, that's nice. Later that day I got a phone call and was told to get down to the station. The newspaper had run a story with my picture and the headline read DJ ADMITS PART IN RIGGED QUIZ SHOW."

At WKMH, Lee found a station struggling in the ratings. "Robin Seymour had a pretty commercial show and that was about it at that time," Alan recalls. "They gave me a lot of leeway on the air and I was able to experiment and do about whatever I wanted. A number of features or gimmicks I used over the years were developed while I was on WKMH."[7]

At midnight, 'KMH put the rock away and aired an all-night jazz show hosted by the extremely urbane Jim Rockwell. "This is Rockwell and these are records," he would articulate as he broadcast his nightly program from the penthouse studio in the Sheraton Cadillac Hotel in downtown Detroit. The rest of the day's programming originated at the Dearborn studios on Michigan Avenue and Greenfield.

WKMH jingle from 1960:

*This is WKMH, 1310, where you're hearing things!*


A SIGN OF THE NEW DECADE at WXYZ was the hiring of that station's first "second generation" disc jockey, Joel Sebastian, to go on from ten to midnight, as Jack Surrell and his piano were phased out altogether, viewed as incompatible with the Top 40 sound.

All the guys on Wixie had sort of invented themselves as deejays by necessity–Fred Wolf from sports, Paul Winter from radio performer, and Fred Weiss from staff announcer. Joel Sebastian was already seasoned as a Top 40 rock deejay, arriving from KLIF, the famous McLendon station in Dallas. Sebastian knew what he was doing and whom he was doing it for and he was about to lead WXYZ charging into the sixties.

A native Detroiter, Sebastian graduated in 1954 from Redford High School. Classmates recall him as a pretty hip dresser who wore his hair longer than most of the other guys. He was attending the University of Michigan, where he originally had planned to study medicine, when he landed his first radio job, part-time at WPAG in Ann Arbor, about 1955. After school came a stretch in the army, where he was assigned to Armed Forces Radio, based in New York. In 1958, Joel was playing the hits at WNHC in New Haven, Connecticut, and then on to KLIF in Dallas.

He had been on WXYZ only a short time when he left briefly for a job at WIND in Chicago. Detroit fans cried loud and Wixie wooed him back. He returned to a hero's welcome, arriving at Broadcast House in a helicopter.[8]

Fred Weiss, who was looked on as having limited teen appeal, was moved to weekends, and Joel was given the entire evening.

Sebastian purred with a rich voice that was both deep and mellow. He became very popular and was able to relate to younger listeners in a far more believable way than his predecessors. Instead of someone who tolerated rock music, he sounded as if he liked it. He had fun on the air but his calling card was an awesome voice, sincere style, and a good amount of sex appeal.

He would really get into the mood of the music, talking soft and low as he introduced teen anthems such as "Angel Baby" by Rosie and the Originals or "Baby, It's You" by the Shirrelles, as if he had a personal understanding of the situation described in the song. Sebastian would also read letters and dedications on the air and pass along some "big brotherly" advice. This approach was decidedly different from that of many of the relentlessly spunky Top-40 disc jockeys across the country, parodied by comedians as "climbing that plattter ladder with stacks of wax." In Detroit, the disc jockeys, in general, were more stylists, who either grew out of the earlier prerock era of radio, such as Clark Reid and Bud Davies, or were influenced by them along with other past Detroit deejays, such as McKenzie, Shorr, and McLeod. Then there was Tom Clay, who arrived in the market with original talent that fit Motor City tastes like a glove.

Sebastian could take time to communicate, talking on the air about the record artists:

> That was really a team effort on the part of two people from right here in Detroit. Jamie Coe, who wrote it, and another talented Detroiter, named Mickey Denton. It's about fourteen

minutes in front of eleven, we'll have news live at fifty-five on WXYZ.

Those are the Paris Sisters and "I Love How You Love Me" and it comes in at number nine on this week's WXYZ Tunedex. It's twelve before ten on the Joel Sebastian Show for a Monday night. [*commercial*] We had the pleasure of talking with our good buddy Del Shannon not long ago and he was showing us some new songs he was considering for his next single and I told him that "Swiss Maid" would be a good break from his last few records, which had kind of a similar sound, so we're happy it's the new single. Let's give a listen on 12-7-0.[9]

Joel Sebastian was a great disc jockey but his song recommendation was questionable, as "Swiss Maid" never made it past the bottom end of the top 100 charts!

If a record was fast, popular, and a novelty, Sebastian wasn't opposed to playing it more than once, evidenced by the night he spun "Norman" by Sue Thompson six times in a row.

The "Swinging Spaniard" did a lot of record hops and broadcast his show on weekends from UAW Hall No. 182 in Plymouth; on the air it was "Joel Sebastian, lookin' for you at Club 182." He did a popular oldies show on Friday evenings (later moved to Sundays): "WXYZ, AM and FM, in good old Detroit. I'm Joel Sebastian and I've got 'Movin' Memories' for you!"[10] At midnight, he offered a very warm and memorable sign-off: "It's a very ordinary world and you're a *most* extraordinary audience," at which time he would play the title line from a song called "I'm Glad There Is You," and close out with "Goodnight, Sweetheart, Goodnight" by the Spaniels. It was part of the sound track of an era. Loyal fans proudly carried their "Sebastian Swinger" cards.

At midnight, WXYZ launched the "All-Night Satellite," with the king of the night people, Don Zee, at the controls. It eventually evolved into his own show as he hammed it up with sound effects and catchy phrases.

Opening at the stroke of midnight with the sound of fluttering bats in the background, Dracula would be heard calling out to Vampira, "Come, fly away vit me!" Then, over some creepy drum and organ music, in a deep voice, Don would announce: "It's time to open that long black box. Welcome in, this is Don Zee, with *two e's if you please,* we've got musical kicks from now until *six!*"

Don Zee was the ultimate late-night deejay, with a voice that radiated "cool" as he operated in the "graveyard shift" six nights a week. He was great company for late-night workers and cruisers as well as younger kids plugged into transistor radios in their bedrooms, trying to stay awake at least long enough to hear some of the nightly rituals. WXYZ promotions included a "Worst Jokes of 1960" contest and a "Why I Like My Mother-in-law" contest, where listeners sent in 1,269 essays.

WXYZ jingle from 1961:

> *Turn your radio on, Turn your radio on,*
> *You'll like the music we play;*
> *Leave your radio on, Leave your radio on,*
> *The music is great, with news up to date*
> *On WXYZ.*
> *It's the right sound, it's the bright sound,*
> *WXYZ Detroit.* [10]

Things had eased up a bit for the WXYZ deejays when Hal Neal was promoted on to ABC in New York. His replacement was John Gilbert. Bob Baker remained program director but the disc jockeys took back much of the control in between records on their programs, although they still worked from a playlist.

"DETROIT'S OWN JACK SCOTT," as the deejays used to say, switched labels to Top Rank and hit the national top five twice in 1960 with the mournful "What in the World's Come over You" and "Burning Bridges." His "Jack Scott's Barn Dance" was a popular destination for Detroit area teenagers.

Berry Gordy started the new decade with another Marv Johnson hit leased to United Artists. "I Love the Way You Love" went to No. 9. In December, Gordy released "Shop Around" by the Miracles on his Tamla label, and it became Motown's first million seller.

As 1961 GOT UNDER WAY, Bud Davies was on in the late afternoon at CKLW and people were tuning in for the latest hits and the "Shafer Bread Quickie Quiz."

Based on the recent number of big crossover hits from the

country charts, such as "Battle of New Orleans," "Waterloo," and "El Paso," CK' went country in the evening hours with a show called "Sounds like Nashville." Disc jockey Bob Staton hosted during the week, Croft McClellan on Saturday.

IN FEBRUARY, WJBK DECIDED TO MAKE CHANGES in its low-rated morning show and hired Marc Avery from station KAIR in Tucson, Arizona. "This is M.A. in the A.M.," he would say each morning between five-thirty and ten. The nickname had been bestowed upon him by the mother of Jonathan Winters. "She ran the station I worked for in Springfield, Ohio, and Jonathon had worked there before going on to Cleveland," Avery recalls. "One day she looked me in the eye and proclaimed: 'You will be M.A. in the A.M.,' just like that and it stuck."

To promote his arrival, the station had Marc telephoning in from somewhere out in the boondocks where he was supposedly lost. Listeners would call in to 'JBK and give him directions to Detroit.[11]

Avery had a great "breakfast table" personality and a way of keeping listeners involved by asking a lot of questions that he would wind up answering himself as he would carry on in his very conversational style about the weather, the wife and kids, and the trials and tribulations of everyday life. He was a sort of one-man "morning zoo." Avery sounded like the kind of neighbor you might bump into on the driveway who says, "Hey, looks like some rain today." He just said it to a lot of neighbors every morning on the radio.

As a perfect family-oriented guy on a mass-appeal radio station, Marc even brought his four-year-old daughter, Kim, to the studios to tape some things he could use on his show. Listeners would hear her reminding her father: "You better get the weather ready" or "Dad, the coffee man is out in the hall."[13] Avery's folksy style caught on and he was able to move 'JBK's morning ratings upward.

"Radio 15" was not as highly formatted as many other Top 40 stations in 1961. "WJBK was very successful," recalls Avery. "About the only directive we really had to follow was that we play as many commercials as we could possibly cram into an hour. I mean we were running twenty-two spots plus two newscasts. That kept it pretty tight."

More than on the show itself, Avery's memories of those days focus on the entertainers that he came into contact with: "I remember going over to see Berry Gordy's sisters, Anna and Gwen. They had their own label, which was called Tri Phi Records. There I met a new artist they were really excited about. He had a record out that was a kind of mellow version of 'Mr. Sandman.' His name was Marvin Gaye and he was quite shy and sort of withdrawn. He was soft-spoken, not at all like people think of him, belting out those big hits later on. That record didn't do anything but Marvin moved over to Berry's company, where things started to happen."

Marc Avery feels strongly that WJBK did an awful lot for the early Motown artists before they became famous: "We really got behind the Temptations and the Supremes, I can tell you that. We promoted something like ten stiffs in a row for The Supremes. We took them out on record hops all the time. I remember one night we were at Saint Christopher's school in southwest Detroit and the Supremes were singing one of these songs and the kids were not very nice. They were throwing pennies at the girls, not a pleasant crowd. Now, waiting backstage or down the hall, I've got Patsy Cline and she has on that wild cowgirl outfit she used to wear. I'm thinking, This doesn't look good. So, like Ed Sullivan scolding the kids in the audience, I stop the music and tell everybody that 'we're going to pack up and split if you can't be a little nicer.' I guess it worked cause the pennies stopped and Patsy wowed 'em."[13]

On Patsy Cline, Avery recalls a great trip he made to Nashville to attend a party for songwriter Harlon Howard, who was responsible for a slew of hits including "Heartaches by the Number." "This was a great experience 'cause I was there with Willie Nelson, years before he became so popular. Roger Miller was there and another songwriter named Hank Cochran and Patsy Cline. Anyhow, the thing I recall is Willie Nelson and Patsy Cline taking me into another room and playing me an acetate of 'Crazy,' which Willie had written. I thought it was just great and they asked me if I would like to take it back to Detroit and have it as an exclusive. I did and it became a huge hit."[14]

Marc Avery could also be seen Saturday mornings on WJBK-TV, where he hosted a kids' show called "Junior Auction."

AFTER A YEAR IN THE TOP 40 RADIO WARS, WQTE management decided there was only so much pimple cream advertising to be spread between five youth-oriented stations and they were not getting their share. At ten o'clock on a Monday morning in June of 1961, the air staff of "Cutie" was called into a special meeting with owners Dick Jones and Ross Mulholland.

According to Dave Hull, it was short and sweet. "Dick Jones said, 'We're changing format and you're all fired. You have five minutes to clean out your desks and leave the building, we'll be waiting at the elevators.'[15] Well, I was young and felt the threat so I went racing to my cubicle and threw a few things together and Morgan was doing the same. Then I looked around and I couldn't find the production guy who we had only recently hired away from a station in Miami. The clock is ticking and I'm looking all over. Finally, I peak in the production studio, which was dark at the time, and down in the corner I see this guy with his arm swinging back and forth. He is holding on to a magnetic degausser and erasing as many tape carts as he can, including commercials. I said, 'What are you up to?' I've never forgotten his response: 'I'm waving my magic wand,'" Hull laughed, adding, "I guess it was his little revenge."[16]

That was it for rock 'n' roll at 560. The station switched to an easy-listening album format so sanguine that it featured soothing harp music to introduce the news. Dave Hull packed up and headed back to Ohio, landing at WTVN in Columbus.

Meanwhile, station management, namely Ross Mulholland, wanted a share of the reportedly "big money" Tom Clay had generated through record hops including the Cobo Hall dances. The always controversial and dramatic disc jockey put out a newsletter in which he defended himself in typical Clay fashion: "How do you write your swan song? Do you wait until the end of the note and very dramatic like, say...."[17] What Clay did say was no way to the station's request and adios as he split for southern California.

IN DETROIT DURING THE SUMMER OF 1961, Lee Alan moved to afternoons at WKMH and, as a replacement, 1310 radio hired Dave Prince for the 7:30 P.M. to 11:30 P.M. slot. Prince, of Sioux Indian background, was born in Fabins, Texas, and was in the first grade with horse jockey Willie Shoemaker. At sixteen, he split for El

Paso, where he went to school and broke into radio. Later, he moved up to WPAG in Ann Arbor and then on to 'KMH.[18]

Frank Maruca was the program director and Dave Prince remembers the meeting where he was hired: "Frank said, 'Be on time and don't get blue on the air,' as in raunchy.[19] That was it. He said I could basically do what I want and play what I want. It was a great opportunity. The station had a three share when I started and I was able to get it up to a fifteen."

Prince created a lot of commotion at WKMH when he started using the nickname "Sangoo." "It was a fluke," he recalls. "The Tokens had just released 'The Lion Sleeps Tonight' and on the flip side there was this silly little song called 'Tina.' The song had some pretty lame lyrics including the word 'sangoo.' I just thought it was funny and we started using it."

Each night, Dave "Sangoo" Prince would bang on trash cans and sound as if he were inside one. "When I was working in Ann Arbor, we had a sales manager named Ken McDonald, and he would sometimes hold a trash can over his head to get an echo effect for a commercial, because the station sure didn't have any equipment that could do that," Prince relates. "I told this story on WKMH and demonstrated by yelling 'sang-goo' with my head in a trash can. Well, people thought this was real wild and then Lee Alan, who also working there, showed me how to thread a tape so you would really get a great echo, and that's what people were hearing when I would do this devilish laugh and yell 'sang-goo!' It was just a crazy thing that really took off. The station told me they wanted to run some promotional ads and I said no. I felt it would ruin the wild image of whatever the listeners thought was happening. It would take off the edge. Even today, people will come up to me and mention that name."

It was a three-way battle for the rock audience in the evening during 1961 and the competition was fierce. Dave Prince was up against the "Jack the Bellboy" show on WJBK and Joel Sebastian on WXYZ. Both Sebastian and Prince lived in Ann Arbor. "I had known Joel for a long time," remembers Prince. "He was attending U of M and would come around WPAG when I was working there full-time. By the way, WPAG stood for 'women's pants and girdles.' This is around 1955 and he started working weekends. We heard that WWJ was looking for an announcer to do a classical program and we both tried out and Joel got the job.

"Anyhow, here we are on against each other a few years down the road. Now, Joel used to tape the last hour of his show in advance and then leave early 'cause he had so far to drive. So I would go on the air and make this big deal about it. 'This is Sangoo and I'm right here at the station and you can call me and talk or request a song. You can't do that with Joel Sebastian because he is on his way home right now, while I'm here live workin' for ya'. If you don't believe me, here's his number at the station.' Kids would call the number and an engineer would answer. They would call me back and say, 'Yeah, you were right.' I mean you would do anything to make some headway in the ratings back then. The only time you really felt like you were having any impact was when you would say, 'Come on out to my record hop' or whatever you had going on and people would actually show up."

While working at WKMH, Dave Prince began a long tumultuous personal as well as legal relationship with fellow deejay Lee Alan. One night after the show, the two stopped off for a beer at a little bar on Michigan Avenue, not too far from the studios. As they were talking and sipping, they focused on how empty the place was. When the bar owner stopped by their table, they struck up a conversation. "The owner happened to be Joe Bonamo, better known as 'Joe Bananas,'" remembers Prince. "We said, 'Hey, it doesn't look too busy in here. If you could do a little advertising on WKMH, I think we could put some people through the door." So we put a deal together to promote dances over there where we would charge a buck to get in and we get the gate. He can charge fifty cents for drinks. The Twist was red hot so we called the place Morey's Royal Twist Lounge, and it really took off. It wasn't the Peppermint Lounge, but Lee and I made more money there than we did from the station, 'cause we were getting four hundred to five hundred people each night," claims Prince. The house band was the Royaltones.[20]

YET ANOTHER "JACK THE BELLBOY" CHECKED IN at WJBK that fall, with the arrival of Dave Shafer, a friendly sounding disc jockey who mixed in a lot of humor, kidding commercials and doing different voices and clever record intros. Shafer liked playing new records and was always asking listeners to "dig this new sound." He was also very good with "drop-ins." These were little funny

lines or sound bites lifted from other sources and used at appropi-
ate times during the show. "I would spend a lot of time listening to
off-the-wall records, especially comedy albums, trying to find
some things that would work," he recalls.[21]

A drop-in that got a lot of mileage on Dave's show usually followed a bad joke or an irritating commercial. It featured the voice
of a rather despairing human being who, in a quivering delivery,
would utter, "Oh, man, I'm sick aw-ready!" Shafer would then try
to console the poor wretch. Then there was a guy who, in a real hep
voice, would pop in and say, "Go big daddy!" Recalling these routines Shafer chuckles. Dave would also enlist the help of comedians who were in town. "I met up with a very young George Carlin
at the Elmwood Casino [in Windsor] and he would come over to
'JBK and cut some very funny voices for me to use."

After starting off his radio career in Dover, Delaware, at, what
else, WDOV, Dave moved to a station in Tucson, Arizona. The guy
that hired him was Marc Avery. When that station changed format,
it left Shafer out of a job, so he got in contact with Avery who had
left earlier for Detroit.

"I went to my boss at WJBK and told him 'I've got a friend who
is very talented and I think you should hire him,'" remembers Marc
Avery. "The only problem was, there were no openings on the air
staff. I said, 'Isn't there something we can use him for?' The boss
said, 'Is he very good at organization? We could use a record librarian.' Well, I called Dave and he wasn't exactly excited but he needed
the job real bad. He was low on funds so I managed to convince the
station to move him all the way from Tucson, Arizona, to work in
the record library," Avery laughs, adding what an accomplishment
that was, because of the thrifty policies at Storer Broadcasting.[22]

Dave Shafer remembers that he had a choice of coming to
Detroit or taking the all-night show at KYA in San Francisco: "My
wife had family not far from Detroit and that's why I took the job. I
worked in the record library and did some production until the
fall, when Harvey Kaye left and I was moved into the "Jack the
Bellboy Show," he recalls, adding: "It's interesting to note that the
guy who took the KYA job was named Bill Drake."

Commenting on the musical content and format, Shafer says:
"There wasn't much in the way of structure, as far as what records
to play at certain times or how or when to use jingles. It was all
pretty much up to the disc jockeys back then, at least at 'JBK. Our

ratings were pretty high, so I guess we were doing something right."[23] The records Shafer and the other guys played, however, did come from the station's approved playlist of about fifty songs put together by program director John Grubbs.

Some of the best record promotion men in the business operated out of Detroit. There was Russ Yerge at Columbia, Tom Gelardi at Capitol, and Harvey Cooper at RCA. WJBK's Clark Reid recalls other top Motor City "hit men," including Sol "Solid Gold" Starr, Sammy "Where am I" Kaplan, Bobby "the Budda" Schwartz, Gordon Prince, and one of the few college grads in the business, Don "Mom wanted me to be a dentist" Schmitzerle.

Detroit was a "breakout market," a town where others measured the performance of new product. If a guy had records in his blood, there wasn't a hotter place to be.

Tuesday was record-meeting day at 'JBK and after eats at the Star Waffle Shop across the street, the deejays would head back to the studios on the second floor above television at Second and Bethune. The halls would be buzzing with fast-talking record promotion men, desperate for one last shot at pitching what was surely going to be the "next number one song, baby!"

"There was always a crowd of these record guys hustling us but I especially recall a fellow named Armen Boladian, who represented Wand/Scepter Records for a local distributor," recalls Clark Reid. "Somehow he would always manage to jump out of the shadows, just as the door was about to shut and get in that last plug."[24]

Behind closed doors, the disc jockeys would listen and vote on new records and John Grubbs would agree or disagree.

Dave Shafer explains how he did break some new records: "I had a feature where I introduced several new records each week called "bell ringers." Kids would vote on these and we would come up with the "bell ringer of the week." Some of the records we started included 'I Will Follow Him' by Little Peggy March and 'It's My Party' by Leslie Gore."

Although the big days of payola had passed a couple of years earlier, there were occasions when a disc jockey could feel a little added pressure to get on a record. One afternoon, Shafer found himself in a restaurant, sitting across from none other than Morris Levy, the president of Roulette Records. "Moishe," as he was known around New York in those days, was a great negotiator and he always had the better end of any recording contract, whether it was Buddy Knox or Sarah Vaughan. He was a heavyweight in the record business and well connected with the bent-nose crowd. In 1957, the trade publication *Variety* had dubbed Levy the "octopus" of the music industry, because of his extensive dealings.[25] What kind of guy was Morris Levy? "If you screw him," said one former friend, "he'll always get revenge."[26]

"Levy was taking a very personal interest[27] in a new record they had out and he says to me: 'What's it gonna to take to get this record on your show?'"[28] recounts Shafer, who, sounding a bit like a boy scout, replied: "I'm not allowed to accept any gifts or gratuities but I will recommend it to my program director and I can probably get it on as a 'bell ringer.'" Hard-boiled Morris Levy didn't really care to hear any more about "bell ringers" or other such nonsense but left feeling that Shafer was positive about the song. Dave Shafer: "The record was 'Peppermint Twist' by Joey Dee and the Starliters, which I could tell was going to be a huge hit without any extra help. It just took off and hit number one pretty quick."

While a deejay for WJBK, Dave did his share of record hops, including a regular gig at Dixie Skate Land in Monroe each week. "As a result of the way I was hired, I was making a lot less than the other guys and I had to practically quit before they gave me a raise," says Shafer. "After getting a little better deal on salary, I negotiated the right to tape my Saturday night show so I could be free for record hops, and it made a big difference."[29]

Like Marc Avery, Shafer took along some of the early Motown artists to the dances. "I met Stevie Wonder when he was just starting out," recalls Shafer. "His parents would bring him to the station and he would sit around the studio with me. I'd pick him up at his house and take him to the hops. The kids just loved him and wouldn't let him off the stage." Martha and the Vandellas and the Supremes also worked with Dave in the early days and he says he has been able to stay in touch over the years.

The most memorable thing about Shafer's show was his opening theme–a real period piece. Starting with pounding drums in the background, a big voice would then announce: "Here's Jack the Bellboy, Dave Shafer." Then, over a driving beat, the chorus would sing, "He's sharp, he's sweet, he's hot, he's a solid old cat" and continue on with, "He rocks, sings, jumps and swings, he's the end, I'm a friend so dig that sound and jump for joy!"[30]

Dave Shafer on the air:

Hello there, everybody, welcome aboard, Dave Shafer, Jack the Bellboy on ever lovin' WJBK [sound of a hotel service bell], getting set to swing away on this wild Wednesday night. Ready to go? Here we go! Okay Dion, *you're on!* [music] That's Dion with his big follow-up to "Runaround Sue" here on Radio 15, it's called "The Wanderer," as we get things under way on the Bellboy show. It's eight past seven and here's another biggie play from our survey, the Angels with "Till." [music] That's in the top 15! "Till" from the Angels, the time is eleven minutes after eight on this warm Wednesday night, twenty-one degrees out there, that's warm! It's going down to fourteen tonight. [WJBK jingle, Cover Girl Makeup commercial] Here's a brand-new up and comin' sound on the Radio 15 Record Review, it's the big beat sound of Sandy Nelson and "Let There Be Drums."

The Pulse rating service ranked Dave Shafer number one in Detroit at night in the fall of 1961 and again in the winter of 1962.[31] He was followed at midnight by Bob Eggington on "Night Beat."

WJBK jingle from 1961:

*Radio 15 will brighten your day,*
*Listening's fun on WJBK*

"JAMIE COE AND THE GIGOLOS" were one of the hottest acts on the Detroit entertainment scene and, like most other bands, they survived by playing the local record hop circuit. In 1959, they were hired to open one of the big stage shows at the State Fair Coliseum, where Bobby Darin was headlining a show that included Jan and Dean, on the charts with their first hit, "Baby Talk," as well as singer Teddy Randazzo. "We got out there and I did a killer version of the Little Richard song 'Miss Ann' and we just tore the place apart," remembers Jamie Coe.[32]

Bobby Darin, who was already thinking of ways to expand his involvement in show business beyond performing, was impressed and became Jamie's manager. He took him to New York, where Coe signed on with Bobby's label, Addison Records. His first release was a Bobby Darin song called "Summertime Symphony." It wasn't much of a hit, but it got Coe a spot on "American Bandstand."

Jamie then started his long trip down record row as Addison was sold to ABC-Paramount. His first release on ABC was

"Goodbye My Love, Goodbye" in the summer of 1960. Toward the end of 1961, he enjoyed a big local smash with "How Low Is Low." "That record was played twice on WXYZ and the next day they had ten thousand requests for it," says Coe. "They were totally taken off guard and the label dropped the ball and the record never made it out of Detroit."[33]

Marc Avery recalls working with Jamie. "He was so popular in Detroit. The kids would be more excited about seeing Jamie and the group than a lot of the national record artists." Later, Jamie became a regular attraction at Club Gay Haven on Warren Avenue. "It seemed like everybody in radio and records would wind up over there at night, he just put on a great show," adds Avery.[34]

ONE OF THE MORE INTERESTING CHARACTERS on the Detroit music scene was a guy named Harry Balk, a sort of road show version of Morris Levy. Although he had early ambitions as an entertainer, he got into the talent-booking end of the business with partner Irving Micahnik. This is after the two had left the siding business.

Balk and company had creative ways of doing business. In 1959, they signed a Toledo band called Johnny and the Hurricanes to their Twirl record label at a royalty rate of 1½ percent and then leased the records to Warwick Records at 8 percent. This resulted in a tidy profit when records like "Crossfire" and "Red River Rock" became big hits. They had the group continue to record reworked versions of songs that were in the public domain and credit themselves as composers to pick up writer's royalties. When this concept had been mined completely, Johnny and the Hurricanes faded fast.

The next artist to come under their influence was Del Shannon, who came from the Grand Rapids area. Del was working in a carpet store during the day and at night was on stage at the Hi Lo Club in Battle Creek. Ollie McLaughlin, the nighttime deejay at WHRV in Ann Arbor, caught his show and was impressed enough to bring him to the attention of Balk's Talent Artists booking agency in Detroit. They heard his songs and saw real potential, immediately locking him up in a tight contract. They recorded what they thought was his best song and leased it to Big Top records in New York. The result was "Runaway," one of the greatest hits from the rock 'n' roll era. It was a number one million seller and was followed by "Hats off to Larry," which reached number five. "Hey, Little Girl" and "So Long Baby" also made the national Top 40 during 1961. When he realized he was still not making any real money, despite these hits, Del left the label and began a decade-long fight with Balk and company over lost royalties.[35]

After Jamie Coe's ABC-Paramount contract ended, he, like others, turned to Balk and Micahnik. Jamie and his group, the Gigolos, did come up with another local hit with "The Fool" before problems set in. "I had the opportunity to audition for the Jackie Gleason show," remembers Coe. "I received a phone call about a week later telling me I had been chosen. I had beaten out Wayne Newton. I was getting ready to do the show and then a few days later the phone rang and someone told me I was no longer on. I found out my great managers, Harry and Irving, got greedy and demanded more money. The Gleason people just said forget it and that was it."[36]

While Jamie was struggling in Detroit, Berry Gordy was going way beyond the local scene as "Please Mr. Postman" by the Marvelettes became Motown's first record to reach number one nationally.

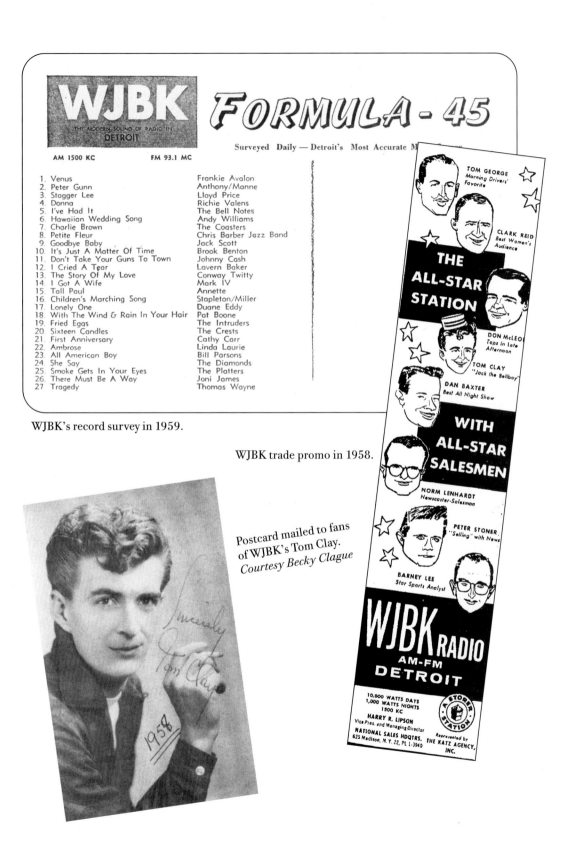

# WJBK FORMULA - 45

THE MODERN SOUND OF RADIO IN DETROIT

AM 1500 KC    FM 93.1 MC

Surveyed Daily — Detroit's Most Accurate M...

| 1. Venus | Frankie Avalon |
| 2. Peter Gunn | Anthony/Manne |
| 3. Stagger Lee | Lloyd Price |
| 4. Donna | Richie Valens |
| 5. I've Had It | The Bell Notes |
| 6. Hawaiian Wedding Song | Andy Williams |
| 7. Charlie Brown | The Coasters |
| 8. Petite Fleur | Chris Barber Jazz Band |
| 9. Goodbye Baby | Jack Scott |
| 10. It's Just A Matter Of Time | Brook Benton |
| 11. Don't Take Your Guns To Town | Johnny Cash |
| 12. I Cried A Tear | Lavern Baker |
| 13. The Story Of My Love | Conway Twitty |
| 14. I Got A Wife | Mark IV |
| 15. Tall Paul | Annette |
| 16. Children's Marching Song | Stapleton/Miller |
| 17. Lonely One | Duane Eddy |
| 18. With The Wind & Rain In Your Hair | Pat Boone |
| 19. Fried Eggs | The Intruders |
| 20. Sixteen Candles | The Crests |
| 21. First Anniversary | Cathy Carr |
| 22. Ambrose | Linda Laurie |
| 23. All American Boy | Bill Parsons |
| 24. She Say | The Diamonds |
| 25. Smoke Gets In Your Eyes | The Platters |
| 26. There Must Be A Way | Joni James |
| 27. Tragedy | Thomas Wayne |

WJBK's record survey in 1959.

WJBK trade promo in 1958.

Postcard mailed to fans
of WJBK's Tom Clay.
*Courtesy Becky Clague*

TOM GEORGE
Morning Drivers' Favorite

CLARK REID
Best Women's Audience

THE ALL-STAR STATION

DON McLEO...
Tops in Late Afternoon

TOM CLAY
"Jack the Bellboy"

DAN BAXTER
Best All Night Show

WITH ALL-STAR SALESMEN

NORM LENHARDT
Newscaster-Salesman

PETER STONER
"Selling" with News

BARNEY LEE
Star Sports Analyst

WJBK RADIO
AM-FM
DETROIT

10,000 WATTS DAYS
1,000 WATTS NIGHTS
1500 KC
HARRY R. LIPSON
Vice Pres. and Managing Director
NATIONAL SALES HDQTRS.
625 Madison, N.Y. 22, PL 1-3940

A STONER STATION

Represented by
THE KATZ AGENCY, INC.

**7th ANNUAL AUTORAMA**
Sponsored by the
Michigan Hot Rod Association

**JANUARY 9, 10, 11**
FRIDAY—SATURDAY—SUNDAY
MICHIGAN STATE FAIR COLISEUM

*"Detroit's Greatest Auto Show"*
● RAILS ● ROADTERS ● CUSTOMS
● DRAGSTERS ● COUPES ● SEDANS
● SPORTS ● FOREIGN ● CLASSICS
*and*

**VARIETY SHOW**
*with*
★ Duane EDDY and His
'Rebel Rousers'
★ The KALIN TWINS
★ The PONI TAILS
★ JACK SCOTT
The BIG BOPPER
*and*
SIL AUSTIN'S BIG BAND
Introduced from the Coliseum stage by
**DETROIT'S GREAT DEEJAYS**
TOM CLAY, WJBK     ROBIN SEYMOUR, WKMH
BEN JOHNSON, WEXL MICKEY SHORR, WXYZ
DON McCLOUD, WJBK RON KNOWLES, CKLW

**DANCING**
FRIDAY-SATURDAY-SUNDAY
9:30 P.M. 9:30 P.M. 9:30 P.M.
**Variety Show**
FRIDAY        SATURDAY        SUNDAY
8:30 P.M.     2-5-8 P.M.   ❊  2-5-8 P.M.
**Auto Show**
12:00 TO 11:00 P.M. DAIL
ADMISSION $1.50

Early publicity photo of J.P McCarthy, who became host of WJR's "Music Hall" in July, 1958. *Courtesy Judy McCarthy*

Ad for a big teen event in 1959.

Clay on stage at one of his popular record hops. 1958. WJBK's Clay attained teen-idol status in Detroit during the late 1950s. *Courtesy Marilyn Bond Legends in Music Collection*

When Clay was featured on Buffalo's WWOL in 1955 he was known as "Guy King." *Courtesy Becky Clague*

Connie Francis directs the attention of Ron Knowles. During the witch hunt over payola, Ron was sorry he had answered the studio line one evening. His conversation with a reporter was printed in the next day's newspaper. *Courtesy Ron Knowles*

GIVE A BIG
LISTEN TO
DETROIT'S
BIGGEST
MUSIC
MAN

BIG
MICKEY
SHORR on the
BIG AFTERNOON
SHOW! MORE THAN 3 HOURS OF
BIG MUSIC
BIG NEWS
NEWS AT :55
WITH TOM WABER
BIG SPORTS
HEADLINES EVERY HOUR AND
HALF HOUR WITH DON WATTRICK

*It All Adds Up to Big Fun!*

3:00 TO 6:15 P.M. WEEKDAYS

WXYZ RADIO

Ed McKenzie (center) lit a fuse with his *Life* magazine article, "A Deejay's Expose." Meanwhile, Ed returned to radio at WQTE along with Detroit broadcasters Eddie Chase, left, and Ralph Binge. *Courtesy Ralph J. Binge Jr.*

In 1959 Shorr became a target in the payola fiasco.
*Courtesy May Shorr*

Newspaper promo for WJBK's "rebel with a cause," Robert E. Lee. 1962.

WJLB promotes their target market to prospective advertisers. 1961.

Joel Sebastian in George C. Scott's production of "Death of a Salesman," at the Will-O-Way Playhouse, Bloomfield Hills, Michigan, 1955. That's Joel's wife, Frances Sebastian, wearing the hat on the far right. *Courtesy Frances Sebastian*

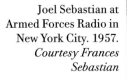

Joel Sebastian at Armed Forces Radio in New York City. 1957. *Courtesy Frances Sebastian*

An aspiring recording artist visits Joel at WXYZ. 1960. *Courtesy Frances Sebastian*

Detroit newspaper promos in 1962.

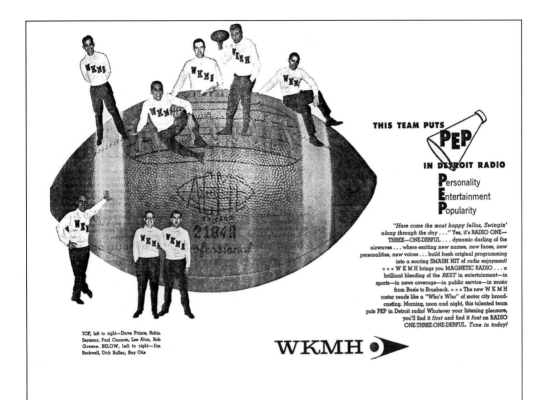

THIS TEAM PUTS

**PEP**

IN DETROIT RADIO

**P**ersonality
**E**ntertainment
**P**opularity

*"Here come the most happy fellas, Swingin' along through the day . . ."* Yes, it's RADIO ONE—THREE—ONE-DERFUL . . . dynamic darling of the airwaves . . . where exciting *new* names, *new* faces, *new* personalities, *new* voices . . . build fresh original programming into a soaring SMASH HIT of radio enjoyment! ★★★ W K M H brings you MAGNETIC RADIO . . . a brilliant blending of the *BEST* in entertainment—in sports—in news coverage—in public service—in music from Basie to Bruebeck. ★★★ The new W K M H roster reads like a "Who's Who" of motor city broadcasting. Morning, noon and night, this talented team puts PEP in Detroit radio! Whatever your listening pleasure, you'll find it *first* and find it *fast* on RADIO ONE-THREE-ONE-DERFUL. Tune *in* today!

TOP, left to right—Dave Prince, Robin Seymour, Paul Cannon, Lee Alan, Bob Greene. BELOW, left to right—Jim Rockwell, Dick Buller, Ray Otis.

**WKMH** ◗

Unique WKMH promo, 1961. Top (left to right): Dave "Sangoo" Prince, Robin Seymour, Paul Cannon, Lee Alan (holding a "round one") and Bob Green. Bottom (left to right): Jazz man, Jim Rockwell, Dick Buller and Ray Otis.

A young Tony Orlando promotes his newest release at a Dave Shafer record hop. 1962. *Courtesy Dave Shafer*

Publicity photo for Dave Shafer, WJBK's "Jack the Bellboy" in 1962. *Courtesy Dave Shafer*

# THE MELLO 9 . . . PLUS 10

### DECEMBER 15, 1962

## YOUR GUIDE TO GOOD LISTENING AND BETTER BUYS
### Compiled By LARRY DIXON - WCHB RADIO - 1440

| | | |
|---|---|---|
| 1. | Upon The Roof ..............Drifters..............Atlantic | |
| 2. | Release Me ....................Little Esther..........Lenox | |
| 3. | Lover Come Back To Me....Cleftones.............Gee | |
| 4. | Everybody Loves A Lover....Shirelles................Scepter | |
| 5. | Zip-A-De-Doo-Dah ............Bob B. Soxx.........Phillies | |
| 6. | You're Gonna Need Me......Barbara Lynn........Jamie | |
| 7. | Jelly Bread .....................Booker T..............Stax | |
| 8. | Anyway You Wanta ...........Harvey...............Tri-Phi | |
| 9. | You Threw a Lucky Punch....Gene Chandler......Vee Jay | |
| 10. | Chains ........................Cookies..............Dimension | |
| 11. | My Man .......................Betty Lavette...... Atlantic | |
| 12. | Comin' Home Baby........Mel Torme...........Atlantic | |
| 13. | Come To Me .................Popcorn Wylie......Epic | |
| 14. | A Wishing Star ..............Jerry Butler........Vee Jay | |
| 15. | Two Lovers ....................Mary Wells...........Motown | |
| 16. | Would It Make Any Difference ....................Etta James...........Argo | |
| 17. | Recipe ...........................Barbara George.....Sue | |
| 18. | Don't Make Me Over.......Dionne Warwick...Scepter | |
| 19. | Fly Me To The Moon........Mark Murphy.....Riverside | |

## MOST MELLO BUYS

I Hope, I Think, I Wish......................Wade Flemons
(Vee Jay)
You're Gonna Need Me.....................Barbara Lynn
(Jamie)
Tweedle Dee.................................Baby Cortez
(Chess)

## MELLO SHOTS

Set Me Free ..............................Larry Bryan
(Vicount)
These Empty Arms.......................Otis Redding
(Volt)
Too Young, Too Much, Too Soon.......Spinners
(Tri-Phi)

WCHB's Larry Dixon published a weekly record survey in his magazine, "Mello-Music Tips," 1962.

Newspaper promo, 1962.

PREMIERES TODAY

JOEL SEBASTIAN

LEE ALAN

CLU
127

Joel Sebastian and Lee Alan teamed on television in 1963. "Club 1270" ran for an hour on Sunday afternoons, before moving to Saturdays.

HITSVILLE 80

DAVE SHAFER

MONDAY thru FRIDAY
3-7 p.m.
SATURDAY
2-6 p.m.

CKLW-RADIO
80

RKO
GENERAL

When Dave Shafer moved to CKLW in May 1963, Terry Knight became the new "Jack the Bellboy" on WJBK.

listen
every night
to
TERRY KNIGHT
on

WJBK

RADIO 15

1500 AM
93.1 FM

"JACK THE BELLBOY" 7 to midnite

J.P. McCarthy, host of the morning and afternoon "Music Hall" on WJR.
*Courtesy Judy McCarthy*

Billboard promo for J.P. during his time with KGO in San Francisco. 1964.
*Courtesy Judy McCarthy*

NAEGELE

EVERYONE LOVES J.P. McCARTHY
6-10 AM
KGO RADIO 81

J.P. on air at 'JR Detroit in 1961. Each day he picked his own records and searched for the winners and losers of the world.
*Courtesy Judy McCarthy*

CA$H FROM WJBK

YOU MAY WIN $15 $150 OR $1,500 IN

(stay tuned for details)

WJBK
RADIO 15

Radio-15's LUCKY LICENSE Contest

15 CHANCES TO WIN DAILY +6 ON SUNDAY

Contests played a big part in the formula for success at Top 40 stations. This one was for WJBK in 1964.

CKLW newspaper promo in November, 1963.

THE HOME OF THE HAPPY FELLAS

TOM CLAY

RON KNOWLES

DAVE SHAFER

JOE VAN

BUD DAVIES

CKLW RADIO 80

RKO GENERAL

PAUL WINTER 11:00 A.M. to 2:00 P.M.

WXYZ 1270 RADIO DETROIT

❞❞ AN ABC OWNED RADIO STATION ❞

FRED WOLF 6 TO 10 A.M.

WXYZ 1270 RADIO DETROIT

❞❞ AN ABC OWNED RADIO STATION ❞❞

WXYZ's "All American" ad
campaign. Fall, 1963.

Tom Clay was working for KDAY in Los Angeles at the time this photo was taken with Natalie Wood. 1961-62. *Courtesy Becky Clague*

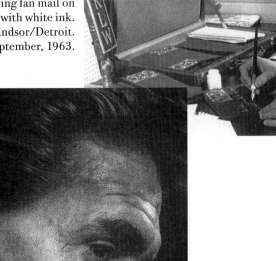

Tom Clay back in the Motor City and again answering fan mail on black paper with white ink. CKLW, Windsor/Detroit. September, 1963.

"I don't like you...I love you." A line that could only have been delivered by Tom Clay. *Courtesy Becky Clague*

The very first "Keener Music Guide."
WKNR featured a shorter list of songs than the other stations.

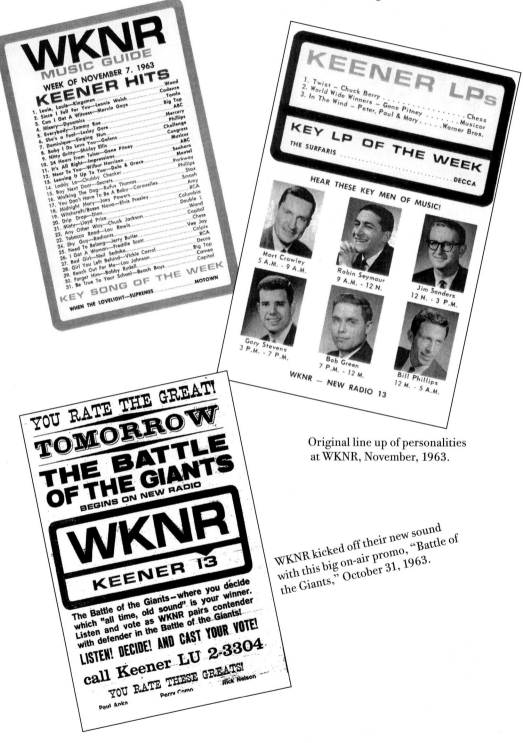

Original line up of personalities
at WKNR, November, 1963.

WKNR kicked off their new sound
with this big on-air promo, "Battle of
the Giants," October 31, 1963.

**WKNR PLAYS MORE MUSIC MORE OFTEN!**

LISTEN TO THESE KEY MEN OF MUSIC

| Swingin' Sweeney 5 AM - 9 AM | Robin Seymour 9 AM - 12 N | Jerry Goodwin 12 N - 3 PM | Gary Stevens 3 PM - 7 PM | Bob Green 7 PM - 12 M | Bill Phillips 12 M - 5 AM |

**IT PAYS TO LISTEN TO WKNR**

Win Cash with WKNR Lucky Match Books
available at all Cunningham Drug Stores

Free WKNR Music Guides at record stores everywhere

Million Top Value Stamp Giveaway

Newspaper promo for WKNR. It seemed like there was always something fun happening on "Keener 13," in 1964.

WKNR disc jockeys celebrate Keener's first birthday. October 31, 1964. Left to right: Bill Phillips, Swingin' Sweeney, Bob Green, Jerry Goodwin, Gary Stevens and Robin Seymour.
*Courtesy Bob Green*

The much talked about "Keener sound" emanated from this studio on Michigan Avenue near Greenfield. Pictured is Bob Green with the "state of the art." 1965.
*Courtesy Bob Green*

Newspaper promo for WKNR's big dance.

Keener had Detroit thinking summer in the winter of 1965.

Detroit's most consistent record survey in the mid-sixties.

**TOMORROW & SATURDAY**

**THE BIGGEST DANCE IN DETROIT!**

FOR THE MARCH OF DIMES!

RECORD STARS! CONTINUOUS ENTERTAINMENT!

JOHNNY NASH
RIVIERAS
SANTO & JOHNNY
DYNAMICS
JAMIE COE & GIGOLOS
THERESA LINDSEY

EDDIE HOLLAND
SUE PERRIN
TIMMY SHAW
DANNY BRICKTA
CORONADOS
TONY CLARKE
DEE EDWARDS

ADORABLES
TOMMY FRONTERA
CHRIS PETERSON
FENDERTONES
GINO WASHINGTON
PAUL LONDON

PLUS—
FORD CUSTOM & EXPERIMENTAL CARS
AND
the WKNR Key Men of Music

★ Robin Seymour    ★ Gary Stevens
★ Swinging Sweeney    ★ Bob Green
★ Bill Phillips

**win prizes, surprises with WKNR's Think Summer Contest!**

THINK SUMMER

Phillips, Jerry Goodwin, Bob Green,
...eeney, Paul Cannon and Robin Seymour)

...ET READY FOR SUMMER!

...a charcoal grill, a picnic basket or maybe even
...of oranges from Florida. To enter WKNR's big
...Summer contest paste the coupon on a post-
...d mail to:

Think Summer
WKNR
...Box 1300

DETROIT

**WKNR MUSIC GUIDE**

WEEK OF MAY 28, 1964

**KEENER 13 HITS**

1. MEMPHIS—JOHNNY RIVERS ............................................ IMPERIAL (8)
2. ANY OLD TIME/WALK ON BY—D. WARWICK ........... SCEPTER (1)
3. I GET AROUND—BEACH BOYS ................................. CAPITOL (5)
4. MY BOY LOLLIPOP—MILLIE SMALL ........................ SMASH (3)
5. DON'T LET THE SUN—GERRY & PACEMAKERS ... LAURIE (12)
6. LOVE WITH ALL YOUR HEART—R. C. SGRS. .... COMMAND (17)
7. WORLD WITHOUT LOVE—PETER & GORDON .... CAPITOL (2)
8. LOVE ME DO/P.S. I LOVE YOU—BEATLES ............. TOLLIE (4)
9. CHAPEL OF LOVE—DIXIE CUPS ............................. RED BIRD (9)
10. IT WILL STAND—SHOWMEN ................................. IMPERIAL (6)
11. JUST AIN'T ENOUGH LOVE—E. HOLLAND .......... MOTOWN (16)
12. SUGAR & SPICE—SEARCHERS ............................... LIBERTY (7)
13. NO PARTICULAR PLACE—CHUCK BERRY ........... CHESS (22)
14. I'll Be In Trouble—Temptations ................................ Gordy (18)
15. Stay Awhile—Dusty Springfield ................................ Philips (20)
16. I'll Touch A Star—Terry Stafford ........................... Crusader (23)
17. Beachcomber—J. Gibson Trio ................................... Twirl (26)
18. What'd I Say—Elvis Presley ....................................... RCA (15)
19. She's The One—Chartbusters .................................... Mutual (25)
20. Yesterday's Gone—C. Stuart/J. Clyde ..................... WA (21)
21. Tears & Roses—Al Martino ...................................... Capitol (29)
22. Remember Me/Just Once More—Rita Pavone ........ RCA (—)
23. Beg Me—Chuck Jackson ............................................ Wand (—)
24. Tell Me Why—Bobby Vinton ................................... Epic (28)
25. People—Barbra Striesand .......................................... Columbia (—)
26. Ain't Love Good—Tony Clarke ................................ Chess (30)
27. Fugitive—Ventures ..................................................... Dolton (27)
28. Milord—Bobby Darin ................................................. Atco (—)
29. Diane—Bachelors ........................................................ London (—)
30. Little Toy Balloon—Danny Williams ...................... UA (—)
31. Gonna Get That Man—Sanshers ............................ Kweek (KS)

**KEY SONG OF THE WEEK**
SHARE YOUR LOVE—BOBBY BLAND ............................ DUKE
Figure in parentheses indicates last week's position.

CHAPTER 10

# "The Cream of the Crop until Twelve O'Clock!"

AT THE END OF 1961, Lee Alan found himself out the door at WKMH and starting a new job at WCPO in Cincinnati. After only a week or so on the air, he received a call from John Gilbert, the general manager of WXYZ. Gilbert told him that the station was making some changes and he asked Lee to come up and talk.[1] Wixie wanted to put Joel Sebastian on in afternoon drive and thought Alan, who had some strong ratings at WKMH, despite a poor signal, could do great things on a better facility. Would Lee be interested in taking over the seven-fifteen to midnight slot? Alan was more than interested. Lee had grown up listening to WXYZ and, like others, viewed it as a legendary station. He had been a huge fan of "The Lone Ranger" and morning man Fred Wolf had been a major influence.

Born and raised in the Motor City, Alan Lee Reicheld graduated from Cooley High School before attending Michigan State. Although his first job in radio had been with WCAR, when it was a small station in Pontiac, he had been exposed to the medium as a ten-year-old, singing and playing piano on the WJR program "Make Way for Youth."

He was already married when he started running records for the disc jockeys at WJLB. After getting out of the service in 1959, he again worked briefly for 'JLB, spinning records for "Frantic Ernie" and doing the all-night show on the weekend. "I was given a tip that WJBK was about to fire their all-night guy [Dan Baxter]," Alan remembers. "I was told to show up for an on-air audition that night. The guy said, 'You go on the air at midnight and the boss will listen. If he likes what he hears, you've got the job.' Well, when I got down there that night, I realized that if I used my real name on the air, someone from WJLB might hear and then if I didn't get the 'JBK job, I could be out on the street. So, at the last minute I transposed my first and middle names and went on as Lee Alan and I was hired to do 'Night Beat' at WJBK."[2]

Now, in February of 1962, the "Lee Alan Show" was about to premiere on WXYZ and it was a "show" in every sense of the word–CinemaScope and Technicolor on radio, as every evening at seven-fifteen, Lee would announce in a booming voice: "From now until midnight in Detroit, WXYZ radio *presents*: [then over a brassy big band version of "Zing! Went the Strings of My Heart"] Lee Alan, '*On the horn*'–and a million dollars worth of talent. We'll call it the cream of the crop until twelve o'clock!" This interplay with the music would continue for another two minutes or so and include such claims as "we've found some of the hottest round ones in this big old town–you find even thirty seconds you like– we'll do it again tomorrow night and call it the cream of the crop until *twelve o'clock!*"[3] Climaxing with a shout of "Oh, yeah!" the theme music would come to a dead stop conclusion and segue into an adrenaline pumper, such as "Palisades Park" by Freddie Cannon, "One Fine Day" by the Chiffons, or "The One Who Really Loves You" by Mary Wells.

The first thing Lee Alan did after arriving at Wixie was to read letters on the air from listeners upset that he was replacing Joel Sebastian in the evening. Everyone was talking about the guy who was reading his own hate mail on the radio–as they continued to listen.

Lee Alan, "On the horn," was thought to refer to a microphone, but soon he introduced a real horn: "It is a seventeen-jeweled, fine-toned Pakistan horn," he would rave on, like a lovable lunatic, claiming that it was "insured for a million dollars with Lloyds of London." He would keep promising (or threatening) that soon he would be bringing out his famous horn, so "stay tuned! " The station ran a contest, having listeners send in a drawing of what they thought the horn looked like and thousands responded.

Lee was always on the lookout for anything controversial. In mid-1962, Dickie Lee recorded a hit record called "Patches." The song told the story of a girl who drowns herself because her father doesn't approve of her boyfriend, who responds, "I'll join you tonight." Lee Alan announced that he would not play the record on his show, because the subject was, as he called it, "teenage double suicide." He then went into great detail about why he objected to the lyric, thus focusing on the subject far more often than playing the record ever would have. Of course, the other Wixie personalities played the song while commenting about Alan's boycott. It was solid publicity for Alan and WXYZ.

Lee ran an exciting and fast-paced show, always promoting ahead. In a dramatic delivery, sounding like some sort of rocking evangelist, he would open the mike: "I want you to do me a favor—go to the telephone and call a friend and tell that friend to call another friend...and tell them to turn on the radio to WXYZ, because *tonight* we have a *very* special announcement to make here on the Lee Alan Show."

This ritual would begin early in the evening and you had to keep listening to find out what the incredible announcement was going to be. By eleven o'clock, Alan would reveal something truly astounding, most likely a new feature he was going to introduce on his show. One such heavily promoted announcement concerned something called "Two for the Price of One." This would involve Lee playing two records without commercials in the middle; of course, he would spend twenty minutes in between making sure you understood what "Two for the Price of One" was all about.

What could possibly follow "Two for the Price of One"? How about "Three for the Price of One"? Obviously, two or three records had been played without commercials before, but nobody had ever made such a big deal about it. You would have thought Lee had just invented fire. One more time, he got people talking and ratings moving up.

For some routines, Alan would use a silly, indignant voice and delivery that would rise at the end of each sentence. Ed Hardy was the heavyset newsman on Lee's shift and when Alan played the David Rose instrumental hit "The Stripper," going into news, he would announce over the bump-and-grind music, "Here comes Ed

Hardy, the *bouncing* newsman, *bouncing* down the hall," and you could sort of visualize this fellow bouncing off the walls like an out-of-control balloon at a Macy's parade. News was something sacrosanct in Detroit in those days. There was no joking or banter between deejays and newsmen, so this sort of kidding of a newsman was ahead of its time and quite funny.

Here is more of what went on between the records:

> Wait a minute, wait a minute! [*Honk*] You see *that?* You hear that? That is the sound of the Lee Alan fine-toned horn, which, of course, is from Pakistan!

> That's "Walk Like a Man," my son, by the Four Seasons on 12-7-0 and it is bound to be a number *one* round one in Detroit!

> It is twenty-five past seven o'clock on a *most* fantastic, *Friday night* in Detroit! Be *sincere,* give 'em the *real* nitty-gritty! Here's Shirley Ellis on Wixie!

> From Detroit, Michigan, baby—let's get it with the *Supremes!*[4]

"Make It or Break It" was originated in 1956, when Mickey Shorr had listeners call in to vote on one new record. Lee brought it back and increased the competition by putting several new releases up against one another. One better-than-average contest put "Sally Go 'Round the Roses" by the Jaynettes up against "Be My Baby" by the Ronnettes. The Jaynettes won the evening but "Be My Baby" went to number one while "Roses" stopped at number three on the Detroit charts. A big loser on "Make It or Break It" in the spring of 1963 was "Please, Please Me" by an unknown English band called the Beatles. Although it probably never really impacted record sales to any degree, "Make It or Break It" made for exciting radio.

In 1962, Alan cut his own record, titled "This Horn Is Going to Set Me Free." The song told a ridiculous story concerning the origin of his famous musical instrument, but the recording was no joke, as it featured Marvin Gaye on piano and Martha and the Vandellas on backing vocals. "There really isn't much to tell regarding how that song came about," relates Lee Alan. "We were over at Motown one day and somebody suggested we do something. I wrote it in about a half hour. Marvin and Martha were there so we just went in and cut it."[5]

The song had a great beat and became a big hit—on WXYZ: "This horn you understand, comes from Pakistan and when you're all alone, if you dig the fine tone, you just wait and see, this horn is gonna set you free!"

Lee tried to have close ties to Motown Records and constantly talked about Motown artists and the *Detroit Sound*. He made it a point to always promote Detroit, and referred to it as a "a great radio and music town."

On July 22, 1963, WXYZ was scheduled to carry the Cassius Clay–Sonny Liston title fight coming over the ABC network. Lee promoted it with a prepared bit built around Clay's poem "I Am the Greatest." Here's what listeners heard:

> [*Clay*] Cassius Clay, the most beautiful fighter in the world today! [*Alan in a loud, mocking tone*] Now, I wonder if he'll be bright and bouncing tonight, or...? [*Clay voice played progressively slower*] He talks in-deed of a punch that's in-cred–i–bly spe-ee-e-dee." [*Alan*] Oh, Cassius went down, aw...[*laughter as he went into a Wixie jingle, after which he put on the hard sell*] We'll find out what happens to Cassius Clay tonight on radio, here on the Lee Alan Show![4]

You would have thought the fight was being held exclusively for his program.

If Lee Alan had never left the studio, he still would have been a huge hit. In the summer of 1962, he arranged to start doing Sunday afternoon record hops at a place called Walled Lake Casino, near the old amusement park on the shores of Walled Lake in far-off Novi. Built in 1929, all the great big bands had played there, including Glenn Miller and Tommy Dorsey. After being out of the limelight for a number of years, new owners Red and Cleo Kramer were trying to make a go of it. When Lee Alan approached them about doing some dances on Sunday afternoons, they had nothing to lose.

The dances started slowly but the crowds grew larger each week, and soon other nighttime hops were added. "I was on the air at night and we were doing the remotes from the lobby of Club 182," Lee remembers. "Joel Sebastian was doing the record hop inside. I started taping the ten to midnight portion of my show so I could do the dances at the Casino. I would race from Plymouth over to Novi and get there just in time for the last show. The place was really taking off and the owners let us know that if the contract for Club 182 ever lapsed, they would sign immediately. Well, that happened and the salesman ran out and signed up Walled Lake Casino. The owners of Club 182 were really mad and sued us."[5]

Besides being a great venue, it was also the remote location that helped make the Casino seem so attractive. It became the biggest dance in the Detroit area and it made Lee Alan the biggest star in Detroit Top 40 radio. Along with top local bands, major recording stars the caliber of Roy Orbison appeared. The sound of Lee on the air from the Casino, with all the background noise, was incredibly seductive, making it the place kids just had to get to.

Lee Alan on the air:

> That's "Surf City" from Jan and Dean. We'll find out what number it is on the new Wixie Tunedex tonight at ten-thirty, when we play back the top twelve on twelve seven-o. It is twenty-three in front of nine, on time. One of the *good things* about Detroit, Michigan, is WXYZ. Let's see, now I have to find the commercial! Say, if you'd rather not lug around great big candy bars, then Mars Junior Bars are for you. Get the teeney weeney candy in the clear polyethylene bag. You see that? Buy Mars! Buy the whole planet, I don't care! [*Tackle commercial, WXYZ jingle*] We're broadcasting live from the stage at Walled Lake Casino, Thirteen Mile and Novi Roads, on the shores of beautiful Walled Lake in Novi, Michigan. Come on out! Lee Alan, "On the horn." Let's check this one out from the Essex, "Easier Said Than Done!"[6]

Alan recalls what it was like on the inside of Walled Lake Casino: "As you walked toward the stage, you could see the glass booth that we built on the left side. That's where the records were played for the dance. We installed two turntables and a mixer and had a better sound than you could find at most places. Then I had a little glass bubble built right on the stage and that is where I would broadcast from; of course, the records heard on the radio were played from back at the station, I just had a mike. We also had a speaker put in there that would pump in the sounds from the dance floor, so even if it happened to be a slow night, and there weren't many of those, it always sounded liked the place was packed."[7]

The Casino was jumpin' with four big record hops a week, Wednesday, Friday, and Saturday nights along with Sunday afternoon. "It got to be an incredible scene out there," recalls Alan.

"Just across from us was Walled Lake Amusement Park, which was owned by the same people who owned Edgewater Park. They saw all the action taking place, so they opened something called the Band Box, which held about a thousand people and they started having dances. There would be people standing out in front of both places, waving you in, much like a carnival barker."[8]

Lee continued to tape the ten to midnight portion of his show for Friday and Saturday nights so he could be free to do the record hop.

One of the biggest nights at Walled Lake Casino came in late 1962, when Lee presented Stevie Wonder for the very first time. Alan had been building and building the appearance up, talking about this "incredibly talented young man, he is blind, only eleven years old, and he plays all these instruments!" Alan wanted to showcase Stevie in the most exciting way he could. Dick Kernen was a production man and record spinner for Lee and some of the other Wixie deejays and remembers the preparation for Stevie Wonder's appearance: "There were two stages at the Casino," Kernen relates. "The main stage was about four feet high and then there was a second, smaller stage at the opposite end of the dance floor. This second stage measured about twelve by twelve and was perched about ten feet high. Lee went out and rented some incredibly powerful spotlights called 'super troopers' and had them facing the small stage."[9]

That evening, according to Kernen, Lee Alan jumped on the main stage and grabbed the mike: "Ladies and gentlemen, Walled Lake Casino and WXYZ are proud to present a great new talent, Little Stevie Wonder!"[10] At that very moment, the blazing spotlights lit up, aimed at the rear stage, and two thousand heads turned at once to face Stevie Wonder at his drum set, bathed in a massive stream of light, ten feet above the crowd.

Another night to remember at the Casino came late in the fall of 1963. Chuck Berry had recently been released from prison and was picking up the pieces of a career that had been put on hold as a result of his Mann Act conviction. (Berry had been found guilty of taking a minor across state lines. He claimed he had hired her to work at his Berry Park in St. Louis and wasn't aware of her true age.) Lee Alan and Dave Prince, who was now a Wixie disc jockey, booked him for Friday and Saturday night appearances at the Casino. In a year when "Sugar Shack" was the top-selling single,

Chuck Berry was the real thing when it came to rock 'n' roll. His reputation only grew larger over time. He was idolized by older kids who bought his records when they were new and by teenagers discovering him for the first time. Besides every band in town performing his songs, Chess Records had recently released the album "Chuck Berry Twist," which was basically a new cover wrapped around classic Berry songs from the fifties. It was the best-selling album in Detroit at the time it was announced that Chuck would be coming to Walled Lake Casino.

Dave Prince recalls that there were problems to be solved before Chuck Berry would perform: "Lee and I had gone to Chicago to meet with Leonard and Phil Chess about hiring Chuck. Now, we knew he wanted to be paid a thousand dollars in cash. We didn't know he would want it up front."[11]

Late in the afternoon, Lee Alan had driven over to a motel to pick up Chuck Berry. As they spun across town in Alan's Corvette, Berry demanded his payment up front and in cash, so Lee made an unscheduled bank stop, arriving at Walled Lake Casino about half past six, just enough time for Chuck to meet the house band and run through a few numbers.

The excitement could be heard over WXYZ radio early in the evening as Lee called Dave Prince to join him in the broadcast booth. As the recorded sounds of "Johnny Be Goode" played in the background, the two made a big deal about Chuck's guitar that was sitting on the stage. Prince, commenting on how exciting it had been a few minutes earlier, witnessed Chuck interacting with the other musicians at rehearsal:

> You know, he says to this one guy, "No, man...on the downbeat, on the downbeat and then a little ba-da-bum and you kick it off with me" and it was really wild and he's ready to get out there and wail! [*Picking up on the momentum, Lee Alan leans into the mike*] You know, we drove out here with him tonight and while you were watching from the other side of the stage, he asked me, "Hey, what time are we goin' on? When we gonna hit?" [*Prince, in his trademark Texan delivery, jumps back in*] Yeah, he's anxious to go. [*Then Lee Alan, moving into a full voice and a fever pitch, takes control of the radio pulpit*] What we're sayin' is that Chuck Berry is at Walled Lake Casino tonight and you better get out here pretty quick, because it is one of the *biggest* nights that I have *ever* seen![12]

Now, claims such as this were not uncommon on the Lee Alan show but on this occasion, there was no need for exaggeration. According to Dick Kernen, who was present, "Berry just rocked the place."

The next night, Chuck was back at the Casino and once again demanding the cash up front. Dave Prince: "Chuck is really giving me a hard time, so I go to the office for the money. They say: 'We don't have any large bills.' I say: 'Give me what you have.' So I carry back this big sack of money and set it down in front of Chuck Berry, who is waiting in the booth where they played the records. Now, while all the kids are screaming for him to play, he's in there counting a thousand bucks in small bills! When he finally finishes and starts moving toward the stage he looks back and tells an associate: 'Count it again!'"[13]

According to those present, Berry performed about forty-five minutes and nobody was disappointed.

The "Lee Alan Show" on WXYZ was at the center of whatever was happening in Detroit or at least it sounded that way. By the spring of 1963, the Hooper ratings showed Lee was registering a whopping 40 percent share of the radio audience available in the Motor City at night. He never let up the momentum, a momentum that he created. While WXYZ had some programming guidelines, they in no way resembled many more highly formatted Top 40 stations around the country; in fact, none of the Detroit stations did. The disc jockeys really carried the ball. If all you had to offer was the time and temperature, you were not going to cut it–Alan had lots more.

In 1963, Lee moved into television, cohosting "Club 1270" with Joel Sebastian. This was the first dance party–style show on TV in Detroit in more than three years. Featuring dancing and record artists lip-synching their latest hits, the show was nothing original, but the two had good chemistry and it was better than average. The Drifters and Dion were guests on the first show.

One of the more dramatic and memorable moments on Lee's radio program came at Christmastime, when he would tell the story of "Michael," the tale of an American GI in the Korean War who is befriended by an angel. As sound effects of wintry wind howled in the background, Lee made it a real heart tugger each year.

In 1959, Frank Sinatra had recorded a moody album called

"No One Cares." One of the classic songs in this collection was the old Bunny Berigan hit from the big band days, "I Can't Get Started." Lee Alan grabbed the song for his closing theme and it gave him the classiest sign-off on radio.

Every night at a few minutes before twelve, Lee would bring the pace down a bit, reading a letter or two and playing something slow and sad, maybe "That's How Heartaches Are Made" by Baby Washington or "Stranger on the Shore" by Acker Bilk. Then, from a studio that a listener would have had to imagine as dimly lit and filled with empty coffee cups and a trail of cigarette smoke wrapping around a microphone, Alan would recount the number of days since his return. On a given night, in the deepest and most intimate of voices, he would say: "It's been 164 days now that we've been back on Detroit radio and somehow...I'm still...a glum one," at which time Sinatra would sing the same opening line to the song. After delivering a few lyrics just ahead of Frank, Lee would then announce: "A long time ago, somebody chose it, so to close it: Mr. Sinatra...."

"I've flown around the world in a plane...." And so the song went as the music floated through the night, into cars with couples parked watching planes taking off at City Airport as well as into those of loners cruising Woodward or Gratiot Avenues. It echoed from speakers in gas station garages and late-night restaurants, and in a few thousand bedrooms across southeastern Michigan. As the song slowly reaches its sad and ironic conclusion, Lee Alan reminds everyone to: "Be sure and drive carefully, and don't turn that automobile of yours into a couple of tons of deadly weapon." Following a reprise of the final line of the song, with the music fading in the background, alone on the radio, he warmly concludes: "If somewhere tonight, you've found even thirty seconds you liked, maybe tomorrow night you'll find thirty-one. Lee Alan...goodnight everybody."

Lee Alan had combined the persuasiveness of Fred Wolf, the "big top" showmanship of Mickey Shorr, and the pathos of Tom Clay and then added a few things of his own along with a dash of arrogance. It was one hell of a style. It was a different kind of act from wild nighttime radio superstars such as Dick Biondi in Chicago or "Cousin Brucie" in New York. Alan was able to break through to a level of intimacy with listeners that others could not or did not care to reach. As Lee might have said, it was a "Detroit kind of thing." Alan was the "entertainer" and his sign-off was cool and sophisticated, creating a certain mystique: how could such a nut be a "glum one"? Listeners would have to tune in tomorrow to try to figure it out–they did.

CHAPTER **11**

# Winners and Losers

IN EARLY 1962, WKMH drew a big crowd to its annual "March of Dimes" rock 'n' roll show at the Light Guard Armory on Eight Mile Road. Unfortunately, they were not getting the same crowd on the radio dial. According to the latest ratings, WJBK and WXYZ were pretty much grabbing all the audience who wanted rock 'n' roll in Detroit. According to Bob Green, who was doing production work as well as a weekend air shift at WKMH, the station had a pretty low share of the market: "WKMH had some good talent but just didn't have a real direction in programming." Dave "Sangoo" Prince was, however, making progress and had the highest numbers on the station. Overall, it was too little, too late.

In April, WKMH threw in the towel and changed format. "Flagship Radio" was their new moniker, featuring, as they called it, "America's best popular music." It was really a bit ahead of its time—a good mix of softer chart hits and album fare by artists such as Peggy Lee and Andy Williams. Robin was still on in the morning, joined by syndicated comedians Bob Elliot and Ray Goulding, for a "Bob, Ray, and Robin Show." Seymour remembers it wasn't a lot of fun doing that show: "Those are some of the worst times I had in the business. The Bob and Ray stuff would arrive on tape and I would have to follow along with a script so I could supposedly

converse with them. It was the sort of thing record companies
sometimes did with record artists so a local deejay could sound like
he was actually interviewing the artist. The difference was I had to
do this every morning for four hours," he groans.[1]

WKMH would find the middle of the road to also be a very competitive area. WJR ruled as the dominant choice for adult listeners,
although Detroit's top morning ratings were still the property of
WXYZ's Fred Wolf, who was racking up twenty-shares and above.
J. P. McCarthy was in hot pursuit with numbers in the high teens,
according to Pulse ratings for January–February 1962.

"This is WJR in Detroit, the great voice of the Great Lakes,
with studios in the Golden Tower of the Fisher Building." So went
the station identification, broadcast by a live staff announcer,
who, every morning at 6:30, would then proclaim: "It's first call to
the morning Music Hall and J. P. McCarthy!"

The opening notes to "Put On a Happy Face" would begin to
pour out of radio speakers all over Detroit and much of Michigan,
Ohio, and Ontario. It was McCarthy's theme as he greeted the
audience: "Good morning world...seems to be a Monday here in
Detroit...and a cold gray one at that. The kind of morning when
you...get the eyes open one at a time. This is J. P. McCarthy in the
Music Hall at WJR."

Like many in the audience, J. P. often sounded as if he too had-
n't yet wiped all the sand from his eyes. It made for a good rapport
with listeners.

McCarthy was in his fifth year at the Goodwill Station. Born in
New York, he grew up in Detroit and got the radio bug while stationed with the air force in Alaska in the early 1950s. He hooked
up with Armed Forces Radio and after performing in an AFR amateur drama, attended broadcasting school in Anchorage and
served as a staff announcer. After discharge, he worked for a
Fairbanks television station and then came back to Michigan and
went on the air at WTAC in Flint.

That station was going through a transition from being an old-
line NBC affiliate to Top 40. The only place McCarthy really
wanted to go to was WJR in Detroit. After numerous auditions, he
was hired as a staff announcer in 1956[2] and rose quickly to take
over the morning show in the summer of 1958, when Marty
McNeely followed CBS to WKMH.

The infamous Sen. Joseph McCarthy and his witch-hunt for Communists was a recent memory, so Joseph Priestly McCarthy was introduced to Detroit as J. P. McCarthy.

J. P. chose his own records, with Sinatra and the Four Freshmen usually at the top of the stack. In between, he would comment on current events in what was becoming a trademark conversational style. At just thirty years of age, he projected a casual but articulate, somewhat sophisticated air persona and was definitely competitive. If Fred Wolf was offering Detroiters "beer and bowling," J. P. was a "late night visit to a piano bar for cocktails," yet he sounded like one of the guys when it came time to talk sports.

Record promotion man Don Schmitzerle remembers calling on WJR: "What I recall about J. P., besides the fact that he was very good on the air, was that he would let me come right into the studio during his show. At most stations you had to line up to see the program director and you never got near the studio. J. P. had the ability to pick his own records and he was so casual and relaxed that it didn't bother him to have me in there."[3]

A former listener recalls McCarthy doing lots of memorable things on his show, including a countdown to the vernal equinox, when he then played "Spring Is Here" by Sinatra.

By the early sixties, McCarthy was searching for the "winners and losers" of the world each day. He could also be heard on the afternoon Music Hall between three-thirty and six.[3]

The rest of the day at WJR resembled the old days of radio.[4] The station still had a staff orchestra, which was featured on live variety programs, such as the "Jack Harris Show" in the midmorning and "Guest House" at seven each evening. Besides the evening show, humorist Bud Guest could be heard for a quarter hour each morning at eight-fifteen. Also on the schedule was "Adventures in Good Music" with Karl Haas and the Jim Wood variety program. There was a heavy news commitment, sports play-by-play, plus Jay Roberts, heading for an imaginary destination on "Night Flight 760." Radio people in Detroit felt that it was almost impossible to program against 'JR because the station broke all the new programming rules and was still successful.[4]

Chasing WJR, but never seeming to catch up, was WWJ, the *Detroit News* station. One of their big stars, Bob Maxwell, departed for New York early in the year. Currently, WWJ featured a lineup that included morning man Hugh Roberts and a strange character called Newt, along with Les Martens, John Lynker, John Hultman, and Bob Allison with "Ask Your Neighbor," one of the earliest call-in talk shows, as well as the "Bumper to Bumper Club" in the afternoon. The station broadcast the various shows from remote studios at Northland, Eastland, and Westland shopping centers.

The other so-called good music station was WCAR. W-car programmed standards by Ella Fitzgerald, Tony Bennett, Sarah Vaughan, and the likes in a fairly tight presentation. Hy Levinson was the somewhat eccentric owner of the station who liked to dabble in everything as well as remind his announcers of how lucky they were to be on WCAR, where "they would be heard by a larger audience than Ethel Barrymore had played to during her entire career." Announcers at the station didn't try to figure him out, they just tried to survive. Voices on Radio 1130 in the '50s and early '60s included Dave Woodling, Todd Purse, Conrad Patrick, Pat Sheridan, Jack Sanders, and Joe Bacarella.

WQTE was finally finding some success with their easy-listening album format. The station originated broadcasts from Greenfield Village.

AMONG THE LIST OF "LOSERS" was WXYZ's Fred Weiss. One of the more infamous moments on Detroit radio occurred in October of 1962 as Fred was about to begin his twelfth year at WXYZ. There have been many accounts of what happened that day. Here is the version given by Lee Alan, who was listening in his car as he drove toward Broadcast House.

"Fred was doing his regular remote in the trailer from Merollis Chevrolet out at eight and a half and Gratiot. Now, in the trailer, the announcer would wear a headset, everything else was handled from back at the main studios. In one ear you would hear the programming, which was the records or commercials, and in the other you could hear the producer back at the station. There was a toggle switch and you could move it into a position to talk on the air, shut off, or to talk to the producer.[5]

"All the guys would always complain that the engineers would keep the programming levels so low you had a hard time hearing what was going on. Anyhow, Fred had just introduced the song "Please Release Me" by Little Ester Phillips, a black singer. Somehow, he had not moved the toggle switch all the way out of the on-air position and his conversation with the producer is going out over the air. It seems they had been discussing the growing popularity of black music, how it was crossing over more and more. As Fred spoke, the automatic gain-control system reacted and sent the music level down so that he could clearly be heard using the 'n' word as he commented how those 'g— d— n—' are gettin' plenty smart.'"[6]

Those unfortunate words were the last ones spoken by Fred Weiss on Detroit radio. After the newscast, a WXYZ newsman finished the last hour of his show. Fred Weiss simply vanished from the dial and from Detroit. According to Lee, Fred Weiss was not known for using that kind of language. "Fred was just a nice guy and I think he was making a complimentary comment in a sarcastic way and it was unfortunate that it went over the air. When I got over to Broadcast House, the switchboards were all lighting up. On Monday, the *Michigan Chronicle*, the black newspaper, was calling for action and the station had to let him go," says Lee.

Dave Prince of WKMH won the job left open by Fred Weiss and was on 1270 radio two weeks later. Lee Alan filled in on the Sunday show and really built things up: "You won't believe who's gonna be the new guy on WXYZ!" and "Wait till you hear who's coming to Wixie next week!" The following Saturday morning Dave Prince was on the air: "Yeah, yeah, this is a wild weekend isn't it? This is Dave Prince and this is my first day, so just remember, if you hear mistakes, they are *not my fault!*"

As to why he did not use the "Sangoo" bit on Wixie, Prince says that it was not his to use: "Back in early '62, when we were still rocking at WKMH, the manager, a guy named John Carroll, stopped me one day and wanted me to sign a release form regarding the use of 'Sangoo.' I had recently had the name copyrighted and when he found out, he was afraid I would take it to another station in town. It was sign or lose my job. I said, 'That's fine. I'll sign but I will eventually leave WKMH and I'm not going to worry about this. You're not going to hurt me by what you're doing,' and that was it."[8]

At WXYZ, Dave Prince did great sans "Sangoo." He was the "Weekend Warrior," "the brave little Prince," and then there was that guy asking for the key in "Fingertips Part 2" by Stevie Wonder. Prince got hold of a miniature harmonica and was soon asking "What key, what key?" over the introduction to many of the hits on the Wixie Tunedex. He signed off his weekend shows with "Last Date" by Floyd Cramer.

WCHB'S ENTERPRISING LARRY DIXON began publishing a music magazine called *Mello-Music Tips*. It listed the top-selling r&b hits, along with pictures and stories of recording artists and was supported by advertising from record labels, distributors, and record shops.

ALSO IN THE FALL OF 1962, former radio star Ed McKenzie surfaced with a new late-night television show on channel 7 called "After Hours." WXYZ-TV general manager, John Pival, the same man who pushed Ed into TV back in 1954, had invited him back. This was no "Saturday Party" but a cultural mecca for insomniacs in the Detroit area as Ed presented a wide range of human-interest subject matter. He focused on the lives, works, and personalities of famous people, such as Adm. Richard Byrd, Henry David Thoreau, Howard Hughes, Socrates, Robert Frost, Benjamin Franklin, and Gandhi. There were no bobby-soxers in attendance.[9]

IN 1962, transplanted Detroiter Casey Kasem was on the air at KEWB in Oakland-San Francisco, after a run at WBNY in Buffalo. "I followed a guy named Bob Hudson who was always leaving the studio in a real mess," recalls Kasem. "So one day I got into there a little early to clean things up. Someone rolled in a tall trash barrel for me to use and it was nearly full of used teletype paper. As I reached for it, my eyes focused on a book that someone had pitched out, lying right on top, and the title caught my eye, *Who's Who in Pop Music in 1962*."[10]

The information inside gave Casey Kasem the idea to start teasing his audience with trivia about records and artists:

"Coming up in a minute, I'll have a song from a group that has had more number one hits than any other," he would promise. He took his new approach on to KRLA in Los Angeles. At that station, he would be part of a legendary air staff that would include someone else who had briefly touched down on the Detroit airwaves, Dave Hull, last seen racing for the elevator in the Brink Building in 1961.

Meanwhile, back on the local music scene in Detroit, Motown was picking up steam with the bombastic performance of the Contours on "Do You Love Me." Mary Wells scored three top-ten hits in 1962, the Marvelettes had "Playboy," and Marvin Gaye and Stevie Wonder made their first appearances on the charts.

There was local talent other than Motown having success. The Volumes were a Detroit quintet that featured a great lead singer named Ed Union. Their hit in the spring was "I Love You," released on the Chex label, and it was a top-ten record in Detroit and reached number twenty-two nationally.

The Young Sisters were area high school girls and their recording of "Casanova Brown" got kids on the dance floor real quick. The song was on the Twirl label owned by Harry Balk and Irving Micahnik and had lots of local airplay but failed to break beyond.

Fortune Records found success in the shadow of Motown when they released two hard-rockin' singles in 1962. "Village of Love" by Nathaniel Mayer and the Fabulous Twilights hit like some kind of rock 'n' roll voodoo. Incredibly raw in sound and content, it nonetheless became one of the top sellers in Detroit and reached number twenty-six on the national charts after being picked up by United Artists for national distribution.

In the fall, Fortune released Nolan Strong's "Mind over Matter." This had to be one of the greatest dance records ever and it shot to number one on the Detroit list. Fortune decided it would try to take this one national itself, but because of their relatively small size, they lacked the ability to distribute and promote their product extensively, and the song, unbelievably to anyone from Detroit, failed to dent the national hot 100. After he had had a number of regional hits with the Diablos in the fifties, this was Nolan Strong's last best chance at the big time. It was a great record and although he was billed as a solo, the group backed him on this classic Detroit hit.

The story goes that Strong was signed to an airtight contract at Fortune that kept him from going with a bigger label. However, according to Sheldon Brown, son of the label's founders, "whenever Strong's contract lapsed, he would just sign up again. He felt it was home and didn't care to leave." Brown also says that Berry Gordy was more than upset at the little label pulling off a number one in his backyard: "Berry Gordy thought it was such a great record that he took the guys who later became the Temptations and they recorded 'Mind over Matter' as the Pirates. Gordy tried to stop our version but his wasn't nearly as good and ours became the big hit."[11]

IN THE SUMMER OF 1962, Edgewater Amusement Park instituted its new P.O.P. policy. As their ever present radio commercials touted, "Pay one price, ride all day, ride all night at fan-tabulous Edgewater Park!" And what Detroiter could forget the questions posed and answered by a local clothier: "Does Louis the Hatter have hats? Louis the Hatter has tall hats, small hats, brown, black and green hats! Does Louis the Hatter have suits? Louis the Hatter has wool suits, sharkskin suits, any suit that suits you." It seemed there wasn't anything that Louis the Hatter didn't have.

The other most memorable commercial on the radio was the mind- bending, heart-pounding spot for Detroit Dragway. Over the opening electric piano notes of Ray Charles's "What I Say," Joel Sebastian and commercial pitch man Rube Weiss let out all the stops as they promoted upcoming races that would be happening "Sun-day, at Detroit Drag-way, Sibley at Dix!"*

IN JANUARY OF 1963, WEXL, which had been a minor player in the market with dated record shows such as "Koffee Karavan" and "Melody Matinee" (and after a brief flirtation with Top 40 à la Hank [O'Neil] Burdick and his kazoo), switched to a twenty-four-hour country format. In contrast to the prevalence of country stations today, there were few in the North that would program the music more than a couple of hours a day. WEXL had, in fact, had a daily two-hour program called "Sagebrush Melodies"on since 1933, hosted for many years by Jack Ihrie. Most stations believed

---

*After 1965 the Detroit Dragway commercials featured Rube Weiss and Robin Seymour.

there wouldn't be the listenership or the advertisers to support the format full-time. Also, a certain amount of snobbery regarding country music was involved. For the Sparks family, who had owned WEXL almost since its inception in 1923, those beliefs meant little when the ratings and then the revenue started to pour in.

For anyone who didn't believe in the popularity of the music, they had only to count the number of "WEXL Country Club" bumper stickers adorning cars all over the Detroit area. Bob Clark, "Big Bill" Samples, Dale Lewis, Bill Mann, Dave "King of Remotes" Carr, and Jim Mitchell were a few of the many voices heard during the sixties on 1340.

WWJ attempted to get a little hip in the evening, when it replaced Faye Elizabeth and her light classical program with the "Music Scene." Smooth announcer Todd Purse played a more varied selection of tunes than were normally featured on the station.

In May, Toby David gave up his radio show at CKLW to devote more time to his television alter ego, Captain Jolly. Bud Davies moved to mornings, and replacing him in the afternoon was Dave Shafer from WJBK, who brought along his theme song sans the reference to "Jack the Bellboy." Shafer also brought along most of the bits he had done at 'JBK and added a new one, "Mr. Show Biz," a fumbling know-it-all who always says the right thing at the wrong time. WJBK hired Terry Knapp from WTAC in Flint and changed his last name to Knight.

In the summer of 1963, WJR was a big loser among radio stations as they watched J. P. McCarthy exit the Music Hall for a job with KGO in San Francisco. His real reason for leaving had been 'JR's refusal to let him augment his income with freelance commercial voice-over work. It was an old policy that the "Goodwill" brass wouldn't back away from.

To fill the void, WJR tried a two-man approach in the morning, teaming Jimmy Launce with Dale McCarron, who came in from WBBM in Chicago. It was a less-than-exciting match: two good broadcasters–little chemistry.

Meanwhile, on the coast, J. P. was doing well, but learning that in San Francisco, there was only one "king of the morning" and the crown belonged to Don Sherwood of KSFO.

CHAPTER **12**

# The Return of "a Guy by the Name of Clay"

IN AUGUST OF 1963, with WEXL playing country round the clock, CKLW dropped "Sounds like Nashville" and started to rock again at night. Tom Clay was brought back to Detroit with great fanfare. "Clay's on CK" proclaimed the ads promoting his arrival to the 7:30 P.M. to 11:30 P.M. slot. He would be going up against Lee Alan at Wixie, on whom Clay had been a major influence when they both worked for WJBK in 1959.

"From now until eleven-thirty, sixty sounds go round and round with a guy by the name of Clay" is how he opened his show on CKLW each evening. In reality, you couldn't count on too many sounds to go round when Tom Clay was on the air. He commented on whatever came to mind, be it love, relations, or social issues. He could build the smallest incident into a major extravaganza as he would attempt to describe a situation that was "beyond description."

In the two years since his departure from Detroit, Tom had been broadcasting on KDAY in Los Angeles, where he had replaced Alan Freed in July 1961. Early on in his KDAY run, Clay went on the air with a variation of his "call Elvis" stunt from Buffalo. This time, he told listeners that Elvis Presley, who Clay said was "a good friend," was in town and they could call and speak briefly with him. Clay said: "Just say, 'Hi, Elvis, I love you.'"[1] He then gave out the number of KFWB, the number one station in town. Clay thought if he could impress them with his pull, they might offer him a job. It backfired, tying up KFWB's phone lines for two days. Tom had to make a public apology to avoid a lawsuit.

During his time on the coast, he pursued the Hollywood scene and made friends with Robert Conrad, who got him a small part in an episode of *Hawaiian Eye*. He also attended several celebrity parties, where he mingled with stars such as Natalie Wood, but, according to Clay, the biggest star sought him out.

During his radio show in September of 1961, Tom was taking calls in between records. A woman phoned in but would not give her name and was hung up on. She called back quite upset and told Clay her name was Marilyn Monroe but not to announce it on the air. After talking on the phone several times, he accepted an invitation for coffee and went to the address she gave. It was indeed the famous Marilyn. Tom Clay wound up visiting her apartment several times over a three-week period, where they talked at length, nothing more. Clay described her as a very lonely woman, who spent a lot of their time together asking questions about his wife and their family life.[2] "That's all he would ever say about the episode," says daughter Kim Tally. "He just had a code about things like that."[3]

Back in Detroit, Tom was trying to recapture the magic from his glory days at 'JBK. Although he had become a bit self-indulgent, many listeners found him charismatic. As he had at WJBK, Tom opened each hour with sizzling production, promoting the great sounds he would be playing and inviting listeners to "try this one on for size!"[4] as he swung into a hit from the "CK' Survey."

After a couple of months, he began to wind down the rock music about ten o'clock and started playing "music for lovers and losers," where in between sad and moody songs, he would muse about the meaning of life or, to be specific, *his* life. "Whatever happened to sitting out on the stoop with friends...in fact, whatever happened to the stoop?" he would wonder out loud.

Turning on a deep echo-chamber effect, Tom would go way down into the vaults at CK' to look for some "dusty musties" to play.

On prejudice, he offered the story of how Nat "King" Cole had been taken to lunch by Detroit record distributor John Kaplan, to a restaurant where "coloreds" were not welcome. The owner came to their table and said, "I'm sorry, Mr. Kaplan, but we can't serve you." Nat Cole supposedly turned to Kaplan and said: "It must be rough to be Jewish."

Clay reached his peak of pathos after the assassination of President Kennedy. A teenage girl sent him a poem she had written about the late president's son, John-John, describing what were possibly his thoughts as he watched his father's casket being pulled during the funeral procession. The poem was titled "Six White Horses" and when an emotional Tom Clay read it on the air over some very dramatic music, he began weeping fifty-thousand-watt tears: "He's in the ground, it cannot be/He should be right here holding me/But Mommy says, I must be good/So I'll just stand here as Daddy would."[5] He had his critics, but even they would agree that during moments such as this, Tom Clay was in a class by himself. A fan once commented, "Tom was such a talented performer...he could read an operations manual for the Toro 206 Weedwacker...and make you cry."

He signed off his show with a haunting, dramatic instrumental version of "That's All," recorded by something called The Aqua Viva Orchestra. Tom Clay: "Well, it's about twenty-six minutes past eleven here on CKLW and we're just about out of time, but before we leave tonight, I want you to know...and I don't care *what* people think: I don't like you...I love you."[6] After a minute or so of music, the ON THE AIR sign lights up:

> So that makes it twelve down and eighteen to go for the month of October, the year 1963. This one has been a Thursday, a day in which some sixty sounds have been round, round, and round with yours truly...just a guy...by the name of Clay.
>
> Right now, we'll take the records, tuck them into their nightgowns, put them to bed and give them plenty of rest, because tomorrow will be another busy day.
>
> Hope you enjoyed two, three, maybe even four of what we had to play. If so...God willing, perhaps...there'll be a Friday.

As Clay concludes, the music erupts in a dramatic crescendo of cascading strings followed by a full orchestral climax. The show is indeed over for another night.

Tom Clay was once heard to say: "I love radio so much I prayed the all-night man wouldn't show up so I could work another six hours."[7]

RECORD HOPS WERE GOING STRONG all over Detroit in 1963. Besides the big dance at Walled Lake Casino, Dave Prince had a regular hop at Notre Dame High School each week, WJBK's Clark Reid ran a Wednesday night dance at the Ambassador Roller Rink in Clawson, Don Zee held forth at the Royal Oak YMCA, and Dave Shafer had started a long-running hop at Riverside Arena in Windsor. These dances would usually feature records along with a local band playing instrumental covers of Ventures-style hits, occasionally throwing in a vocal or a Chuck Berry tune. The dee-jays would often secure a recording artist to appear, lip-synching their hit for promotion purposes. A record promotion man could cover a lot of miles during an evening, attempting to take his act to as many of these dances as possible.

Sometimes, things just didn't work out as planned. Joel Sebastian was hosting a record hop at the State Fair one evening and had moved far out of the way after introducing a singer named Ed Bruce, who was promoting his new single called "See the Big Man Cry." After doing a pretty credible job of lip-synching through half the song, the needle in the little turntable at the foot of the stage started to skip and there was poor Ed: "See the Big Man, See the Big Man, See the Big Man." Joel Sebastian leaped off another stage and bounded through the crowd. His arm out-stretched to the max, he reached for the turntable arm and the PA system reverberated with the sound of a needle sliding across the grooves. "Hey, everybody, let's give a big hand for Ed Bruce!" exclaimed a breathless Sebastian.[8]

A good sign that a record hop was about to wind down was the requisite fistfight, followed by the arrival of the police.

Detroit Top 40 stations continued to sharpen their image, with WXYZ promoting their disc jockeys as the "All-Americans." Meanwhile, WJBK was the "Home of the Good Guys." CKLW, which tended to be a little off the mark, decided to call their jocks the "Happy Fellas," making them sound as if they might be fitted in straitjackets behind the microphone.

WJBK Jingle from 1963:
*All the Good Guys say, stay with us all day*
*Having you as our guest, makes us feel at our best*
*Keep listening as we lead the way,*
*Radio 15–WJBK*

In 1963, Martha Jean "The Queen" hit the airwaves at WCHB and became a sensation with a sassy style. Until this point, most women in radio were relegated to homemaker types of programs. Although she inherited that kind of show, the kitchen cooking soon took a back seat to cookin' with rhythm and blues.[9]

Things also continued to cook at Hitsville U.S.A. Although Stevie Wonder's first release, titled "Contract on Love," had some modest success the previous year, his incredible live recording of "Fingertips Part 2" became a megahit across the country in 1963. Martha and the Vandellas debuted with "Come and Get These Memories," followed by "Heat Wave" and its follow-up, "Quicksand." Marvin Gaye had "Hitch Hike" and "Pride and Joy," while the Miracles did "Mickey's Monkey." All these great hometown acts could be seen together on stage at the famous Motortown Christmas Review at the Fox theater.

A local non-Motown group named the Dynamics had a two-sided smash in the fall with "Misery" and "I'm the Man," released on Big Top Records. "Misery" just missed the national Top 40, stopping at number forty-four.

BY THE FALL OF 1963, WXYZ's John Gilbert had moved on and had been replaced as general manager by Charles Fritz, who was happy to inherit such a good situation with a winning station. Fred Wolf was still number one in the morning, and midday man Paul Winter was in his twelfth year at the station. Like other Wixie personalities, his voice and delivery were unique. As a former philosophy teacher, he was fond of quoting the great philosophers during his midday show.

Winter, like others, made use of drop-ins on his show. The difference was he never knew what was going to be dropped in. His producers would wait for an appropriate moment and hit him with something that he would react to in a totally spontaneous way.[10]

On one show, he had paused to air one of the Flair reports from ABC. The subject being discussed by a Mr. Golden had to do with the philosopher Plato's take on the meaning of everlasting love. When Paul took the show back locally, he could not resist commenting on what had just aired. After spending a minute or so of Top 40 radio time explaining to Detroit listeners about what Plato had "really meant when he spoke of everlasting love," he was interrupted by a tough, rude-sounding voice: "Hey, you know, this show ain't nothin' like the book!" As a record begins to play, Winter comments: "Well, if you *read* Plato, you'd *know* what the book's about, but I don't have time to go into all that jazz...Mr. Bobby Rydell is in love! [music] He's got Bonnie? You've got Paul Winter...like it or not. The WXYZ easy-listening time is nineteen after eleven and you're where the fun is on 12-7-0."[11]

Paul Winter's performance had wit, humor, and charm along with an infectious chuckle, and it's doubtful that anything even remotely like it was airing on any Top 40 rock station, anywhere.

The rest of the day was top-rated at WXYZ, with Joel Sebastian in the afternoon and Lee Alan the center of attention at night. Sebastian and Alan continued to promote a "Brother Joel" and "Brother Lee" relationship on radio and TV that benefited them both. The commercial logs were loaded and things were going just fine at Broadcast House in October of 1963.

CHAPTER **13**

# The Keener Sound

FOR A YEAR AND A HALF, WKMH had tried to attract an audience to its souped-up middle-of-the-road format, but by the fall of 1963, nothing was working. The syndicated Bob and Ray features had been dropped from the morning show, and, with its ratings at an all-time low, Knorr Broadcasting decided to let "Flagship Radio" sink. "We jokingly claimed that we were number eleven in a ten-station market," laughs veteran WKMH deejay Robin Seymour.[1]

Radio consultant Mike Joseph was hired to come into the market and figure out what to do with the station. Joseph was a pioneer in what at the time was a very small field of consultants and was kept on retainer by a number of stations across the country. He had done work for WKBW in Buffalo, taking it Top 40 in 1958 and for WABC in New York when it made the switch in 1960. He had recently been successful modernizing WLAV in nearby Grand Rapids.[2] "The station paid Mike Joseph fifty thousand dollars to come in and set up a new format," recalls Robin Seymour. "Many of the things he did had been brought to the attention of management by others at the station including myself. It wasn't until things had gotten so bad that they took action and paid him all that money."[3]

After sitting in a motel room listening closely to Detroit radio,

Joseph decided that even with three Top 40 stations in the market, he could take 'KMH back to rock and jump ahead of them all.

Top-rated WXYZ was viewed as vulnerable on several fronts. Because they were owned by ABC, they were forced to carry network programming that did not fit the image of a station targeting a youthful audience. Every morning when Fred Wolf ended his show at ten, the music stopped for an hour as WXYZ broadcast "The Breakfast Club" from Chicago. It was a somewhat schmaltzy, old-time variety program, popular with older listeners, and had been serving up corn on the air since 1933. Music resumed at eleven but through the day there were network lifestyle features called Flair Reports, and hourly network and local news and sports. Afternoon drive was crowded with news commentaries by Lou Gordon and Dick Osgood show-business reports. In the evening WXYZ featured an hour and twenty-five-minute block of news, sports, and commentaries, the result being that from 5:50 to 7:15, there was no music available on the number one music station! On Saturdays, Notre Dame college football was carried. WXYZ sounded more like a "full service" radio station than a rocker.

CKLW was a pretty disjointed operation in 1963. Starting the day with farm news and a paid program sponsored by the UAW called "Eye Opener," morning disc jockey Bud Davies didn't get on the air with music until 6:45. CK's broadcast day included drab newscasts and stops for Bill Kennedy's Hollywood news and Mary Morgan's features for women. At seven in the evening there was a thirty-minute block of news commentaries before Tom Clay had to pick up the pieces at seven-thirty. At the conclusion of Clay's shift, music stopped yet again for a paid religious program called "The World Tomorrow," providing a not very strong lead-in for all-night man Ron Knowles.

While WJBK didn't stop its format for any long periods, it did have its share of clutter, with news on the hour and half hour and Detroit Public Library book reviews and other assorted public-service features all day and a fairly relaxed, homey approach to Top 40. The station also suffered from a weak signal at night.

On Sundays, all the stations were loaded with religious and public-service programming. Contemporary music was available only in the afternoon.

As for the music itself, all three stations featured long playlists that the disc jockeys could program from. WJBK had close to one hundred records, the WXYZ Tunedex was made up of seventy, and CKLW had more than eighty tunes listed.

Mike Joseph felt he could fine-tune WKMH to program successfully against the above situations. However, one thing neither Joseph nor anyone else could do anything about was WKMH's signal. At five thousand watts, their transmitter power was equal to WXYZ's, but there was a big difference as to where that signal went. In the daylight hours, WXYZ transmitted a nondirectional pattern and at night they made just a slight adjustment to the west to avoid interfering with another station on the 1270 frequency. All in all, WXYZ covered the metro Detroit area twenty-four hours a day. CKLW, with its fifty thousand watts, covered much of Michigan, Indiana, Ohio, Pennsylvania, and Ontario in the day, and at night their sky wave skipped down the eastern seaboard.

WKMH, on the other hand, had extreme directional patterns both day and night. In the daytime, their signal formed the shape of a cloverleaf, resulting in some dead spots here and there. At night, it switched to a teardrop formation, with the base of the pattern forming north of Toledo and curving in when it hit downtown Detroit. The result was that the station came in loud and clear on the west side and in the northern suburbs while at the same time, people across town in Grosse Pointe and much of the east side were unable to hear it at all. At sundown, WKMH would simply disappear from the dial. To overcome this signal disadvantage, the new station would have to do double duty where its signal could be picked up.

The first decision was to drop the WKMH call letters, which had been in place since the station's inception in 1946. This practice is commonplace today but in 1963 it rarely happened. At midnight on Halloween, October 31, 1963, WKMH 1310 became WKNR, New Radio 13. The new call letters were a tribute to the station's founder, Fred Knorr, and lent themselves nicely to a new nickname, "Keener." Until now, the Top 40 stations in town had sort of eased into the format. This was the first time a completely new station and sound would come on the air with the flip of a switch. Teaser ads ran in the newspaper for a week or so, leading up to a big full-page ad the day before the changeover.

For the first twenty-four hours, WKNR broadcast ghost stories with no commercial interruptions. Every few minutes an announcer would remind listeners that in so many hours and minutes the "Battle of the Giants" would begin.[4]

To WKNR personnel, the "Battle of the Giants" described what was about to take place as Keener challenged the competition. To listeners, it would be an opportunity to call and vote for their favorite song as million-sellers like "Runaway" by Del Shannon, "Only the Lonely" by Roy Orbison, "Save the Last Dance for Me" by the Drifters, and other monster hits were pitted against one another, the winner played over and over until a challenger received more votes. No commercials were played, just back-to-back million-sellers interspersed with catchy station breaks and jingles singing about Keener 13.

At the conclusion of the "Battle of the Giants," there was no letdown as regular programming got under way. Gone were the Mutual network newscasts, evening news blocks, Van Patrick sportscasts, and the all-night jazz show. Mike Joseph instituted a short thirty-one-record playlist, guaranteeing that only the top hits would be heard. Keener had budgeted close to $130,000 for advertising and promotion, which included bumper stickers and the printing of some fifty thousand Keener Music Guide surveys that were shipped to area record stores every week. The number one song that first week was "Louie, Louie" by the Kingsmen, and Keener kept banging it out.

There also was a musical pattern for the disc jockeys to follow, tailored for each hour. As an example, a plan might call for an up-tempo top-ten song, to be followed by a slow-to-medium tempo song from the bottom half of the survey, then an up-tempo record from the top twenty followed by an oldie, and so forth. Joseph also scheduled a "Keener top 13 countdown" to air, with no commercials, just as WXYZ would go into "The Breakfast Club" or their evening news block.

WKNR's newscasts were scheduled at the unorthodox times of fifteen and forty-five past the hour, and deejays never signed off their shows but simply introduced their last record, which would segue into a station break and then the first record of the next show. All this created an illusion that the station never stopped playing hit music.

A reverb system was installed that gave Keener a distinctive sound on the dial. More than just an echo chamber, it made the words and the music jump out of the speaker. Jingles selling "WKNR, Keener 13, more music more often" were featured. Jingles had been a part of the programming at the other stations in town for years, but were never used to the extent that Keener used them. There were jingles for weather, sports, and community notes. There was even a jingle to introduce the news: "With first person news alive [*staccato Morse code sound effect*] at fifteen and forty-five [*sound effect again*], WKNR Contact News."

The new deejay lineup began with sardonic morning man Mort Crowley, formerly of WLS in Chicago (sister station to WXYZ). On the air, Crowley could be somewhat abrasive, a sort of mix of wacky Jerry Lewis and Jackie Mason. He was the wildest voice on Detroit morning radio. Robin Seymour reinvented himself in his new nine to noon slot. Jim Sanders, another holdover from 'KMH, followed from noon to three, soon replaced by Jerry Goodwin.

Keener made a bold move in hiring a wild nighttime disc jockey named Gary Stevens from WIL in St. Louis and putting him on in the important three to seven afternoon drive shift. Stevens cooked with an energy level seldom heard on Detroit radio. In a raspy but youthful voice, he shot out words like a fighter throws left jabs, his voice sometimes cracking in midsentence, making him sound like Henry Aldrich on steroids. A grunting sidekick called the "Wooly-Burger" provided comic harassment, eating everything in sight and then letting out with a decidedly gross belch. Stevens would feign disbelief and then throw that rude little "Wooly-Burger" out of the studio!

Originally from upstate New York, Steven's first job in radio was at a tiny station in Conneaut, Ohio, and he liked all the gimmicks Top 40 radio had to offer. To put the spotlight on listeners in a particular town, Gary produced a concoction of strange noises that would be released over the air whenever he fired his "zap gun," as in : "Hello to everyone listening in Wyondotte! ZAP!"[5]

From seven to midnight, Keener featured Bob Green, coming from WQAM, the Storz rocker in Miami. Green, originally from Rochester, New York, was doing his second tour in Detroit, having been with Keener's predecessor in 1961. He had a catchy way of mixing up the order of words, so you might find yourself listening to the "Greenie Bob Show."

Aside from his on-the-air duties, Bob Green was Keener's resident production wizard. He could be found spending long hours, locked deep away in the Keener production studio, buried amid reams of audio tape–double and triple tracking, speaking, singing, and screeching about the latest WKNR contests and promotions: "Here's the number one song on this week's WKNR Music Guide!" There were few faster on the draw with a razor blade and splicing bar. The results were some of the brightest and most exciting promotions on Detroit radio. Green was followed on the air at midnight by Bill Phillips.

Bob Green had arrived in Detroit a couple of weeks before the changeover so that he could record lots of promotional spots and everyone could get ready to go. "None of the staff was really happy about many of the things Mike Joseph wanted to do," recalls Green. "There were some good ideas but he wanted things like lost doggie reports and other service-type featurettes. So as soon as he left town, Frank Maruca, who was program director, and a few of us got together and put some ideas on the table that we thought would work and much of what Detroit listeners started hearing had been influenced by that as well as my time with WQAM in Miami. We used a very similar approach and we achieved a sound that just kept Keener moving along in a very exciting way."[6]

What was the "Keener Sound"? According to Frank Maruca in a 1960s article, "It's everything we do and the way we do it. It can't just be the music we play because others play the same music."[7]

The "Keener Sound" kept the big personality sound while at the same time tightening up and adhering to format techniques that added consistency without rigidity. Everything was presented at a faster pace than the other stations as Keener moved Detroit radio ahead at warp speed. Listeners were exposed to a combination of bells, whistles, tones, jingles, and promotions that made the station sparkle like some sort of audio amusement park. More than any other station in town, WKNR branded everything:

> Okay! That's it! Keener hit number one! "Dancin' in the Street" from Martha and the Vannnnn-dellas! [tone] WKNR time is twenty-one past four on the Gary Stevens Show and the Keener temperature is forty-two. [WKNR jingle] I just saw something creeping by the studio window and it looked like

the Wooly-Burger." We'll find out what he's up to in a few minutes. Right now on Keener 13, here's Bobby Jameson with number five on the WKNR Music Guide, "I'm Lonely!"[8]

Also helping WKNR stand out from the pack was that for the first time in Detroit, listeners could call a radio station and be put on the air to request a song or participate in a contest. "Okay, on the phone for 'Keener Pick and Play,' we have Susan from Ferndale. Susan, what song can we play for you today?" Susan: "I want to hear 'She Loves You' by the Beatles!" Gary Stevens: "Thanks Susan, no sooner said than done!"

Listeners were amazed that a song could be found so quickly, but with only thirty-one records on the list it wasn't that difficult.

While Detroit had never been a spectacular contest town with big prizes and huge sums of money given away, Keener always had something going on. "Keener DJ Baseball" let listeners call in and guess whether one of the jocks would hit a single, double, triple, or home run, with small amounts of cash awarded. If nobody guessed correctly, there was always the highly regarded "Keener ballpoint pen." According to Bob Green, there was no delay system with the phones in the early days: "We just went on the air live with the contests and somehow we never had a problem with bad language or practical jokes. I doubt if you could do that today."[9]

Bob Green also recalls another of Keener's attention-getting contests: "We were having just one of the worst winters in Detroit, very, very cold and lots of snow and ice. It seemed like the sun never came out, so we came up with a contest called 'Think Summer.' We had special jingles and a song recorded around the theme and we gave out thousands of 'Think Summer' buttons. Listeners sent in entries from the newspaper and we had prizes like a basket of Florida oranges, a charcoal grill, and other things associated with summer. It was probably the most successful promotion we did."

When it came to promotions, Keener was in a class by itself. Each year the station released a full-length album of oldies with great cover art featuring station personalities, the proceeds going to charity.

The news department produced a "year in review" record that was provided to Detroit area schools. News presentation was another area where WKNR excelled. News director Phil Nye led a seven-man team that moved like seventy as they covered Detroit. WKNR news had a very authoritative sound that eschewed the "over the top" sensational gimmicks featured in newscasts on the Storz and McClendon stations and consistently won journalism awards. Adult listeners had no need to tune to another station for information.[10] Some of the voices on Keener newscasts over the years included George Hunter, Bill Bonds, Dick Buller, Erik Smith, Ed Mullins and John Maher.[10]

The top-hit records, great deejays, contests, promotions, jingles, exciting production, and the famous reverb system, plus award-winning news and total consistency of sound, all came together and lifted WKNR from the bottom of the ratings to the top in a very short time. All over Detroit, kids were talking: "Have you heard that new station, Keener?" The resounding answer: "Yes!"

WKNR jingle from 1964:

*W—We're always around*
*K—Keep Keener, the action sound*
*N—News at fifteen and forty-five*
*R—Ready, come on and swing*
*With WKNR, Keener 13*[11]

## CHAPTER 14

# Beatle Boosters, Morning Madness, and Other Weird Tales

As 1964 GOT UNDER WAY, WKNR saw its rating share consistently moving up from 2 to a 6, to a 14, and way beyond.[1] At the end of sixty days, Keener was number one in most time periods and second in the rest. Shares of 25 and 30 were not uncommon. Bill Gavin, who published an influential record tip sheet, called Keener the "miracle baby" of the industry. The other stations were reeling, trying to figure out just what had happened.

Keener wasn't the only thing new on the radio in 1964. There was the British invasion led by the Beatles. Tom Gelardi was in charge of Capitol Records' Detroit office and remembers his first involvement with the group: "Capitol was owned by EMI in England and they requested us to release 'I Want to Hold Your Hand' by a new group called the Beatles. I didn't think much of it and I was already under a lot of pressure, so I kinda lost my cool one day and threw that record across the floor, yelling, 'I have enough problems trying to get our American artists on the radio,' like, 'leave me alone!' Anyhow, we finally got behind the song and the next thing I know, there is a company memo 'thanking Tom Gelardi for the great job breaking this huge hit record by their new group.' That was the last time I made such a presumption," confesses Gelardi.[2]

AS THE BEATLES EXPLODED ON THE SCENE, every radio station was trying to ride in their wake. WKNR, arriving at about the same time, tried to stake a claim on the group, but the competition was formidable.

When it was announced that the Beatles would be appearing in Miami, WXYZ's Lee Alan booked a flight, with plans to grab an exclusive interview. Bob Green, who was with WKNR at the time, recalls what happened: "A friend of mine who worked for Capitol Records in Miami called to say that he had been told that Lee Alan was on his way down to meet the Beatles. Things were very competitive, so I asked him if he had anything we could use to beat Alan on this and he happened to have some sort of generic interview material the Beatles had cut somewhere in Europe. He sent it up the line and I was able to edit the material and conduct an interview with The Beatles on Keener before Lee Alan got off the plane! We really promoted the heck out of it. Later, I found out Lee wasn't too happy," he laughs.[3]

Alan did, however, get his interview with the group and some other folks who came into contact with them, including a cab driver. The whole adventure was released on a record called "A Trip to Miami to Meet the Beatles."

At CKLW, Tom Clay was playing all Beatle songs during the first half hour of his nightly show and, of course, claiming to have all the latest inside information on the group. Before long, he was making plans to stage a "Beatle Booster Ball" to raise money to bring the Fab Four to Detroit. Clay asked fellow CK' deejay Dave Shafer if he wanted to split the costs of staging this event: "I thought Tom was crazy and I didn't want to get involved," remembers Shafer. "Then Tom found another partner and they held it at the Michigan State Fairgrounds and just thousands of kids showed up. I was surprised."[4] Tom Clay reigned over his "Beatle Booster Ball," passing out records, pictures, and any other free promotional materials he could come by.

After this success, Clay informed Dave Shafer of his plans to travel to England to meet the Beatles in person. "I told him, 'Tom, you're never going to get near them,' recalls Shafer. "I spoke too soon. Clay manages to spend hours and hours with them and he collects all this stuff to bring back, supposedly personally used by the Beatles. He's got hairs, cigarette butts, tissue, you name it."

Clay also turned the trip into a great promotion, holding a contest, with the two winners accompanying him to England.[5]

Back on the air, Tom Clay is telling listeners to send in one dollar and he will send them back something personal from the Beatles–over forty thousand letters arrive within three days. Meanwhile, the second "Beatle Booster Ball" draws thousands more paying fans. Dave Shafer remembers visiting Tom Clay's house while all this was going on: "It was some scene over there. In this one room, there were all these bags of money and girls counting it out. Then, out in the garage there were girls sorting all this crap he was giving away. It was a major operation. You wouldn't believe it, I think the money involved was something like $185,000," he adds. (Others have put the dollar figure as high as $300,000.)[6]

Ron Knowles remembers seeing bags of mail piled up at the station and wondering what was going to happen to it all. Knowles also recalls seeing Tom in the production studio late into the night, sorting though all sorts of raw tape he brought back of his interviews with the Beatles. "He had so much and would edit it every which way for playback on his show," says Knowles.[7] In addition, Clay put some of the interview material on a record entitled "Remember, We Don't Like Them...We Love Them!"

Soon, complaints were coming in from listeners less than enthusiastic about a cigarette butt and from those claiming to have received nothing. Dave Shafer: "Out of nowhere, Tom gets this great job offer out in California and he's bailing out of CK' fast. On the air he tells listeners that he's going off to "travel with the Beatles" and that "Dave Shafer will be taking over the 'Beatle Booster Club,' so long!" One evening, after I get off the air, I'm on my way to do a record hop for Father Bryson at Notre Dame High School. As I am coming out of the Windsor Tunnel, I'm pulled over and arrested. The police serve me with papers accusing me of involvement in international fraud and then they haul me off to jail! All this because Tom Clay has supposedly left this Beatle booster thing in my lap. I had to use my phone call to contact Father Bryson: 'I'm sorry, Father, I can't make it tonight, I'm in jail.'"[8]

CKLW bailed Shafer out later in the evening and then informed Tom Clay he had better get back to Detroit and clean up this mess. "I went on the air and apologized," recalls Shafer. "I said I had nothing to do with this situation and I think I said something unflattering about Tom. Well, when he gets back to town and hears about it, he gets all upset, like, 'Gee, Dave...I'm hurt,' but that was typical of Tom," Shafer quipped.[9]

ANYONE TUNING IN TO WKNR one strange morning in March got a real surprise on the "Mort Crowley Show." Before joining independent WKNR, Crowley had been employed by ABC as the morning man at WLS in Chicago, where he aggravated management. Fellow Keener deejay Bob Green remembers the Detroit incident: "We had been running all kinds of phone contests along with our song request line. So many people were calling in that we were shutting down phone exchanges left and right and the phone company was raising hell. The station had agreed to hold off doing any more contests until we could find a solution. Now, on this particular day, management had left a memo for Mort not to take any requests or to give out the contest phone number on the air. I don't know what happened but Crowley went berserk and locked himself in the studio."[10]

Here is some of what WKNR listeners heard as Mort ranted and raved: "You know, I worked for a big company too long. I lost my sense of values, I lost my sense of dignity. Now I got it back. It's gonna cost me my job, but I got it back. Here's the Keener Key song from Johnny Nash, very apropos this morning, it's called 'I'm Leavin.' [music] That's Johnny Nash on WKNR. Well, I have a responsibility to you people for the last hour and a half of the show, so you're gonna get up happy!"[11]

He then continued his tirade, which was directed toward the phone company and station executives, whom he saw as giving in to pressure from a monopoly. When it was time for the newscast, he announced: "Now you talk for five minutes." The newscaster, obviously affected by what was happening, stumbled over a few words but, by the end of the newscast, was in good spirits and instead of announcing the standard exit line, "Now, more music with Mort Crowley," he offered. "Here's more of the 'Mortacular.'"

Crowley started right in again:

We are reduced to one phone line today because they have

frightened all of our executives. The only number I am supposed to give out is Luzon 2-4481. I won't give the other. This
is because of the the phone company in its tremendous mag-
nificence and its great surge of power tells us not to, because
we're jamming the lines. That's wrong. *That is wrong!* We got
enough shook up people around here. What the heck do you
wanna shake 'em up some more? This has come to a head *right
now!* We are living in fear and this isn't the way it should be.
Everyone should be happy. This is not the concept of the
country. Who gives Ma Bell the authority to threaten to take
our phones out? This is the big utility company talking to the
small group of people–"You do as I say!" The Octopus has
struck again, ah-hah! We have reacted with typical radio forti-
tude–we got scared. That is, they got scared, I'm not. I don't
care. I don't. We had a nice thing but who wants to work under
those conditions? Anyone would be a fool who did that. I come
in at four-thirty this morning and find this stinking memo–it
makes you wonder who the executives are working for. I would
like to say bon voyage, it's been nice.

When nine o'clock rolled around, Mort got up, unlocked the
door, and walked out, as if it were no big deal. He was then
escorted out of the station. It was the end for "Crowley and
Company" in Detroit.

WKNR replaced Mort with the more jovial Frank Sweeney
from Cleveland, better known to Keener listeners as "Swingin'
Sweeney." Jim Sanders also departed about the same time, and
Jerry Goodwin, formerly of KBOX in Dallas and most recently
WQAM in Miami, became Keener's high-profile noon-to-three
personality. "Welcome, welcome, welcome into a *Tues-day* Jerry
Goodwin Show,"[12] he would say in his very big, hip, soulful voice.
Goodwin had a bag of regular sayings that became well known to
Detroit listeners, the most familiar being a very heartfelt "Thank
you, so much" and along with every phone contest he would
remind listeners: "You've got thirteen minutes from the *toot,* to
collect the *loot.*" He also would refer to dollars as "rubles." The
records he played were "out of sight sounds!" or "brand-new for
you." The number two song was always "the runner-up song on
the Keener Music Guide!" On a good day he could rattle the windows with his vocal acrobatics.

Each year, Goodwin served as the station's point person for the

Danny Thomas Teenagers' March to raise money for St. Judes Children's Hospital. Now, Jerry had a reputation for being, at times, a bit moody both on the air and off. One year he found himself having trouble raising enough volunteers to sign up to march, and after an on-air plea from Danny Thomas, Goodwin chided his listeners: "I have no doubt that we will reach our quotas, but frankly...you're drivin' me a little cra-zy, right now, friends." Of course, this was the same day that he opened his show with the observation: "People who live in glass houses shouldn't get stoned."

Jerry Goodwin fit right in with the "cartoon" flavor of what people in the industry were calling the "Keener Sound," which could be heard all over Detroit in 1964. Stores, restaurants, and service stations all seemed to have their radios tuned to Keener 13, the station that sounded like it had the most music, best deejays, and contests. Strangely, the other Top 40 stations were slow to react.

CKLW continued to rely on its massive signal to bring in the business. Media buyers were less sophisticated back then and booked lots of business on the station because, besides delivering lots of listeners in Detroit, CK' could be heard far beyond the metro area. WJBK stayed the course with its long playlist and personalities including Robin Walker on the "Jack the Bellboy Show." Although they were fighting back with new jingles, production, and money giveaways, they just didn't have the pizzazz that Keener offered. WJBK also had some bad luck about the time Keener came on the air. "They were doing some construction work near our towers down in Lincoln Park," recalls Marc Avery. "Anyhow, a bulldozer knocked over a couple of our towers and we were off the air for quite a while. This is on Halloween of '63, when 'KNR came on. When we finally got things operating again, we were reduced in power to 250 watts and you couldn't pick up the station."

Paul Winter recalls that the feeling around WXYZ regarding Keener was one of extreme anxiousness: "We felt they were doing what we were doing, only doing it much better!" Winter found relief from the building pressure in a job inquiry from a station in Boston: "For whatever reason, they expressed an interest in me, so we taped a couple of hours of the show and mailed it off. I was careful to do more of what I thought they wanted to hear on that tape,"[13] Winter confides. In March of 1964, after his fortieth birthday and thirteen years of service, Paul Winter resigned and moved to Boston to do mornings for WEEI, which became one of the early talk stations. Dave Prince shifted to middays and Don Zee, tiring of the all-night grind, took over weekends.

ONE NIGHT EARLY IN APRIL, Lee Alan was cruising home in his Corvette, after working late at the station. Ignoring the advice he passed on to listeners each night, he was traveling too fast. Just ahead was a huge semitrailer truck making a sudden stop. Alan swerved but the 'vette skidded on ice, flipped over, and rolled into a ditch. Lee crawled away as the gas tank exploded behind him. He suffered a broken back that kept him off the radio. Beaumont Hospital was flooded with get-well mail as Lee Alan lay in traction.[14]

After returning to the air some weeks later, he found himself in trouble of a different sort. WXYZ management had been told that Lee was shaking down the owners of Walled Lake Casino for more money, threatening to pull his remotes and the record hops that he and Dave Prince both did.

"Lee stopped me in the hallway one day and told me he was having a problem of some kind with management," recalls Dave Prince. "Lee said, 'I may need your support.' I said, 'Okay.' Later on I was called into a meeting with Charles Fritz [general manager] and Bob Baker [program director] and these guys are asking me why I have been threatening the owners at the Casino. I said, 'Hold on, I don't know what you are talking about.' They said that the owners of the Casino say that Lee says that 'both of you would pull out if they didn't come up with more money.' I said, 'Lee does not speak for me and I never threatened anyone.'

"Now, I wasn't making what he was out there, but I was doing okay. I got about $125 a dance and I think Lee was getting like $350 and we're doing like three or four a week. I had no problem with the arrangement. Then they told me, 'You better get out of here [as in Broadcast House], because we're going to fire Lee today.' So I left and there has always been this spin on it that I somehow double-crossed him and it just wasn't so. In fact, I had supported Lee on many other occasions when he would get himself into trouble. When Lee was let go from WKMH, I spent my whole evening show bemoaning that he had been fired. He was a very bright guy and wanted his ideas to prevail. A lot of the time he was right, but you have to watch how you act."[15]

Lee went on to deny the charges, explaining that he had only asked the Casino owners to increase his fees back to where they had been before he had voluntarily taken a cut from three hundred fifty to two hundred fifty per dance, to help out with renovations. Despite this explanation, WXYZ fired him in late May. One year earlier, Lee Alan had been the kingpin of Detroit radio. Now a triple punch of Keener, the car accident, and the Walled Lake casino accusations left his career in ruins.[16]

In June, WXYZ hired Texas deejay Russ "the Weird Beard" Knight to replace Alan in the evening. At KLIF in Dallas, Knight had enjoyed great popularity; in Detroit, no one cared. Keener was too hot that summer and Wixie had lost momentum. Also, kids were tuning in another Knight on Radio 8-0. Terry Knight had left his 'JBK gig to return to his hometown of Flint. CKLW brought him back to replace Tom Clay when he left for California.

At only twenty, Knight was roughly in the same age-group as his audience. An incredible communicator, he promoted ahead in a style like Lee Alan's, trying to keep listeners hooked as long as he could by giving out tickets and exclusive information. He was in peak form when the Beatles were coming to town: "Okay, it is time for the announcement we promised. This Sunday, we will be doing a record hop at Windsor Arena from two until six in the afternoon. I have secured the *last three tickets* in the city of Detroit or probably anywhere else to see the Beatles in person at Olympia Stadium in August. These tickets are for the fifth row from the stage. Three people will be selected at Windsor Arena on Sunday and will be given the *last* available tickets to see the Beatles, *in person!*"[17]

After this grand announcement, he sequed into "Things We Said Today." Despite the hype over the Beatles concert, Knight set himself apart from the radio crowd of Beatle fanatics by getting behind the Rolling Stones when their first records came out.

In typical Detroit fashion and in what had to have been the most maudlin sign-off in radio, Terry Knight closed his show each evening with Jerry Lewis warbling "I'll Go My Way by Myself."

CKLW jingle from 1964:

*CKLW, Ra-di-o 8-00000!*

WHEN IT WAS FINALLY ANNOUNCED that the Beatles were coming to Detroit, WKNR made the most of it in promotion, including a deal to have reports filed from the Beatles' plane by a fellow named Larry Kane, who was traveling with the group. Bob Green remembers meeting the Beatles when the plane landed in Detroit: "When we arrived at Executive Airport, we were surprised that none of the guys from the other stations were there. Then we found out they had all gone to Metro [Airport] by mistake, so we had some exclusive time with the Beatles and covered their news conference."[18] On August 16, 1964, Bob Green and the other Keener deejays were on stage with the Beatles at the Olympia.

Beatlemania was everywhere in 1964. Stations had Beatle exclusives, Beatle countdowns, and contests to choose a favorite Beatle. Things reached absurdity when a local club group called the Headliners grew their hair long and billed themselves as the "American Beatles."

CHAPTER 15

# Cruisin' the Sixties

FOR TEN MONTHS, it had been a four-way split of the Top 40/rock audience in the Motor City, with Keener the new powerhouse. In late August, people punching in to WJBK for the latest Beatles hit were greeted by "The Sound of Just Beautiful Music," as Radio 15 bid farewell to good guys, bellboys, and rebels.

"It came out of nowhere and I was just devastated," remembers Clark Reid. "I thought it was a terrible idea. One day we're playing the Beatles and Motown, then, all of the sudden, they had us tracking instrumental album cuts by the 101 Strings. They were the sort of cheap albums you could buy for forty-nine cents at the gas station. Everything we said was written out on cards. We would have to announce: 'The smiling time on WJBK is 4:15' or 'The safe crossing-the-street time is...' it was ridiculous."[1] After a few months, Clark left the beautiful music behind and departed Detroit for a program director's job that started out in Philadelphia but, because of an ownership exchange, took him to KYW in Cleveland.

In the same month of 1964, WXYZ fired longtime program director Bob Baker and promoted David Klemm from sales and promotions, giving him the new title of director of operations. ABC was blaming Baker for the station's fall, implying that he had not worked hard enough at maintaining the format guidelines put into place by Hal Neal way back in 1959. In other words, he hadn't been tough enough with the disc jockeys in enforcing a tight format, but who had cared? WXYZ had been high in the ratings, thanks to the on-air talents of Fred Wolf, Lee Alan, and a lineup of professionals, without whom Wixie would not have been much of a power, as the station really lacked exciting on-air promotion and modern production. WXYZ still employed staff announcers as late as 1963. These were announcers separate from the disc jockeys, who read station breaks, live commercials, and public-service announcements after newscasts and during network programming blocks. Aside from having the slogans and call letters recited so many times between records, it had pretty much been a situation of handing the deejays the records, commercials, and station jingles and having them put it all together in an entertaining and exciting presentation. Now all that had changed with the sweeping success of WKNR. Keener made Wixie sound like the past.

David Klemm had almost no credibility with the Wixie staff and the news of his promotion was not well received. Klemm let everyone know that things were going to change. The pace was going to pick up and WXYZ was going to get very aggressive.

The "Weird Beard" was having no success in the evening race for the ratings, and in October, Russ Knight was given his walking papers. No big deal. In the radio biz, there is no guarantee that what plays in Dallas will work in Detroit.

The British invasion was still hot, so Wixie came up with an attention-getting two-week promotion featuring an English disc jockey named John Benson, broadcasting on WXY-Zed, as the British pronounce it.[2] Trying to figure out what to do at the end of Benson's run, Wixie management consulted with its former boss Hal Neal, now at ABC in New York. Neal advised that the person they really needed was right there, working on another floor at Broadcast House.[3]

Neal was referring to Lee Alan, who, after being let go and sitting out for a couple of months, had been offered a booth-announcing job in the morning on WXYZ-TV. It had been a big comedown, but financial and personal problems caused Alan to welcome the employment. Now Dave Klemm was buzzing Lee Alan in television and offering him the chance to go back on the radio from 7:15 to 10:00 each evening. Alan did not hesitate in accepting the offer.

According to Jim Hampton, who was called in to play the records that evening, Alan's return was a real surprise to everyone including himself: "I was handed a tape cartridge and at 7:15 I put it in the machine and Lee's old theme started to play and then he walked into the studio. It was very exciting and a real morale booster having him back on the station."[4] Listeners in Detroit were once again hearing "Lee Alan, on the Horn." Pat Murphy split the evening, going on from ten to one.

Aside from bringing back Lee Alan, Klemm made a strong move in hiring a very talented radio and commercial producer from Norfolk, Virginia, named Bruce Miller to serve as production director.[5] Although Miller's job included writing and producing commercials, he was also responsible for creating more excitement on the air by producing new show opens, contests, and promotions built around WXYZ's new "Radio a Go-Go" jingle package from the innovative Dallas jingle company called PAMS.[6]

Formed as an ad agency by Bill Meeks in 1951, the letters PAMS originally stood for Production, Advertising, Merchandising, and Sales. After finding out that jingle production alone could be extremely lucrative, the agency dropped all other activities and focused solely on creating the catchy musical logos for stations across the country.*

Now, after newscasts, listeners would hear:

Jingle chorus: *"Let's go, go, go, go, go"*
[each go sung progressively higher]

Miller: *It's a good time for the good sound of "Radio Go-Go" on WXYZ and the Joel Sebastian Show!*[7]

Other new production included special chart position intros and contests:

Jingle chorus: *The Super Hit Sound of Wonderful WXYZ*

Miller: Today this song is Super Hit number 2,2,2! *Go-go* for your fling at a fortune, in the WXYZ secret word Sweepstakes! Be listening every day! You could win a thousand dollars, yes,

---

*As WXYZ had the exclusive rights to PAMS material in Detroit, WKNR used the services of CRC (Commercial Recording Corporation), also based in Dallas, until PAMS became available and then Keener switched.

*one* thousand dollars if we call your name and you know the secret word. It's the WXYZ secret word sweepstakes! Now—that's strictly Wixie![7]

Also, WXYZ's record list was cut back to forty songs and renamed the Detroit Sound Survey.[8] At the expense of listeners being exposed to fewer artists, WKNR had proven that you could attract an audience by playing a shorter list of familiar songs.

WXYZ jingle from 1964:

*Wherever you go, go-go with swingin' 12-7, WXYZ.*

GOOD BUDDY MICKEY SHORR WAS BIDING his time in southern California in 1964, since being blown out of Detroit in the payola explosion of 1959. "It was for something I didn't do. I was black-balled for five years. No one would talk to me,"[9] Shorr related in a later interview.

In California, he survived, peddling from a car loaded with cookware and tools. He did some theatrical productions and was involved with the making of a novelty hit record called "Ben Crazy," which was a parody of the popular television medical drama.[8]

One day the phone rang and it was Leonard and Phil Chess on the line from Chicago. They were trying to come up with a format for their new FM station. Remembering Mickey as the guy with ideas, he was invited to come to a meeting in Chicago. Shorr hopped a plane with nothing really in mind but during the flight he came up with a wild concept. The Chess brothers said yes and made him their program director. The Chicago station became an early FM success, programming light jazz with sexy female voices doing taped lead-ins.[9] The announcing staff included future NBC news correspondents Norma Quarrels and Linda Ellerbee, who went by the air name Hush Puppy.[10] The station was WSDM, which stood for "smack dab in the middle," and that's just where Mickey Shorr liked to be.

IN THE SUMMER OF 1964, Keener deejay and master promoter Robin Seymour approached CKLW-TV with an idea for a new weekly show. "I was not entirely happy at Keener since they had forced me off my commission structure and on to a salary. I was making a lot less money, so I was looking for ways to offset that," remembers Seymour. "I went to Ed Metcalf, who was vice president and general manager of CK radio and TV, and said, 'I've got a great idea for a half hour show on Saturday that can make you some money.' That got his interest. I told him that we could bring some business right on board from Federal Department Stores, 7 Up, and the Stevens Modeling Agency. He gave us five hundred dollars a week to produce the show, so in the fall we came on with 'Teen Town.'

"We had a hit right off with the salute to a different high school each week and the set with the bleachers. I give it to our production crew. We were just two-camera black and white but those guys gave it a network look. They never missed a shot of someone coming on or going off. We were proud of all the shows but people tend to remember the Motown specials we did, including the one devoted to the Supremes. I think I made a whopping hundred and fifty bucks from 'Teen Town,' but I got a million dollars worth of exposure that I was able to parlay into some great deals," Seymour stated.[10] Airing Saturday afternoons on channel 9, it was another chance to see record artists lip-synch their hit records and to see kids do the latest dance. Footage of Stevie Wonder and the Supremes taken from this show pop up on rock documentaries from time to time.

ALSO ABOUT THIS TIME, Larry Dixon became the first black disc jockey in Michigan to host a dance party-style show on television, when "Club Mellow" premiered on Detroit's newest television station, WKBD, channel 50 (Jack Surrell had hosted a variety show on channel 7 in the mid-fifties). According to Larry, it lasted only a few weeks: "The station received some complaints after a black and white couple were seen dancing across the screen and management came up with a different reason for taking us off the air."

Dixon, who had also departed WCHB, after eight years, found a microphone available at WGPR, a low-profile station on the almost invisible FM dial. Larry again broke new ground as he sold Pepsi-Cola on sponsoring an hour each day. It was the first advertising they had ever done on FM.[11]

IN DECEMBER, Terry Knight announced that he was leaving CKLW and radio. Knight was an aspiring musician and was supposedly going off to hang out with the Rolling Stones while he pursued a music career. Listening to the dramatic closing to his final show, one would have thought he had been on Detroit radio for twenty years. In fact, his combined time at WJBK and CKLW totaled less than two years, but with so few stations attracting such large audiences, it was possible for a hustling disc jockey to achieve the kind of awareness in six months that in today's crowded market might take five years.

Terry Knight had made his mark at an early age and was getting out. After talking about his plans on the air for almost ten minutes, he made the most of this last radio sign-off:

> It is exactly twenty-eight minutes past eleven o'clock. It is Friday, December 18th, 1964...and it is time to say good night. [*As the closing theme music eases in, there for the last time is emotional Jerry Lewis singing*] "I'll go my way by myself." [*Terry solemnly interjects*] Tonight...I'll be by myself. [*Lewis*] "I'm by myself alone." [*Terry*] But by myself only for the one second that I forget you're there, and when I remember you're there, then I'll know, I'll never be by myself again...good night, sleep tight, and remember that I love ya the most, bye, bye.[12]

Then, a deep-voiced staff announcer intoned: "This is CKLW, AM and FM, in Windsor," as the opening notes of American Airlines' "Music till Dawn" took to the air.

CKLW slogan from 1964: This is CKLW, small enough to know you, but big enough to serve you.


MOTOWN HAD SOME LOCAL COMPETITION in 1964 with the emergence of Golden World and Ric-Tic Records, owned by Eddie Wingate and JoAnne Jackson. Despite being a black-owned record company, Golden World hit national pay dirt with a white group called the Reflections, who had a huge top-ten smash with "(Just like) Romeo and Juliet." Tony Micale was their lead singer.

Gino Washington was one more young black kid growing up in Detroit with dreams of becoming a recording star. At thirteen he was showing up at "Frantic" Ernie Durham's amateur talent shows. "I kept losing," he recalls. "Ernie was just a great guy and when he saw how upset I was, he said, 'Come back and watch the performances, that's what gets the attention.' I did and after that I started doing the splits and they would call me 'Jumpin' Gino Washington.'"

Although failing to make the national charts, Gino's first record, "Out of This World," was a big local hit. "We released it on a local label called Mala and hired Tom Gelardi from Capitol to do promotion and it went to number four in Detroit," Gino recalls. "My next hit was 'Gino Is a Coward,' which I had written a couple of years earlier and recorded again for Ric-Tic and it became a huge local hit."[13]

Gino remembers being one of the biggest draws on the local record hop scene in the mid-sixties. "I would be running all over to do three or four dances in one evening. I did hops with Dave Shafer, Joel Sebastian, Lee Alan, and Tom Clay. I remember show-ing up at a lot of them with Stevie Wonder and some of the other Motown acts."

Aside from Berry Gordy's ego, Motown was not hurting in any way from local competition, holding their own nationally as the British invasion swept the country. "My Guy" by Mary Wells, "Dancing in the Street" by Martha and the Vandellas, "Baby, I Need Your Lovin'" from the Four Tops, along with three consecu-tive number one hits from the Supremes, made 1964 a staggering year for the Detroit label.


THERE WERE A LOT OF NEW SOUNDS on the air in 1965–hard rock and folk rock: "Like a Rolling Stone" by Bob Dylan, "Turn, Turn, Turn" by the Byrds, "Eve of Destruction " by Barry McGuire, "Satisfaction" by the Rolling Stones, and "We've Gotta Get Out of This Place" by the Animals. There was also "Wooly Bully" by Sam the Sham, "Downtown" by Petula Clark, "The In-Crowd" by Dobie Gray, and "Help Me Rhonda"by the Beach Boys, all going into the Top 40 mixer and onto the radio airwaves.


TOM SHANNON WAS HIRED by CKLW to fill the evening hours vacated by Terry Knight. A popular disc jockey on WKBW and WGR radio in his hometown of Buffalo, New York, Tom had also hosted "Buffalo Bandstand" on WKBW-TV. Besides broadcasting, he dabbled as a songwriter and along with his partner, Phil Todaro, penned the top-ten instrumental hit "Wild Weekend," recorded by the Rockin' Rebels.

The tune had originally been used as a theme song for Shannon's weekend radio shows in Buffalo. When a local group played its version for Tom, he immediately arranged for the group to record it, and "Wild Weekend" became a local hit in upstate New York in 1959. An executive for Swan Records bumped into the song several years later and contacted Tom, who owned the master, and it was rereleased. This time it became a hit across the country.[14]

Shannon arrived in the Motor City in the middle of December 1964. His memories of CKLW are vivid: "It was fifty thousand watts in a top-five market and that was about it. The format, if there was any, was quite loose and you could put things together pretty much to your own tastes. It was a much looser operation than we had in Buffalo," says Tom, who was able to roam around CK's eighty-record list, looking for goodies.

Shannon came across a record called "96 Tears" that had been recorded by a group from Saginaw called "Question Mark and the Mysterians" and had been released by a tiny label called Pa Go-Go. "I heard this thing and it had that great grunge rock sound and I knew it could be a smash. I have to admit that I leaned on it a little, which wasn't hard to do in those days, and we were really getting a good reaction. I pitched it to Neal Bogart, who back then was running Cameo-Parkway out of Philadelphia, and he took it national. It sold a million and they gave me a gold record for it," Shannon remembers.[15]

Record hops were still popular, and Tom, being an enterprising fellow, decided that more is better, so he started the "Shannon Caravan," enabling him to hit up to three places in one evening. "Probably the biggest dance I had back then was at a place called Surfside 3 in Kingsville, Ontario," says Shannon. "Lots of Michigan folks vacationed in the area and we had huge crowds all summer." The "Shannon Caravan" was not to be confused with "Dick Clark's Caravan of Stars," which toured the country in huge buses. "No, we didn't have any buses and there were no vans around back then, so I would rent the biggest station wagon I could find to be able and carry some talent with me," Tom remembers. "We had Paul Revere and the Raiders crammed in there a couple of times and Bob Seger's band when they were starting out. It was a great time and we had a lot of fun."[16]

By mid-1965, CKLW was upgrading their sound with new jingles, production, and a reverb system of their own.

Tom Shannon on the air:

> "With These Hands, Small But Mighty" from Bobby Blue Bland on the Tommy Shannon Show at four before nine. Seventy-nine degrees for a Thursday in the Motor Cities of Windsor and Detroit. How low tonight? Fair and warm it'll be with a low of seventy. Partly cloudy and warm on Friday and Friday night. Everything well with you? Good, I'm glad, 'cause we've got something *good* for you! [*Jingle: Listen here, a CK' replay from Radio 8-0*] I met him on a Sunday and my heart went blip! The Crystals on CK! [*Nine o'clock news intro*] Listen here now, this is CKLW radio newsman Barry Sharpe. [*Newscast*] The CK international temperature is seventy-nine degrees. Listen minute by minute for CK radio news. [*Jingle: From the Home of the Happy Fellas, here comes Tom Shannon*] [*music*] There you have the Contours on "hit-packed CKLW," passing out some good advice, "First I Look at the Purse."

> This is Tommy Shannon and I'll be looking for you coming up on the fifteenth of August out at the Note at Ruggles Beach, right on the shore at Lake Erie, located at Routes 2 and 6, just east of Huron, Ohio, for a big night with the Kingsmen. Bring a friend, bring a girl, bring one for me, but be sure to be at the Note. We still have a Honda to give away out there. That's the Note, your teen host from coast to coast, each Wednesday, Saturday, and Sunday night from eight to twelve midnight, located at Ruggles Beach on the shores of Lake Erie! We have seventy-nine degrees in the Motor Cities and a reminder that "the sun never sets on the Shannon empire!" [*Jingle: It's C-K-L-W Radio 8-0, the station that's all heart!*][16]

The last half hour of Tom's nightly show on CKLW was called "Bear Skin Rug." Shannon would dim the lights and read poetry, prose, and a bit of philosophy over some soft music. His parting words were "above and beyond all else...later."

THERE WERE MANY INSTANCES where disc jockeys would be asked to change their air name to something that sounded more attractive. Larry Morrow, working at WKHM in Jackson, Michigan, in 1963, bragged to a friend how he would never work under any name but his own. He then joined WTRX in Flint, where the deejays were called the "Jones Boys" and he became John Paul Jones.

A year later, Morrow accepted an offer to jump into the big time at CKLW. "I was hired and ready to go on the air in Detroit," recalls Morrow. "Then, the general manager, a guy named Bob Buss, called me into his office and told me they had a great idea for a name they wanted me to use on the air. Here, I'm back in my hometown and all excited that people I grew up and went to school with would be able to hear me and the station wants me to use another name! I told Buss that I didn't like the idea, for these and other reasons, but he said, 'It's for the good of the station.' What could I do but go along."[17] So, Larry Morrow was transformed into radio nobility as "Duke Windsor" on CK's all-night show in 1965. For lovers of trivia, Larry was part of Jack Scott's back-up group in 1960 and sang the bass line on "What in the World's Come over You."

ON THE AIR, WXYZ was sounding more aggressive and putting up a good fight. However, behind the scenes, they were operating in a great deal of turmoil in 1965. Morning man Fred Wolf was at odds with operations director David Klemm. Wolf had always been given quite a bit of leeway regarding music and content during his morning show. He had fought and won the right to replace the ten hardest records from Wixie's survey with his own selections. (If Fred Wolf had been allowed to play only one record on his entire show, it might well have been "Sugartime" by the McGuire Sisters.) With ratings dropping across the board, however, Klemm was relentless as he hounded Wolf regarding format violations, such as talking longer than twenty seconds between records and not giving the call letters often enough, and about his choice of music. Fred Wolf was not happy. On the air, his dry sense of humor was turning downright sarcastic:

> It's twenty-nine minutes past eight o'clock, the sun is shining. Gale Garnett says the Wigloo's "A Lovin' Place." It is?

> That's Al Steiner Ford, the granddaddy of them all. [*WXYZ weather jingle*] We got the sun shinin' on the Fred Wolf Show,

every mornin' between six and ten o'clock, yes, sir! The Sunshine Kid himself, who's perc-o-latin' all the time. Oh...what a line of baloney that is.

[*A United Theaters of Detroit commercial ends with "Dick Osgood speaking."*] [*Fred Wolf speaking*] Oh, you speak too much, keep your mouth shut." It's twenty-five in front of nine o'clock in the morning, WXYZ Big Time.[18]

Engineers were ordered to tape Wolf's show at various times so that Klemm could review it later and have proof of his transgressions. Fortunately, Fred Wolf commanded a lot more loyalty from the engineering staff than Dave Klemm and would be warned when they were ordered to roll tape. Fred had been at or near the top in the mornings in Detroit for fifteen years and resented the harassment. He complained to WXYZ station manager Charles Fritz, threatening to bolt if he didn't get Klemm off his back. Typical of management, both parties were asked to get along.[19]

While WXYZ worried about keeping its morning star in place, afternoon favorite Joel Sebastian announced in April that he was leaving for an afternoon slot at WINS, the Westinghouse station in New York that was home to high-profile deejay Murray "the K." Sebastian's last show on WXYZ was filled with testimonials from well-wishers, including Wixie management. It was obvious he had been highly regarded at Broadcast House during his five-year run.

Dave Prince was tapped to take over from Sebastian not only on radio but also on channel 7's Club 1270. Unsure of Fred Wolf's future, Wixie hired WJBK's morning man, Marc Avery, to come over and do middays in preparation for a possible morning opening. "Both Fred Wolf and I were real golf nuts," recalls Avery. "One day Fred called and asked me to play a round at his club, Lochmoor, in Grosse Pointe. At lunch, Fred suddenly puts down his menu and staring across the table says to me: 'How would you like my job?' I was sort of stunned, but without missing a beat, I dropped my menu and said, 'Sure.' Fred told me he was thinking about retiring and he was going to talk to ABC about hiring me."[20]

Detroit lost to New York for a second time in the same month of April when WMCA grabbed Keener's afternoon powerhouse, Gary Stevens, for evenings, replacing fast-talking B. Mitchell Reed, who returned to the West Coast. Stevens was accompanied to the Big Apple by the Wooly Burger!

CHAPTER **16**

# The Purtan Principle

AT A FEW MINUTES BEFORE NINE, WSAI's morning disc jockey was wrapping up his last show on the Cincinnati station.[1] On the air, he was talking with a few coworkers who had gathered in the studio to wish him well in his new position, one, which he kept reminding everyone, he was "not at liberty to divulge." Then, someone else came in and said: "Good luck in Detroit." The show's host sarcastically responded, "Thanks a lot."

Paul Purtan had been developing a somewhat droll, satirical on-air persona, but on this, his final show, he was quite sincere as he thanked the audience for listening, and rather than close with a predictable hit from WSAI's Top 40 survey, chose a sentimental cut from a Peggy Lee album recorded several years previously. The song was an ode to peace, love, and happiness titled "The Folks Who Live on the Hill." Purtan probably didn't realize it at the time, but in Detroit, he would not only be able to live on the hill— he would just about own it.

Paul Cannon was the all-night man at WKNR in 1965, and being that radio stations dislike having disc jockeys with the same name, Paul Purtan once again became Dick Purtan on his new ten-to-one late-night show in Detroit. He had also had to make a name change in Cincinnati, where there had already been an announcer with the same first name on that station. There wasn't much said about his arrival in Detroit, all the promotional hoopla having been showered on Scott Regen, hired for the seven to ten shift that preceded Purtan. On the air, Keener had been tracking Scottie as he "skate boarded in from Kansas City." An enthusiastic rock jock, whose sentences were peppered with teen jargon such as "Sock it to me" and "out of sight!" Regen made lots of noise as he hit the airwaves with a sort of radio teen magazine. Dick Purtan had to catch up:

> As you know, Scott Regen has a song on the survey called "Skate Board Song," because they had a big contest...so I had to come to town and nobody has ever heard of me and I might add, there are still people in this town who haven't heard of me. So I've come up with my own contest called the "Picture Contest," which was a very creative title I found in an old radio manual. So, what you do is, draw a picture, oh, I'm screwing this up. Make a drawing of what you think I look like and mail it to Picture, WKNR, Box 1300, Detroit 31, Michigan. Do that for me right now and the winner gets a cheap Japanese transistor radio!

On the same Memorial Day weekend show, Purtan conducted yet another big contest:

> Okay, everybody, we got up to five yesterday, so if you have had an accident or you are planning on having one, call and let us hear about it and we'll send a Keener news crew out to cover it and maybe you'll win our "Keener Top-13 Auto Accidents of the Weekend."[2]

There were more than a few listeners thinking, Is this for real?

Paul Richard Purtan grew up, as an older brother to two sisters, in Kenmore, New York, a suburb on the north side of Buffalo. His father was a manufacturer's representative, and as an eight-year-old, Dick (as he was always called) accompanied his parents on a sales trip to the Motor City. "I thought it was a very exciting place," he recalls. "Hey, this was the big city, tall buildings and all that, the memory stuck with me and I always wanted to live in Detroit someday."

Before getting to the Motor City, Purtan had some other stops to make. At Syracuse University, he earned a Master's Degree in

Radio/TV, while working part time as the "Buckaroo Sandman" at WOLF. His first full-time job was at station WWOL in Buffalo. "They called it Happy 1120 and I worked there under the name of Guy King," Purtan remembers. "It was a daytime-only operation, with ethnic programming until noon and music with Guy King from noon to sign-off, which varied. A fellow named Frank Ward had been Guy before me, and Tom Clay had the job even earlier."

After a six-month hitch in the army, it was back to "Happy 1120" for a short run and then off to a station in Jacksonville, Florida. In late 1961, Purtan moved to WSAI in Cincinnati, a well-known Top 40 station that was a springboard to the major markets.

Known to Cincinnati listeners as "Lovable, Hugable Paul," Purtan's biggest memory from his time in Ohio's Queen City centers on the Beatles. "I was talking to the program director of WIFE in Indianapolis, who were sort of courting me at the time. That station was presenting the Beatles concert locally. He asked me if the Beatles were booked for Cincinnati. I said that I didn't think so and he said, 'Hey, you should look into it, they only want $12,500 up front and another $12,500 at the concert,'" Purtan relates. "I got right in touch with their representatives, NEMS ltd. in London: 'This is Paul Purtan at WSAI radio in Cincinnati and I wanted to inquire if there was some way we might be able to book the Beatles?' and they said, 'Sure, you can have the Beatles. We just need a cashier's check for $12,500 sent to us right away.' It was just that simple. Now, being that I didn't have quite that amount of money laying around, I went to four of the other disc jockeys at the station and they all kicked in a share and suddenly we're in the promotion business. I called Cincinnati Gardens and booked the space and that was it."

On August 27, 1964, the Beatles came to Cincinnati, and thirty-five years later, Purtan, sounding like a seasoned promoter leaning back with thumbs tucked under suspenders, can still reel off all the vital statistics. "We had a crowd of 13,500. Tickets were priced at $7.50 and $5.50. We each made a profit of $2,200,"[3] he sums up with pride! And yes, he still has the videos taken of himself with the "Fab Four" in the dressing room at Cincinnati Gardens all those years ago.

In the spring of 1965, Purtan telephoned disc jockey Gary Stevens at WKNR in Detroit, whom he had previously met. "I told

Gary that I wanted to get up to Detroit real bad and he told me to send a tape to Keener's program director, Frank Maruca, and I did." It was good timing, as Stevens himself shortly announced that he was leaving the station. "One day Frank Maruca called and I flew up to interview for Stevens afternoon shift from three to seven," remembers Purtan. "Keener was rocking pretty hard back then and Gary Stevens had a giant reputation. I felt I wouldn't fit because I had been doing mornings in Cincinnati, so when he offered me Gary's slot I actually turned it down and went back home. A few days later, Frank called back and said, 'How about coming up to do seven to ten in the evening?' Again, I said, 'No thanks.' Finally, a day or so later, he called and offered me ten to one at night. I thought, How bad can I screw up at that time of night? So I accepted and went on the air at night at WKNR on May 24th of 1965."[4]

As he related in a late-sixties interview, Dick Purtan adhered to a simple principle: "Everything about my show is a put-on. I try never to say a serious word on the air."[5] When Purtan would drop in teen slang, such as "groovy," "my bag," or "sock it to me," listeners knew it was a straight send-up.

He made fun of music, movies, politics, and local celebrities. Along with the creative help of Tom Ryan, who started out as one of the switchboard crew at Keener, his show at night satirized the popular family film *Mary Poppins,* serving up a "Mary Poppins fan club" with Ma and Pa Poppins. Ryan provided a sort of Maude Frickett voice for Ma, who would banter with Purtan. "I hope the little kids take it seriously and the older crowd gets a kick out of it," Purtan said at the time.[6]

Tom Ryan also showed up on Dick's show, portraying a swarmy children's personality called Captain Happy, who sold gadgets to kids for three hundred dollars, and explained to Dick and the kiddies how they could be creative with things around the house, such as an empty beer case. Of course, there was Purtan himself, smirking his way through pimple cream commercials, record hop promotions, and chart numbers from the "Keener Music Guide": "This is the 'DP get-together' and we're gonna swing and make the scene with the record machine from now until the news machine," he would say with tongue in cheek.[7]

Dick Purtan went against everything that Top 40 radio and

Keener in particular were being successful with, including tight, clean, on-air production. Surrounded by peppy promos such as "Hey! You're swingin' on W-K-N-R!" and jingles, including one that introduced him as "a guy whose really got the drive!" Purtan would hit the airwaves during his early shows, fumbling with controls, cueing up records over the air, and ridiculing contests and commercials. The "anti–disc jockey" had arrived and followers began to gather along the radio dial. Sweeney was still swinging in the morning, but how long could Keener ignore what was happening at night?

WKNR station ID:

> *WKNR, AM and FM, Dearborn, offices in the*
> *Sheraton Cadillac, Detroit*

WKNR'S "SWINGIN' SWEENEY" WAS PLAGUED by a severe case of insomnia, and more than once on the air had been transformed into "Sleepin' Sweeney."[8] According to Keener's Bob Green, one morning after introducing "I Got You Babe" by Sonny and Cher, the morning disc jockey's head began the slow descent, eventually resting on the console beneath the microphone. As the record finished and the needle continued to circle the empty grooves over and over, Sweeney snoozed. When he awoke, WKNR let him know he was on notice. Management was happy with the response Purtan was getting at night and they were making plans to move Sweeney to the position of assistant program director and have Dick take over mornings in late August.

On a Saturday morning about a week later, Sweeney had finally managed to get to sleep at home. Now the problem was waking up. For some reason, midday deejay Jerry Goodwin had been doing the all-night show that morning and was more than ready to go home at six o'clock. After Sweeney's late arrival at a little past seven, a fight broke out in the Keener studios. When the records and tape cartridges had stopped flying, Sweeney was sent swingin' on down the road and Dick Purtan was moved into the important morning drive hours two weeks ahead of schedule. Frank Sweeney survived, landing a program director spot at WOHO in Toledo.[9]

Inside the mind of Dick Purtan, successful morning disc jockey, lurked the soul of a frustrated comedy writer, who proudly wore the wounds of rejection, having had a script he submitted to

the "Dick Van Dyke Show" turned down.[10] Hollywood's loss was
the Motor City's gain as Purtan honed his writing skills, cranking
out an endless stream of Polish jokes and other off-the-wall material. "I think my audience knows that I am only kidding," assured
Purtan, who spent about four hours a day at home with a type-
writer, jotting ideas down as they popped into his head.[11]

Dick began to hit his stride, setting up satirical vignettes
revolving around public figures, such as controversial council-
woman Mary Beck, Gov. George Romney, and Mayor Jerome
Cavanaugh, who provided plenty of grist for the mill when his
name showed up in the infamous "little black book" of a questionable character doing business in the Grecian Gardens restaurant:
"Our movie this morning stars Mayor Cavanaugh and twelve
bikini-clad meter maids in 'Manoogian Mansion Beach Party,'"[12]
Purtan quipped.

He skewered channel 4 news anchor Dick Westerkamp's
nightly attempt to close his newscasts with an amusing little story
that always seemed to fall flat. There were promises of incredible
upcoming features: "Be sure to tune in to the Dick Purtan show
tomorrow, where we will be showing Van Patrick's baby pictures in
Cinerama" (Patrick was the cherubic TV sportscaster).

Purtan came across an old record called "Hamtramk Mama,"
and ran a contest to find someone to star in a movie of the same
name. Along with starring in the film, the winner was to receive a
"1967 Studebaker," which, of course, was no longer being produced.

Another contest, exclusive to the "Dick Purtan Show,"
revolved around Detroit police commissioner Ray Girardin. Every
time Girardin was interviewed on a newscast, he seemed to be
stopping to cough between every other word. Purtan made a
recording of it and ran an "imitate Ray Girardin cough contest."
The winner would have the privilege of naming the new police
commissioner. Among the many contestants calling in one morning was Ray Girardin himself, who coughed on the air and
remained in his job.[13]

Tom Gelardi of Capitol Records remembers taking Dick a copy
of an album recorded by an extremely out-of-tune female vocalist
who gained dubious notoriety in the mid-sixties as "Mrs. Miller."
This California woman, who physically resembled Mrs. Nikita

Kruschev, was under the impression that she possessed a delight-
ful voice. Someone thought she was quite funny and had her
record an album for Capitol, doing contemporary hits, including
an excruciating rendition of "Downtown." As Gelardi played some
of this incredible shrieking noise, Purtan sat forward as if experi-
encing a revelation. "Gee, this is great, Tom, I'm going to play this
stuff every morning for the next thirty days," he promised.[14]
Purtan had an almost sadistic gleam in his eye, adding: "I'm going
to play this until the listeners are begging for mercy." Gelardi says
that "as a result of Purtan's fascination with 'Mrs. Miller,' we sold
a hundred thousand albums right out of Detroit." As for "Mrs.
Miller," she parlayed her success into an appearance on the Ed
Sullivan Show and a second and final album.[14]

Dick Purtan's irreverence was a welcome change on Detroit
radio and, as hoped, he was pulling in lots of adults as well as teens.
WXYZ watched their morning ratings drop to fourth place as
Keener moved up behind WJR in the morning drive hours. How
close was Purtan to J. P. McCarthy? "It got pretty tight," Dick
recalls. "WJR had shares around 22 to 25 and we were hitting
around 20. Of course, the rest of the day Keener was racking up 30
shares and higher."[15]

When Dick Purtan moved to the morning show in August of
1965, his ten to one slot at night was filled by the "J. Michael
Wilson Pop-a-Shoo," as only Wilson could refer to it. He arrived
from KBTR in Denver and before that, had been with KOMA in
Oklahoma City, a fifty thousand-watt station that had beamed his
show over much of the Southwest. Wilson was a favorite among
peers as he weaved his way in and out of records and commercials
with an assortment of quips and asides few others could have
pulled off. J. Mike sounded as if his brain were wired directly to
everything that went over the air, making all the components of
the station, including himself, perform in a certain peculiar
rhythm.

As a spot for a new movie played, the commercial announcer
repeated the chilling title several times in a threatening voice:
"*Psychopath, Psychopath,*" and in the background was Wilson, in
his flat but crisp delivery, uttering: "At your service" and "Who do
you want strangled?"

Here are some other Wilson-isms:

That was "Theme from A Summer Place." That's really a bit misleading. That was actually taken from the sound track of that great psychedelic Western of a few years back: "Freak Out at the OK Coral."

Here's Richard and the Young Lions. [*pause*] "Open Up Your Door," [*pause*] I'm gonna sell you a Britannica.

Okay, wax lovers, like to send this next one out for Dick Purtan who just went on a diet. Old pudgy Dick–just lost twenty pounds–cleaned out his ears. Here we go![16]

Deadpan J. Mike had a squeaky-voiced sidekick named "Rodney the Wonder Rodent," who would pop in from time to time:

[*Wilson*] How 'bout a golden oldie? [*Rodney*] Squeak, squeak, how about Mr. Ugly by Herman Munster? [*Wilson*] How about Mr. Lonely by Bobby Vinton? [*Rodney*] Squeak, whatever you say, kid.

[*Rodney*]. Squeak, yoo-hoo, J. Michael Wil-son-ski! [*Wilson*] What is it, Rodney? [*Rodney*] I've got a joke here, it's from my Plum Street dictionary. [*Wilson*] Oh, really, this ought to be good. Let's hear it. [*Rodney*] Okay! What's the definition of an orgy? [*Wilson*] I don't know. What is it? [*Rodney, giggling*] An orgy, that's a catered love-in.[*Wilson*] Oh, that's beautiful.

The voice of Rodney was recorded by Wilson himself on a variable-speed tape machine during a record and then played back over the air with Wilson going on live with the rodent.

The line up at WKNR in the fall of 1965 included Dick Purtan, 6-9; Robin Seymour, 9-12; Jerry Goodwin, 12-3; Bob Green, 3-7; Scott Regen, 7-10; J. Michael Wilson, 10-1; and Paul Cannon, 1-5 in the morning.

WKNR jingle:

*Music, that's our middle name,*
*WKNR, Keener 13.*

## CHAPTER 17

# "Detroit Swings While Joey Stings"

ON JUNE 30, 1965, crusty Fred Wolf informed the management of WXYZ that he was leaving in thirty days, he didn't need the aggravation any longer. Fred Wolf, in the land of "Radio a Go-Go," just didn't jell. He was tired of the early hours, the music, and the format restrictions imposed by David Klemm. It was the end of a tradition in Detroit radio. There would be no more old "per-co-lator" broadcasting from a "wandering wigloo."

Billboards around town announced that Marc Avery (pictured in a red-striped suit, straw hat, and cane) was taking over the morning franchise established by Wolf back in 1950. It was hoped that Avery's calm but more contemporary style would hold on to Wolf's audience and, at the same time, appeal to the younger listeners that Keener was attracting. The lineup at Wixie now included Marc Avery, 6-10; Steve Lundy (another Texas recruit), 11-2; Dave Prince, 2-6; Lee Alan, 7:15-10; Danny Taylor, 10-1; and Pat Murphy, 1-6 in the morning.

When Lee Alan had been doing booth announcing on channel 7, he had been approached by WXYZ-TV's innovative general manager John Pival about hosting a new youth-oriented show he was planning for national syndication. Pival was calling it "The Swingin' Kind." This show would have top-notch production values and be taped live at various attractive locations around the Detroit area. "The Swingin' Kind" would feature Lee Alan introducing an artist from high atop the Ferris wheel at Edgewater Amusement Park, Marvin Gaye singing to a downtown audience along the Detroit River, Stevie Wonder on the sand at Metropolitan Beach, and so forth.[1]

The show looked great and several half hour installments ran successfully in Detroit in 1965, but plans to go national were shut down by corporate bosses at ABC in New York with whom John Pival had fallen out of favor.

IN THE SPRING OF 1965, Robin Seymour's "Teen Town" went on hiatus. Ed Metcalf from channel nine called Robin to a meeting at Little Harry's, a restaurant on East Jefferson, where he asked if Seymour would be interested in doing a new show every day during the summer. They were going to call it "Swingin' Summertime." Robin Seymour remembers the special conditions that CKLW-TV offered him: "They were more than accommodating at channel 9, offering me a big boost in salary and the go-ahead to cross-plug my shows. That meant when I got off the air at noon on WKNR, I would say, 'See you on channel 9 this afternoon' and at the end of the TV show it was, 'Join me on Keener radio tomorrow morning.' It couldn't have been a better situation. Unfortunately, Walter Patterson, the general manager at Keener, was bothered by my TV work and would tell me, 'Robin, all you think about is TV, TV, TV.' One day he told me that it has to be one or the other. Now, this was during the summer run and I still had no guarantee that we would be picked up for the fall. In other words, it looked like I could wind up out in the cold. For whatever reason, they didn't force the issue and it sort of went unresolved for a few months, but all was not well."[2]

"Swingin' Summertime" turned out to be a ratings hit and in the fall stayed on the air as "Swingin' Time." There was Robin five days a week, whipping the studio audience into a frenzy: "Come on now, everybody, let's swing, all right, hey!"[3]

Toward the end of the year, Walter Patterson came to Robin Seymour with the latest rating report and the same old argument: "You need to decide if you want to be on Keener or do that TV show, because your ratings are suffering," he charged. Robin grabbed the ratings book from Patterson and scanned down the numbers. "Walter, I have the highest numbers on the station and I'm sure the cross-plugs have something to do with that," countered Seymour. Patterson wouldn't back down this time. "I believe he just wanted me out and that's how it ended after nineteen years with Knorr Broadcasting. Now that I was free from Keener, CKLW wanted me to go on the radio for about three months as a promotional move, as we were on their TV station," says Robin. "CKLW radio was very loose and they offered me the position of program director. The problem was that a very dear man named John Gordon held that job and had for a long time. I said, 'What happens to John Gordon if I take the job?' and they said he was going to be let go. I just couldn't be the guy responsible for that, so I passed. A couple of months later they hired Hugh Frizell for the job."4

At the end of three months, at a few minutes before midnight, as Robin was wrapping up his last radio show, he was joined on the air by CKLW's all-night deejay, Duke Windsor, piped in from another studio. Windsor wished him luck, telling listeners how Seymour had been a big influence on him and other disc jockeys who came up during the fifties. Robin said so long and played "Cryin' Time" by Ray Charles and that was it.

SWINGIN' HAD BECOME SOMEWHAT OF A MISNOMER in the mid-sixties. While the term "rock 'n' roll" was definitely passé, adults and kids as well as the media referred to Top 40 stations as "rock," even though their playlists included everything from "Hello, Dolly!" and "Dominique" to records by James Brown and the Beatles.

In the program director's office, Top 40 stations identified themselves as "rockers" and conversation could focus on whether another station was going to "go rock." On the air, though, the same stations were loath to use the word. Thus, deejays were "swingin' guys" as opposed to "rockin' guys" and stations played "swingin' sounds" not "rockin' sounds." Top 40 stations still thought the word *rock* evoked images of gangs, motorcycles, and trouble. Seeing themselves as having mass appeal, the "swingin'" description was viewed as hip but less offensive. For someone beaming back in time, it would all seem rather strange.

ON THE LOCAL MUSIC SCENE IN 1965, Edwin Starr had a national hit on the growing Detroit Ric-Tic label with "Agent Double O'Soul." It went as high as number twenty-one.

Members of the Detroit Symphony Orchestra, who had provided string accompaniment on many Motown hits, recorded an album of their own on Ric-Tic, under the name the San Remo Golden Strings and pulled off a national top-thirty hit with the instrumental "Hungry for Your Love." In Detroit it reached number three.

The Reflections had a top-five follow-up to "Romeo and Juliet" on Golden World with "Poor Man's Son," although it failed to break nationally.

Billy Lee and the Rivieras were a very hot local band. Formed at the old Village club on Woodward in 1963, they played a lot of gigs at Walled Lake Casino. Billy Levise was their drop-to-the-knees lead singer and Jim McCarty played a wicked lead guitar. WXYZ's Dave Prince brought them to the attention of record producer Bob Crewe, who was impressed and brought the guys to New York.[5] Rechristened "Mitch Ryder and the Detroit Wheels," their first hit, "Jenny Take a Ride," hit the charts in November.

Motown was big time with the Supremes, Temptations, Four Tops, Martha and the Vandellas, and Marvin Gaye all scoring consistently on the national charts and appearing all over the world. The Supremes did, however, headline the band shell show at the Michigan State Fair in August. Their opening act was pop crooner Jack Jones.

BATMAN CAME TO TELEVISION in January of 1966 on ABC, and an onslaught of marketing and promotion swept the country much like the Davy Crockett craze in the fifties. WXYZ radio, seriously in need of a boost, proclaimed itself "Bat Radio." Special jingles were recorded tying the bat theme to everything. There was WXYZ Bat Weather, Bat Time, and there were appearances by the Batmobile around Detroit.

After a couple of months, batmania subsided and with no real leadership present, Lee Alan sold himself as the programming savior at WXYZ and was promoted to program director. Former program director Bruce Still was shifted to an operations position that centered mainly on public service.

Lee got right to work, writing and producing a series of new custom jingles, featuring the Anita Kerr Singers. They were built around the theme "Personality Plus, that's us, WX (the Detroit Sound) YZ."[6] Alan made an arrangement with WCFL in Chicago to carry its comedy spoof of superheroes, "The Adventures of Chickenman," in two-minute installments, several times per day. Wixie would also be the first station in Detroit to have traffic reports broadcast from a helicopter. For a time, Lee Alan did the reports himself from the "Wixie Whirlybird Watch." Also brought in as part of the new sound was the last of the big Top 40 nighttime deejays to hit Detroit, Joey Reynolds.

Sensing that his peak of popularity was passing and more concerned with programming responsibilities, Lee wanted to cut back his airtime, going on from 7:15 to 9:00 each evening and he searched the country for something really different, really hot to put on in Detroit from 9:00 to midnight.

Joey Reynolds was one of the most talented as well as outrageous people in the business. As a teenager, he started his radio career as an intern, helping a fellow named Dick Purtan at Buffalo's WWOL back in 1958. "I was doing the Guy King show and in the summer Joey would come with me when we did remotes from Crystal Beach," recalls Purtan. "His job was to stay with the equipment on the beach while I went frolicking in the water. Anyhow, I thought he was a talented kid and he moved right along careerwise."[7]

After early success at WPOP in Hartford, Reynolds moved back to Buffalo and the evening show on WKBW, the top station in town. While at 'KB he was named the number one disc jockey in the country by *Billboard* magazine. In Buffalo, he also hosted a weekly television show. Feeling underpaid, he complained on the air about how celebrities Frank Gorshin and Forest Tucker had been paid ten thousand dollars to host a charity telethon that he had been forced to work on for free. For this, the station fired him. Before checking out, and moving to a station in Cleveland, Reynolds nailed a pair of shoes to the door of the general manager's office, with a note attached that read "Fill these, you asshole!"[8]

In Cleveland he found more success, taking a low-rated rocker called WIXY to number one. After spending time in Cleveland, listening to Reynolds's show, Lee Alan was convinced that this was the guy who could help him put WXYZ back on top.

Joey was only twenty-four when he hit the Detroit airwaves. His opening theme song was recorded by the Four Seasons to the tune of "Big Girls Don't Cry"–"Jo-ey Reyn-olds," with words that included "Swing, Joey, swing (Burn, baby!)."[9] While his very swingin' theme music played, the "Royal Order of the Night People" would get under way. As Wixie's new resident "attack dog," Joey would open up with a sort of stream of consciousness monologue, throwing out opinions on politics and pop culture. It was stand-up comedy on radio. Ego played a big role in his show as he verbally assaulted celebrities. Reynolds was painly funny without relying on the tee-hee factor of sexual references.

A listener called on air to remind Reynolds that J. P. McCarthy was supposed to be the best disc jockey in town. Joey responded, saying, "What's so great about him?" as he proceeded to do a dead-on impression of the WJR star.[9] He referred to WKNR as the "Keener wiener." Bob Green, who was with WKNR, recalls hearing Reynolds talk to a girl on the phone who was telling him some good things about Keener and that they were going to present the Beatles and so forth. "Joey told her we were all liars and none of it was true. I became obsessed and after remembering her name, I went to the phone book and called ten people with the same name and then I found her and invited her to the concert to meet the Beatles. It was a small victory," laughs Green.[10]

It wasn't only the competition that got roasted, as Joey turned on his fellow Wixie disc jockeys, harassing Pat Murphy that he was "on his way out" and calling Marc Avery "boring." When Lee Alan gave up his airtime to Reynolds, to devote more time to programming, Joey was merciless on his boss, telling listeners: "He's old, it's over. It's about time he got *off* the air and let me do the job I was hired to do!"

Records and commercials also received special treatment:

That's "Say I Am" from Tommy James and the Shondells, the follow-up to "Hanky Panky"–Aye! It's worse! It's twenty-five before...I like that though, it's got more of a melody. Anyhow, it's twenty-five before nine on WXYZ. Welcome to "rate the records," friends. You notice I don't have a panel, I just tell you what *I* think.

Hershel Electronics, yes there are five locations and for as low as fifty-four ninety-five, you know what you can get? A bill for fifty-four ninety-five! For fifty-four dollars and ninety-five cents you can get a receipt and also you can get a stereo with four speakers that go in your car–of course it costs four hundred dollars to install 'em. No, really, you get a good deal. Hershel's is the place to go. I don't know why you even bother listening to Michigan Mobile commercials![11]

Off the air, Reynolds was equally wild. When Joey arrived, WXYZ general manager Charles Fritz had asked Fred Wolf, who was off the air but still had a relationship with the station, if he would do him a favor and see if he could make arrangements for Reynolds to stay temporarily at the Detroit Athletic Club where Fred was a member. After two weeks, Wolf was on the phone to Fritz: "What have you guys done to me? You've gotta get him outta here. I'm a disgrace!"[12]

According to Marty Greenburg, who was part of the sales staff at WXYZ, things went from bad to worse: "We had a guest room that was located on top of the cafeteria at Broadcast House, so Joey moved in. It was one big party up there and they really tore the place up." Greenburg went on to say that Reynolds was "one of the most creative personalities he had ever heard" despite the bad-boy behavior.[13] Jim Hampton, who returned to WXYZ as a disc jockey, after establishing himself at WAMM in Flint, followed Joey at midnight. He proved to be a good match for Reynolds as they jousted on the air in a good-natured way. It was an exception.

Joey Reynolds had offended a lot of people both on the air and off, without any real benefit in the ratings. Listeners had tuned in to hear the bluster and then went back to their normal listening habits. By the end of the summer, Joey Reynolds was history and Wixie brought back Danny Taylor from weekend exile.

According to Lee Alan, who was Joey's boss, the reasons for Reynolds's departure had nothing to do with his on-air performance. "Joey had been involved in the music and record business for a number of years. He also was very talented in that area," relates Alan. "When he came to work at WXYZ, he had to comply with ABC rules that required him to cut all ties with record companies. After a few months, there were rumors that he was doing some things in that area. One day we had a big meeting scheduled for all the sales and programming people. All the ABC brass were in Detroit for this and Joey did not show up. We found him in a downtown recording studio, and for that, I was forced to fire him. I still believe that he was and is just the finest talent and it is amazing how after only six months on the air in Detroit in 1966, so many people remember him."[14]

More than Reynolds air work, the problem at WXYZ stemmed from the fact that they were still handicapped by having to carry ABC network programming, which would always kill any momentum that had been built up. While WXYZ was airing almost an hour-and-a-half news block in the early evening, Keener and CK' were playing music. In addition, many of the on-air changes that Lee Alan had instituted, although of high quality (such as station breaks, jingles, newscasts, and traffic reports), tended to make the station sound more adult-oriented and softer, at a time when the competition was going the opposite direction.

WKNR continued to dominate the ratings and financially was making a killing, with advertisers lining up to get on the station. In the morning, Dick Purtan was entertaining commuters with his own traffic reports that included conditions on the "Robin Seymour Freeway," which corresponded to the alley running behind the Keener studios on Michigan Avenue.[15]

In the early evening hours, Scott Regen covered all the bases when it came to being on top of the music scene in Detroit. Scottie knew all the local talent and they would record customized versions of their hits just for his show. He interviewed the Supremes and Stevie Wonder on the air and debuted the latest Beatles releases, including album cuts. He wrote liner notes for Motown LPs and did a teen column for the *Detroit News* as well as hosting "Motown Mondays" at the Roostertail nightclub.

Born in New York, Scott (real name Bob Bernstein) had attended Alan Freed's big stage shows in the fifties, where he caught the fever. He was on the radio in Florida at WLCY in Tampa and WFUN in Miami and then on to WCPO in Cincinnati and WHB in Kansas City before coming to WKNR in May of 1965.

Daily Drive-in Restaurants honored him with the immortal "Regen Burger."[16]

CKLW WAS IMPROVING their overall sound in 1966, having finally gotten rid of all paid programming that interrupted the flow of the station. Hugh Frizell was the new program director replacing John Gordon, the old-line RKO man. The big promotional push at Radio 8-0 was a reminder for listeners not to worry, because "Wherever you are, you're still in CK' Country!"[17] Celebrities visiting the Motor City would be featured in these promos recorded over music from *The Magnificent Seven*. The choice of celebrities was questionable, with one promo featuring Eddie Fisher! For a while the station also referred to itself as "Giant CK."

By August, CKLW, for reasons unknown, let veteran Bud Davies go after twenty-nine years of service. Taking over Bud's morning show was Dusty Rhodes from WSAI in Cincinnati. "I really couldn't figure out why they wanted me," Rhodes recalls. "I had been a nighttime disc jockey for five years in Cincinnati and I knew Bud Davies to be pretty good. But one of the salesmen from 'SAI went to work at CKLW about a year earlier and talked me up to management and the next thing I know, I'm doing morning drive in Detroit!"[18]

Despite changes in production and format techniques, CKLW still featured an eighty-record playlist, and, according to a 1966 interview with Dave Shafer, the deejays were pretty much free to program their shows from the list and Shafer stated he leaned toward "newer, up-tempo records."[19] Dusty Rhodes found the "CK' Survey" pretty strange: "I got to CK' and I couldn't believe they had such a long playlist, there were close to a hundred songs on there and it seemed to me that the bottom half of the list was getting real heavy airplay. I thought this was possibly due to the fact that there were a lot of local artists on there that were doing hops with the deejays."[20]

CK's lineup in the fall of 1966 included Dusty Rhodes, 6-9; Joe Van, 9-noon; Ron Knowles, noon-3; Dave Shafer, 3-7; Tom Shannon, 7-12; and, after a go at the insurance business, Don Zee, back in the graveyard shift with all his familiar trappings, from midnight to 6 in the morning.

THE ERA OF THE RECORD HOPS at venues such as skating rinks was winding down by the late sixties. There were still high school dances but the big commercial dances at rinks and various-style halls and churches were being replaced by teen nightclubs such as the Hideout, the Chatterbox in Warren and Allen Park, and the Crow's Nest at the corner of John R and Gardenia. These were densely packed, cavern-style clubs featuring small dance floors and loud bands playing covers of Beatles, Stones, and Byrds hits and performing some original material.

There were three Hideout locations, including two in Southfield and in Clawson on Main Street north of Fourteen Mile Road. Eddie "Punch" Andrews ran the clubs and managed Bob Seger and the Last Heard, who frequently played there. Also appearing at the Hideout in 1966 were the Kingsmen and the Tidalwaves. It was a fairly intimate atmosphere with low ceilings and a crowd usually about three hundred per night. For teens with club memberships, admission was a dollar, nonmembers paid a dollar fifty. Two bands rotated from one stage.

SPORTING A PRINCE VALIANT HAIRCUT, Terry Knight returned to Detroit radio on record in May, as the leader of a new rock group called "Terry Knight and the Pack." Knight and his fellow musicians from the Flint-Saginaw area had landed a recording contract on the Lucky Eleven label. Their first release, "Better Man Than I," went top twenty in Detroit as did the follow-up, another socially relevant song called "A Change on the Way." Both records failed to dent the national *Billboard* charts. Their third single was a reworking of the Ben E. King hit from 1963, "I (Who Have Nothing)." Featuring a spoken-word section delivered in a dramatic fashion by Terry, the song became their biggest hit, climbing to number six in Detroit and number forty-six nationally, thanks to its release on Cameo-Parkway Records out of Philadelphia.

Besides Motown, which was really a national label, 1966 produced a bumper crop of records tied to the Detroit area by artist or label. The Shades of Blue were a mixed gender white group from Livonia, discovered and produced by Edwin Starr. Nick Marinelli was the lead singer in the group that featured three guys and one female. They recorded Starr's "Oh How Happy" for Harry Balk's

Impact label. It went top five locally and reached number twelve on the national charts. Starr himself recorded one of the greatest records to come out of the Motor City with "Stop Her on Sight" (S.O.S) on Ric-Tic and enjoyed a local smash, while the record stalled on the national list at number forty-eight.

"Wait a Minute" was recorded by a group from Allen Park with the not-so-macho name of "Tim Tam and the Turn-Ons." This record featured a driving beat and a lead singer with a falsetto that could challenge Frankie Valli. Released on a Detroit label, Palmer Records, it was written by Tom DeAngelo, a deejay at WTRX in Flint, and was a springtime smash in the Motor City.

"The Man in the Glass" by the Shy Guys from Grosse Pointe, was another local top-ten hit on the Palmer label.

Deon Jackson, born in Ann Arbor, recorded some sides for Ollie McLaughlin's local Carla label. Two years after he cut "Love Makes the World Go Round." It was leased to Atlantic for national distribution and the song went to number twelve across the country. The Capitols were another McLaughlin act, who hit the national top ten doing the "Cool Jerk."

Ann Arbor also produced a quartet composed of two sets of twin brothers. Students at the University of Michigan, they called themselves The Arbors. After securing a contract with Date Records, a subsidiary of Columbia, they released a syrupy ballad called "Symphony for Susan." It became a top-twenty hit around Michigan and reached number fifty-one on *Billboard*.

Detroit nightclub favorite Jamie Coe, still chasing that elusive national hit, made another run at the charts and received some local airplay with "Greenback Dollar."

Bob Seger charted his first local top-ten record with "East Side Story." Billed as "Bob Seger and the Last Heard," it was released on the Hideout label, named after the rock music nightclubs where Seger often performed.

Another great Michigan rock band was the Rationals. The Ann Arbor group reworked r&b hits such as Eddie Holland's "Leavin' Here" and Otis Redding's "Respect," which went top five in Detroit.

Mitch Ryder and the Detroit Wheels continued their string of national hits, coming out with "Little Latin Lupe Lu" and the megahit "Devil with the Blue Dress On/Good Golly Miss Molly."

A new rock music venue opened in October, founded by a Detroit teacher named Russ Gibb. The "Grande Ballroom" was at 8952 Grand River and was more about listening than dancing. The first band to take the stage were five guys from Lincoln Park who played very loud and called themselves the Motor City Five, soon modified to MC 5.

Toward the end of 1966, WXYZ looked back in frustration. The Joey Reynolds fiasco still had the station reeling and Lee Alan's programming changes had not stopped the ratings decline. It was felt that Marc Avery had failed to hold on to the audience in the morning, his warm folksy style losing big to Dick Purtan's humor-intensive approach at Keener. Avery contends that management was overreacting.[21]

General manager Charles Fritz decided to make changes himself, wooing the WKYC Cleveland morning team of Martin and Howard for mornings. The word leaked out and Marc Avery approached Fritz: "I hear through the grapevine that you are planning to hire Martin and Howard. Is this true?" Charles Fritz hemmed and hawed and would neither confirm nor deny. "He was obviously trying to keep me in tow until he had a firm answer from Martin and Howard," recalls Avery. "I asked him again, and got the same response so I just up and quit, 'See ya' later.'"[21]

Charles Fritz was almost giddy with anticipation as he awaited the arrival of what he thought would be the one-two punch of Martin and Howard. After a few too many drinks in the lounge at Oakland Hills Country Club one day, he bumped into J. P. McCarthy and supposedly told him that WXYZ's new morning team was going to knock J. P. and WJR out of the top spot in the ratings. It has been said that McCarthy then informed Fritz that he was not acting like a gentleman by saying these things and that he didn't think WXYZ was going to hurt him.[22]

During this same period, Fritz also hired Joe Bacarella, the ultracool afternoon disc jockey and program director at WCAR, to come over and head the programming department. Bacarella seemed an odd choice to program a Top 40 station, one that already had an operations manager and a program director in place.

On January 16, 1967, Bacarella came to work at WXYZ along with the new morning team of Martin and Howard and a fellow named Ray Koeppen, who wrote material for the duo. WXYZ was paying the two personalities $48,000 each, with another $20,000 going to their writer.[23] It was a big investment. The next day, on a trip to New York to meet ABC brass, Specs Howard was surprised to find out that WXYZ was about to change format and go middle of the road. A feeling of dread took over as he wondered how their material would play within the new sound and as to what other surprises awaited in the Motor City.

Upon returning to Detroit, Bacarella and Lee Alan butted heads. It was a clash of two very strong personalities and Bacarella had the mandate. So, for the second time, Lee was fired from WXYZ. Soon, the "Detroit Sound Survey" was gone and all references to the station as "Wixie" along with it.

WXYZ was now promoting itself as the "Sound of the Good Life," which was probably meant to evoke images of backyard barbecues, station wagons, and lots of spendable income. Musically, it was a mixing of softer rock hits by artists such as the Association, Mamas and Papas, and Simon and Garfunkel, with album cuts by more adult artists such as the Ray Coniff Singers, Andy Williams, and Nancy Wilson, along with jingles and personality deejays.

For Martin and Howard it was disastrous. They were not allowed to do much of the material that had made them so popular in Cleveland, such as their "Congo Kurt" skits. People listened, waiting for the funny stuff that had been promoted, but got only two "nice guys." It was a rough year as ABC closely monitored the progress of the station. The air staff was under constant pressure. Pat Murphy was let go, followed a few months later by Danny Taylor.

DETROIT WAS NOW DOWN TO TWO TOP 40 ROCKERS, although there was still great r&b to be found on the dial. The former daytimer WCHB had received authorization for full-time broadcasting by the mid-sixties and they absolutely cooked twenty-four hours a day. Deejays such as "the Demon," Jay Butler, Jack "the Ripper" Springer, "Butterball," and his successor, the incredible "Rockin' Robbie D" made "Soul Radio 1440" the spot on the dial most likely to experience a meltdown.

"D," in particular, rapped and rhymed at a hundred miles an hour, drenched in an bottomless pit of echo: "Hey ! Baby! This is me! Rockin' Robbie D on WCHB! I make flowers die–I make babies cry–I take candy from babies and give dogs rabies and if that ain't bad–the rain don't fall and that ain't all–biscuits ain't bread! Right now it's a James Brown breakdown–'Cold Sweat!'"[24]

"Rockin' Robbie" was only twenty during his heyday on "Soul Radio," where he was "makin' with the shakin'" between eight and midnight. WCHB's primarily black audience was slightly blown away to find out a white guy could have so much soul! Robbie D had offers to go elsewhere, including the fifty thousand-watt NBC station in Cleveland. He chose to stay with 'CHB.

CHAPTER **18**

# "You're Gonna Like It... I Bet-cha!"

CHOOSING NOT TO STAY AT WCHB in 1967 was Martha Jean "The Queen," who packed up and moved over to crosstown competitor WJLB.

Martha Jean Steinberg had arrived in the Motor City in November of 1963. A black woman who acquired her last name by way of marriage, she came from WDIA in Memphis, the South's premiere black-formatted radio station.[1]

Before her entrance to broadcasting, Martha Jean Jones had taken the usual path for young women like herself. After high school she went to nursing school, then got married and proceeded to have five kids.

By the mid-fifties she was doing some volunteer work around WDIA radio, which was right at the center of black entertainment in the region. One day the station had a contest to choose a new female announcer, so she tried out and lost. "The stations back then usually went with teachers when they were looking for female air talent," remembers Martha Jean. "One day, the station manager came to me and said, 'I know we didn't select you but you're a natural.' I didn't even understand what he meant, but when he told me they had a weekend shift open and wanted me to have it, I grabbed the opportunity."[2]

Things started to happen fast when the woman who had won the talent contest was forced to leave for family reasons. Martha Jean took over the "Nite Spot" show for thirty minutes, each evening at nine.[3] The original reason for airing this program had been to provide a bridge, or transition, from an early-evening gospel show to the wild antics of Rufus Thomas, the Memphis musician who doubled as a late-evening disc jockey. However, when Martha Jean took to the the air, she became an overnight sensation, using a sultry tone of voice as she delivered sexy double entendres, between hot r&b records. So much for transition as WDIA went directly from the "Hallelujah Jubilee" to "Honey, I've got somethin' right here, I just *know* you're gonna like!"

The response from listeners was so strong that management created a new show for her at noon on Saturdays called "Premium Stuff," where she would introduce the best in new releases. Her tall good looks, coupled with a smoldering on-air style, caused listeners to associate the name of the program not with the records but with her. She would have the men howling and whistling at public appearances, like the WDIA Revue at Memphis's Ellis Auditorium in 1956, where she came on stage dressed as "Princess Premium Stuff," during an Indian-themed skit.[4]

Eventually, Martha Jean was called on to take over the station's highly rated daytime women's program, "Tan Town Homemaker's Show," when Willa Monroe, the program's original host, became too ill to carry on. Powered by WDIA's fifty thousand-watt daytime signal, Martha Jean's fame really spread. All of the sudden she had a weekend show, a nightly rhythm and blues program, and a daily woman's hour. "The daytime program was full of household tips and information on food preparation," she recalls. "Being that I didn't know much about preparing food, I tended to play more records mixed in with light talk and a little cooking information."

Whether it was homemaker tips, gospel, or the blues, Martha Jean's sassy style made her very popular in a very short time. In 1963, while driving through Memphis on their way to a convention, Dr. Wendell Cox and his wife, part owners of WCHB, Detroit's black-owned and operated station, heard her show. "They invited me to visit the station in Michigan, so I did. I met with the other owner, Dr. Haley Bell, who was a fascinating man and thought it would be a good move. I was also coming out of a divorce and the chance of moving to a new city was very appealing on the personal level," she confides.[5]

Martha Jean came on board replacing Trudy Haynes, who, like most other women on radio, was relegated to hosting cooking and lifestyle programs. Martha Jean took to the air from 10:00 to 11:30 each morning with a show like what she had done in Memphis, a heavy amount of music and personality with a dash of recipes.

Martha Jean "The Queen" was a huge hit in the Motor City with her "Blue Collar Salute" and payday reminder for wives to "get down to the factory and get that check!"[6] "Some of the men would get really mad at me because I would tell the ladies that they needed to get their 'vacation money,' she laughs. Her trademark was a firm: "I bet'cha," tagged on to all her commercials, most of which she announced live.[7]

Although WCHB had a primarily black audience, few people in Detroit were not aware of her presence. Martha Jean believes her notoriety stemmed from the fact that there were not a lot of influential blacks at the time, such as judges and other politicians: "Blacks who were well known within the community were usually either in labor or in entertainment," she comments. Her status was evident when she was chosen to be master of ceremonies for Martin Luther King's visit to the Motor City.

Being a black woman on the radio who spoke her mind gave her a great deal of power and she gathered a long list of sponsors. Still, radio was a man's domain for the most part. "There were a few guys who didn't care for my success," she recalls. "I was able to break quite a few hit records but I never got the credit because the men were more connected with the trade magazine chart reports, but that's just the way it was back then," she says without any trace of bitterness.

The first couple of years in Detroit, Martha Jean pulled her own music but then the station started moving to more of a Top 40 approach. "I remember some of the guys saying, 'You'll never be able to keep up,' says Martha Jean, "but I did okay."

Some of her best memories from WCHB revolve around the big Motown Holiday Shows staged at the Fox theater each year: "We always emceed the shows and I had the chance to introduce all the Motown greats like Marvin Gaye, Smokey Robinson and the Miracles, just everybody."[8]

By 1967, Martha Jean was tired of driving out to WCHB's Inkster location each day and was interested in moving to WJLB, who she felt would give her a larger presence. In the past, the Booth station had not shown that much interest, but now they were moving into cable TV and needed cash. Martha Jean had become so successful that WJLB was losing a good deal of business to her. Once John Lord Booth realized where the money was going, he decided he would be better off having her on his station. A deal was struck, with one condition—Martha Jean requested to be paid a commission on all the commercials aired on her program. Booth agreed. Roughly, only four other radio personalities in Detroit had had such a deal, one that was struck in the late forties–early fifties: Ed McKenzie, Ross Mulholland, Fred Wolf, and Robin Seymour. This sort of arrangement simply was not being done in 1967. Martha Jean's show was expanded to four hours each weekday and she became more popular than ever.

Along with the big shows, Martha Jean did a lot of club work in the Fireside Room of the Twenty Grand, where she hosted something called the "Monday Night Swing" with drinks for fifty cents. She also held forth at the popular Chit Chat Club on Twelfth Street: "The guys from the Motown staff band moonlighted at several clubs, including the Chit Chat," Martha Jean recalls.[9] "The nucleus of this group was leader Earl Van Dyke on piano, James Jamerson, the wizard of the bass, with Benny Benjamin on drums, and Robert White on guitar. On the road with the Motortown Revue and on a record album they were billed as the Earl Van Dyke Sextet, but behind the scenes, if you needed the absolute hottest players for a session, you would send for the Funk Brothers."[10]

Martha Jean also stayed active in the community and devoted a half hour of her show each day to discussing things of a social and spiritual nature. During the summer riots of 1967, she spoke out on the air, asking that everyone be calm and let firemen get into the area to put out the fires.

Along with Martha Jean "The Queen," Bristoe Bryant and "Frantic Ernie" were still on the air, joined by LeBaron Taylor and Tom Reed, "the Master Blaster," as WJLB attempted to update its sound, calling it "Tiger Radio," as in ferocious, not the baseball team.[11] Greek and Polish language programs were still aired in the early evening hours, and Jack Surrell played jazz all night.[11]

CHAPTER 19

# Ladies and Gentlemen: The "Big 8"

IN MARCH OF 1967, Paul Drew arrived as the new program director at CKLW, coming from WQXI, a hot Top 40 station in Atlanta. He would be working under the direction of West Coast radio guru Bill Drake. Drew a Michigan native, lived next to Drake while growing up in Georgia.

After moving back to Michigan, Drew had worked for record promoters, hustling discs to Detroit deejays such as Robin Seymour and Ed McKenzie. His first radio job was at WHLS in Port Huron in 1955. Later he returned to Georgia, where he again crossed paths with Drake, who, like Drew, was another young radio guy with a lot of ambition.

Bill Drake was born Philip Yarbrough in Georgia in 1937. He got hooked on radio early on and had a job as a teenage deejay on a small local station. After a short time, he left that position to attend Georgia State Teachers College, where he spent a year before jumping back into radio full-time. After a stint with WAKE in Atlanta, he headed to San Francisco, where he did the all-night show at KYA in 1961 and found greater success as program director. A few years later he hooked up with Californian Gene Chenault to form a consulting firm.[1]

In California, Drake had been so successful programming stations in Fresno and San Diego that he was hired by CKLW's parent company, RKO General, in 1965, to turn around KHJ, their low-rated middle-of-the-road station in Los Angeles. Drake and company created a tight, fast sound they called "Boss Radio" and with high-caliber disc jockeys such as Robert W. Morgan and "the Real Don Steele," they quickly overtook the formidable competition from KRLA and KFWB, going from twelfth to number one in less than six months. Now, two years later, it was time for a major makeover at CKLW.

By 1967, WKNR had become a money machine, bloated with commercials, up to the legal limit of eighteen minutes per hour. As they had done for some time, a jingle was played before and after commercials. What had sounded so exciting in 1964 had begun to sound a bit cluttered. The so-called Drake Format was designed to be clean and streamlined. The week of April 1, 1967, CKLW introduced the new sound that featured short a cappella jingles performed by the Johnny Mann Singers. The disc jockeys followed  a "hot clock," which indicated certain times that elements of the sound would be run. These elements were current hits, oldies, new releases, and commercial clusters.

Anyone listening in those days can no doubt remember the famous hourly station breaks voiced by  Bill Drake himself: "And the hits just keep on comin'" or "Ladies and gentlemen, the beat goes on!"  followed by the chorus singing "CKLW, the Motor City." As one record would fade out, an a cappella jingle would make the transition to the next record: "More music, CKLW." Over the intro to the song, the deejay would be limited to one or two sentences or pieces of information such as "The Big 8, with a chance for you to win big money in the Black Box contest, coming up!" Upon exiting a song: "Those are the Esquires, hitbound with 'Get on Up,' It's 7:09, CKLW Big Wheel time on the Tom Shannon show." One short a cappella jingle was played after a commercial, setting up the pace for the next set. Brevity was the operative word. The station was tight, aggressive, and seemed to leap forward, the deejays at times sounding as if they were broadcasting at gunpoint.

CKLW went into their new format with no commercials at first and then restricted the number of commercial minutes they would play each hour to thirteen. Drake had convinced RKO management that fewer commercials would result in higher ratings whereby they could charge higher rates. It worked. The sound was fast, tight, and seamless, a literal conveyor belt of hits. During the first four months of the changeover, the station was referred to as "Radio 8" and "Fun Radio 8," before the final transformation into "The Big 8." For the air staff and board operators, it was like going from piloting a Piper Cub to a jet aircraft. CKLW was the fastest thing on radio.

Tom Shannon and Dave Shafer stayed on while longtime veterans Ron Knowles and Joe Van, along with recent addition Dusty Rhodes, hung up their headphones. "Drew asked me to go on nights and I said, 'No.' He fired me a couple of weeks later," recalls Rhodes.[2]

Ron Knowles moved to the television side at channel 9 and Joe Van, who wasn't happy in the new format, moved to Montreal, ending a ten-year run. Tom Shannon remembers the changeover: "Paul Drew came to Dave Shafer and myself and said that he thought we could make the transition; others at the station didn't fare so well, and it was kinda sad. At the same time it was exciting to feel the energy level rise along with the ratings."[3]

Dave Shafer remembers it a little differently: "For whatever reasons, Paul Drew didn't really like me, but on an earlier occasion, I had been able to meet and spend time with the president of RKO and we hit it off. Through him, I also met Bill Drake. When the president of the company said good things about me to Drew, it provided some protection...for a while."[4]

Although the new sound of CKLW was very tight, Tom Shannon says there was room for personality: "I think the talk rule for exiting a song when you were going into spots was something like eight seconds, but because I had been established there for some time, they gave me a little more leeway in my comments. I felt anointed," he laughs.[5]

The name and look of the new CKLW record survey also evolved during the first few months, premiering as the "Hit Parade" and then the "Big 30." Under either name, it was a radical departure from the old days of a list that stretched to eighty-three titles. Now there were just thirty heavily controlled and in-demand chart positions available along with a couple of "hit-bounds." Although they had a strict and rigid format to follow, the CKLW disc jockeys were still in charge of rotating the records on their shows. In other words, if the clock called for a top-ten record, the deejay would choose that record rather than every record being programmed.

CKLW grabbed a lot of attention playing back the Motor City's "All-Time Top 300" over the first weekend in May. They launched a "Million Dollar Weekend" every Friday afternoon at 3:00, where every other record played was a huge hit from the past. CK' also used oldies creatively in midday hours during the week, where the audience from 9:00 A.M. to 3:00 P.M. had been shrinking at Top 40 stations, as rock 'n' roll continued to harden. To attract more housewives, CKLW started to program a few oldies each hour that dated ten to twelve years. These were the songs that the housewives of 1967 were listening to when they were teenagers. Brought back from extinction were moldy oldies such as "Come Go with Me" by the Del Vikings, "Diana" by Paul Anka, "Little Darlin'" by the Diamonds, "Yakaty Yak" by the Coasters, "Since I Don't Have You" by the Skyliners, and lots more. Midday ratings shot up.

The Big 8 featured "20/20 News" at twenty past and twenty before the hour, enabling the station to run a forty minute music sweep. Veteran news director Dick Smythe, along with Byron MacGregor, Grant Hudson, Don Patrick, Don West, and Joe Donovan, were among the powerful voices reporting. Newscasts were shortened to three and a half minutes, concentrating on hard local news stories delivered in a breathtaking dramatic style. Over the sound of a pounding Teletype machine, listeners would hear the announcer practically chewing up the microphone: "It's twenty minutes before nine! Windy tonight, mild tommorrow. This is *Byron MacGregor,* C-K-L-W *Twenty Twenty* News!"[6]

According to former CK' deejay Mike Rivers, one of the hallmarks of 20/20 news was the incredible style of writing. "I remember driving along one Saturday morning, listening to Grant Hudson relate the grisly details of a car-pedestrian fatality. The victim, according to Hudson, 'was strained through the grille of a '65 Cadillac...' I had to pull over," Rivers concluded.[7]

On another newscast, the announcer reported a triple murder by using the rhythm from the nursery rhyme "Baa Baa Black Sheep," as he headlined : "Bodies, bodies, three bags full." Other reports described run-ins with "gun-toting, knife-wielding thugs in Detroit streets drenched in blood."

As another blistering newscast concludes, the newsman would announce: "That's what's happening today, June 15, 1967!" This would be followed by the sound of an explosion and then the deejay would give the same date of a previous year and blast into a million-selling oldie from that year.

CKLW's flawless production was almost hypnotic. It didn't happen by chance. Inside the CK' studio were two special phone lines. One enabled Bill Drake to call from wherever he was and monitor CKLW, as he did with all his stations. The other was an ominous red telephone, with no dial on it. It was connected to a very bright red light bulb and when it rang, there was no ignoring it. On the other end of this instrument of terror was program director Paul Drew, who was not calling to say "good show." Dave Shafer: "You would be on the air trying to concentrate and here would be Drew calling to harass you: 'What the hell are you doing?' 'That was wrong,' 'You talked too long,' or some other complaint. So, when he would call from his mobile phone, I would pick up the receiver and say, 'Hello? Hello?' There would be Drew, who had this very nasally little voice, screaming at the other end, but I would continue to say, 'Hello? Hello?' as if the phone were not working and I couldn't hear him," Shafer gleefully recalls.[8]

Dusty Rhodes remembers Drew warning the staff in a threatening tone that he was "listening twenty-four hours a day" and how nobody wanted to see that light go on. "He was just a nasty little man but I do give him credit for really pulling that station together," Rhodes adds.[9]

Marc Avery, who by this time had returned to do middle-of-the-road mornings at WJBK, remembers a very strange dinner he attended with Paul Drew and, of all people, actor Tony Randall: "I don't quite recall exactly how it came about but Tony Randall was in town to promote something or another and we were having dinner at Mario's. I'm on one side of the booth and Drew is on the other with Tony next to him and we're making some small talk. Now, Drew is sitting there at the table with two earphones sticking out of his head. He is monitoring CK' on one side and I guess the competition on the other. It was really rude. Tony Randall leans forward and says to me in that articulate way of his: 'Isn't *he* quite the asshole?' I think Drew even excused himself so he could get on the phone and ream some poor guy back at the station," Avery adds.[10]

The saddest story at the new CKLW concerned the fate of Don Zee, who was somewhat older than the new crowd. He was given the opportunity of staying but Paul Drew hated that name. He favored those all-American boy-next-door names, so Zee was forced to bear the indignity of going through a name change. They turned it into a promotional opportunity, with deejays telling listeners to "listen as Don Zee reveals his real name!" For a couple of weeks he became Don Z. Williams and then the middle initial was dropped. Don continued on in the nine to noon shift for a little while longer and then he was gone.

It was a blip on the screen of success as CKLW forged ahead, swamping Keener with attention-grabbing contests such as "Where Is Location X!" and "CKLW's Quicksilver Giveaway." The air staff that departed was replaced by a new breed of disc jockey. Johnny Morgan was the first new high-energy voice on the station, in the afternoon from three until seven, soon replaced by Mike (Let's power up!)Rivers, arriving from Tulsa, Oklahoma, where he had been working on KAKC, a station also consulted by the Drake-Chenault team. Rivers crammed as much personality as he could into the precious seconds of airtime allotted and built his reputation on getting away with what, at the time, seemed somewhat raunchy, blue material.

Other 1967 deejays included Gary Mitchell, Billy Mack (Kris Erick Stevens), and Jim Edwards, along with Shafer and Shannon. It didn't take listeners any time to find out that the old CKLW had shed its skin. "The Big 8" effectively ended Keener's four-year reign.

When CKLW first went with the so-called Drake format, the music selection was pretty much dictated by RKO's national music director, Betty Breneman, working with Bill Drake in Los Angeles. Back at CK', Rosalie Trombley had started working as a switchboard operator in 1967. When a position opened in the station's music library, Ted Atkins, who had replaced Paul Drew as program director at the start of 1968, gave her the job, and it soon became obvious that she had great skills in music selection, especially when it came to the needs of the local listening audience.

As CKLW's music director, she developed a reputation for being extremely knowledgeable about the product that would go on her station. "We did an exhaustive two-day survey, every week," says Trombley. "We talked to all the stores plus the rack jobbers and one-stops that supplied product to the retail outlets. Also, we recognized Detroit as a unique market. There were a lot of hit records, both hard rock and r&b, that we broke in Detroit that would never make the charts in places like Boston or out in Los Angeles."[11]

Tom Gelardi, who ran Capitol Records in Detroit all through the sixties, remembers calling on Rosalie to plug his latest releases: "Rosalie had a feel for the street retailers and would always be loaded with information on how product was doing," he recalls. "It was no use bullshitting her. If you didn't have an accurate and honest story to tell, you were better off not even talking about records." Gelardi also remembers that CK' played more r&b than many other Top 40 stations, including Keener: "That station [CKLW] responded to the makeup of their market and was very good at finding those r&b songs that would work well with all the audience and it was a very fine line." "Soon, the walls of Trombley's office were lined with gold records. Rosalie's music selection and the Drake format were a dynamite combination. Not only was "The Big 8" number one in Detroit, they were also beating the local competition in Cleveland and Toledo.

It was total victory. CKLW had the audience and, just as important, they had the power to keep them: fifty-thousand watts.

CHAPTER **20**

# "Busted in Baltimore— Dawn in Detroit"

As CKLW's RATINGS CONTINUED TO CLIMB, Dick Purtan recalls that a feeling of impending doom was spreading throughout the offices and studios of WKNR: "We were called into an emergency meeting at ten o'clock on a Sunday night with the station's consultant, Mike Joseph, and were told that, from now on, no more than ten seconds of talk would be allowed between records. The next morning I went on the air and did the show the way I always did it. Later I got called in by Joseph, who was threatening me: 'You better do it my way or hit the road' is basically what he said. I left and went home. The next morning I did my regular style and again Joseph hit the roof."

This battle of wills went on all week. Finally, on Friday, Dick Purtan was called into a showdown with both Mike Joseph and station manager Walter Patterson. "They got tough with me real fast," says Purtan. 'Dick, you better do what we ask because this man [Joseph] can make or break your career,' warned Patterson. "Wait a minute, you are telling me that Mike Joseph can make or break my career? I don't believe he can," countered Purtan.

"At that point, I got up and said, 'I'll take my chances' and walked toward the door. Just before I turn the handle, Patterson says, 'Now, hold on there. Please sit down.' Then, as if refereeing a juvenile argument, he says, 'Dick, this is going to be your station from 6 to 9 in the morning and Mike it's your station from 9 A.M. to 6 A.M.,' and that is how that whole mess turned out," explains Purtan.[1]

Things did not turn out as well for Bob Green, who had boy-cotted the Sunday night staff meeting. "I was just really upset that Patterson brought Joseph back in a panic. He had been out of the picture for a long time. I just couldn't make myself attend that meeting. I knew the kind of stuff he was going to be doing," Green commented.[2]

By December of 1967, Keener was not only losing listeners but also the billing. To lighten the bottom line, deejays Ted Clark, Jerry Goodwin, Bob Green, and Scott Regen were let go in one fell swoop and replaced by more reasonably priced talent. Dick Purtan and J. Michael Wilson remained. Purtan was really the last line of defense at Keener, his morning ratings still holding until nine, when the station took a nose-dive. WWJ made an offer to Dick Purtan in the fall of 1967: a three-year contract at twenty-eight, thirty, and thirty-two thousand-dollar steps. WKNR matched the offer; Purtan stayed.[3]


On a December afternoon, at the 1090 position on the AM dial, Santa Claus could be heard taking phone calls from children: "Okay, what's your name? Karen? That's a very pretty name. So, Karen, what would you like Santa to bring you for Christmas?[4] On closer listening, the voice of Santa was eerily familiar. It was soft and intimate, sort of like Tom Clay. Hey, it was "that guy by the name of you know what," back again on Detroit radio, this time on talk station WTAK. During the past three and a half years, Clay had bounced around several stations, including KBLA in Los Angeles and a second tour at KDAY in L.A., where he served as program director. Now he was in a format that suited him perfectly. Paul Winter had also found a home at the Garden City station as its resident liberal voice.


Musically, everything was rocking harder in Detroit in 1967. Bob Seger was back with two more local top-ten hits, "Persecution

Smith" and "Heavy Music." Cameo records out of Philadelphia picked up his Hideout releases for national distribution, but they failed to find much action outside of Michigan and Ohio. Cameo was also releasing the Rationals. A band called the Wanted had a rock version of "In the Midnight Hour" on the Detroit Sound label and it hit number three in the Motor City.

The Scott Richard Case had their first chart success with "I'm So Glad." It was released on Jeep Holland's local A Square label and went top ten in Detroit. They became better known as SRC.

The Unrelated Segments released "Story of My Life" on the HBR label.

Motown Records, smelling money, decided to get in on some of the local rock action and signed one of the hottest bands in town, the Underdogs, to their new V.I.P label. Although "Love's Gone Bad" entered the top five in Detroit, the Motown machine wasn't able to break it nationally.

Ric-Tic Records continued to have success, scoring two local top-ten hits with "To Share Your Love" by the Fantastic Four and "You've Got to Pay the Price" by Al Kent.

"Sock It to Me" became the last big hit for Mitch Ryder and the Detroit Wheels. Producer Bob Crewe decided to separate Mitch from the group and have him wear a cape and sing "What Now My Love." It effectively ended his and the group's career.

Although not originally from Detroit, George Clinton and friends had moved to the Motor City from New Jersey because of the music scene. As the Parliaments they recorded "(I Wanna) Testify" for the local Revilot label. It was a smash in Detroit and nationally went to number twenty pop and number three r&b. In the summer of 1967 they appeared in a ten-day revue staged by Robin Seymour at the Fox theater. Martha Reeves and the Vandellas headlined the show, which featured other Detroit (but not Motown) performers Deon Jackson and J. J. Barnes.

Robin Seymour recalls one particular show: "It was a Sunday matinee and I will never forget it. We had been getting huge crowds but this particular Sunday we only had about five hundred people and we wondered what was going on. Well, we found out when the police arrived to warn us about the riots that were breaking out all around us. Martha Reeves was just great, she got on stage and was telling everybody to be calm and for the kids not to worry, we would get them to their parents. That's what I think of when I think about Motown. A lot of heart, it was so important to Detroit."[5]

CKLW-TV didn't show a lot of heart as they dropped Robin as host of "Swingin' Time." The show had been channel 9's biggest moneymaker, netting a million dollars annually. Seymour was replaced by Tom Shannon, who they thought had more youth appeal. "I think channel 9 just started to think I was getting too old, recalls Seymour. The funny thing was, business quickly dropped off and after a few weeks they changed the name of the show to "The Lively Spot" and then it died. I have to admit, I had some sad times around then, but then they called me back to do a weekly show and we sort of hung on, for a while."

WKNR's SCOTT REGEN PRESIDED over the most surreal musical event of the year as he emceed a concert headlining the Monkees. The opening act was a new group from England: the Jimi Hendrix Experience.[6]

Jim Jeffries was Keener's all-night disc jockey and, like the station's other deejays, he put listeners on the air live, for song requests, without benefit of a delay system.[7] One Saturday night at a little past twelve, Jim went on the air with a pleasant-sounding young man who was very complimentary about the station and seemed to like all the disc jockeys. After his song request, he shared one more thought with Jeffries on the air:

Listener. "Oh, Jim?
Jefferies. "Yes?"
Listener. "F— you!"

IN FEBRUARY OF 1968, Dick Purtan arrived at Topinka's Country House to have lunch with WXYZ's program director, Joe Bacarella. It seemed the station was desperately in need of a boost. The ratings showed the once mighty Wixie down to a 4 share in the morning and not much better all day. Bacarella invited Purtan to come and do afternoons at the middle-of-the-road station, with Martin and Howard's morning show as the carrot. The money was great, $40,000. Purtan's answer: "No, I'm a morning man." A

Tom Clay signing autographs at the "Beatle Booster Ball," State Fair Coliseum. March, 1964. *Courtesy Becky Clague*

Tom Clay with the Beatles in England. April, 1964. (l-r) Tom Clay, George Harrison, contest winner, Paul McCartney and John Lennon. *Courtesy Becky Clague*

CKLW newspaper promo for Dave Shafer and Tom Clay, 1964. The two became entangled in a Beatle Booster brouhaha.

When the Beatles finally arrived in Detroit, Tom Clay was gone. Keener's Gary Stevens, Bob Green and Robin Seymour detain Ringo Starr for an interview with WKNR newsman George Hunter. August, 1964. *Courtesy Bob Green*

CKLW deejays Joe Van, Dave Shafer and Tom Shannon backstage with Keith Richards and Brian Jones of the Rolling Stones. 1965. *Courtesy Dave Shafer*

Record surveys from CKLW and WJBK. 1964.

KNORR BROADCASTING CORPORATION

A young man who knows how to please his audience, Jerry Goodwin, who came to WKNR from WQAM in Miami, Florida, where he was a top rated personality. His 12 Noon to 3 P.M. air show enjoyed number one ratings in Miami. In addition to his air show, Jerry was Music Director of WQAM and later Program Director. Before going to Miami, Jerry was in Dallas, Texas, where he was a featured personality on KBOX.

Jerry grew up in Boston, Massachusetts and graduated from English High School. While in high school, Jerry became a proficient musician, specializing in percussion instruments. He later studied at Boston Conservatory and became a member of the Junior Symphony Orchestra of Boston.

A veteran of the Air Force, Jerry attended West Texas State College in Amarillo and studied Psychology. During his final year, he was a psychiatric therapist at the Rehabilitation Center at Amarillo Air Force Base.

Even with his busy schedule, Jerry finds time for community activities and he teaches radio announcing classes three times weekly at a Detroit radio school.

Jerry and his wife have a daughter, Robin. The Goodwin family raises German Shepherd dogs.

Two happy people and why not! Danny Thomas and Jerry Goodwin are smiling over the success of the Teenage March Against Leukemia, a charity in which both are deeply interested. This year, almost 18,000 teens marched, all recruited by announcements on WKNR.

*Jerry Goodwin Show*

WKNR
THE STATION THAT
KNOWS DETROIT

Personality profile of WKNR's Jerry Goodwin. Second photo shows Jerry with Danny Thomas. Jerry organized the Detroit effort to raise funds for St. Jude's Children's Hospital yearly.
*Courtesy Tom Shannon*

CKLW's Tom Shannon arrives in style, 1965.
*Courtesy Bob Green*

Detroit disc jockeys visit Brenda Lee at the Elmwood Casino in Windsor, 1964. Left to right: Gary Stevens/WKNR, unidentified fan, Dave Prince/WXYZ, Paul Cannon/CKLW, Brenda Lee, second undentified fan, Marc Avery/WJBK, Ron Knowles/CKLW and Dave Shafer/CKLW.
*Courtesy Ron Knowles*

Paul (Dick) Purtan and fellow WSAI disc jockeys pooled their resources and brought the Beatles to Cincinnati. April 1964. Left to right: Bob Harper, Paul Purtan, Dusty Rhodes and Steve Kirk. Harper and Rhodes would later work for Detroit radio stations. *Courtesy Dick Purtan*

LISTEN
TO THE
BRIGHT
HAPPY SOUND
OF
LOVEABLE

**WXYZ**
1270 RADIO
DETROIT SOUND

WXYZ's weekly record survey. 1964.

**WXYZ** 1270 RADIO
DETROIT SOUND

## WEEK OF OCTOBER 27

| | This Week | | | Last Week |
|---|---|---|---|---|
| | 1 | AS TEARS GO BY | MARIANNE FAITHFUL | 9 |
| | 2 | LEADER OF THE PACK | SHANGRI LAS | 1 |
| X | 3 | I'M GONNA BE STRONG | GENE PITNEY | 8 |
| X | 4 | BABY LOVE | SUPREMES | 2 |
| SS | 5 | WHY | CHARTBUSTERS | 7 |
| SS | 6 | SCRATCHY | TRAVIS WAMMACK | 5 |
| | 7 | ASK ME | ELVIS PRESLEY | 13 |
| | 8 | COME A LITTLE BIT CLOSER | JAY & AMERICANS | 6 |
| | 9 | RINGO | LORNE GREENE | 25 |
| X | 10 | GONE GONE GONE | EVERLY BROS. | 20 |
| X | 11 | MOUNTAIN OF LOVE | JOHNNY RIVERS | 24 |
| X | 12 | REACH OUT FOR ME | DIONNE WARWICK | 12 |
| X | 13 | Needle In A Haystack | Velvelettes | 4 |
| | 14 | Time Is On My Side | Rolling Stones | 18 |
| X | 15 | Everything's All Right | Newbeats | 26 |
| | 16 | She's Not There | Zombies | 3 |
| | 17 | Here She Comes | Tymes | 23 |
| | 18 | Walking In The Rain | Ronettes | 28 |
| | 19 | Crazy | Emanuel Lasky | .. |
| | 20 | Mr. Lonely | Bobby Vinton | 36 |
| | 21 | You're Bad News | Headliners | 30 |

| | | | | |
|---|---|---|---|---|
| X | 22 | Ain't It The Truth | Mary Wells | X |
| SS | 23 | The Boy From Crosstown | Angels | 33 |
| | 24 | Over You | Paul Revere | 40 |
| SS | 25 | The Jerk | Larks | SS |
| SS | 26 | You Should Have Seen The Way | Dixie Cups | 27 |
| | 27 | Don't Ever Leave Me | Connie Francis | 29 |
| | 28 | Too Many Fish In The Sea | Marvelettes | 35 |
| | 29 | Pushin A Good Thing Too Far | Barbara Lewis | 34 |
| X | 30 | Big Man In Town | Four Seasons | X |
| | 31 | California Bound | Ronnie & Daytonas | 37 |
| | 32 | Rhythm & Greens | Shadows | 38 |
| | 33 | Run Run Run | Gestures | 39 |
| | 34 | Dance Dance Dance | Beach Boys | .. |
| | 35 | Oh No, Not My Baby | Maxine Brown | .. |
| | 36 | Little Queenie | Joe South | .. |
| | 37 | Big Boy Pete | Olympics | .. |
| | 38 | Goin' Out Of My Head | Little Anthony | .. |
| | 39 | The Wedding | Julie Rogers | .. |
| | 40 | Walk Away | Matt Monroe | .. |

X—Former Exclusive
SS—Former Spotlight Sound

**MEET JOEL SEBASTIAN**
WXYZ SPOTLIGHT PERSONALITY
2:00 P.M. - 6:00 P.M.

**WXYZ SPOTLIGHT SOUND**
ALWAYS SOMETHING THERE TO REMIND ME—SANDIE SHAW

WKNR deejays paint Happy Birthday to Keener, November 1966. Left to right: Jerry Goodwin (on ladder), Jim Jeffries, Scott Regen, Ted Clark, Dick Purtan (holding pallet), Bob Green (above), J. Michael Wilson and Paul Cannon. *Courtesy of Bob Green*

Fifty thousand guides were printed every week and available at area record shops.

WKNR promotion for morning personality, Dick Purtan. Second photo: Dick Purtan hangs out with Napoleon Solo (Robert Vaughn) 1966. *Courtesy Bob Green*

DETROIT

# WKNR
## MUSIC GUIDE
### WEEK OF SEPTEMBER 1, 1965
## KEENER 13 HITS

1. EVE OF DESTRUCTION—BARRY McGUIRE..............DUNHILL (1)
2. UNCHAINED MELODY—RIGHTEOUS BROS. .............PHILLES (2)
3. HUNGRY FOR LOVE—S. REMO GOLDEN STRINGS RIC-TIC (9)
4. LIAR, LIAR—CASTAWAYS .........................................SOMA (7)
5. TREAT HER RIGHT—ROY HEAD....................BACK BEAT (21)
6. LIKE A ROLLING STONE—BOB DYLAN.............COLUMBIA (4)
7. HOLD ME, THRILL ME, KISS ME—MEL CARTER....IMPERIAL (10)
8. YOU WERE ON MY MIND—WE FIVE..................A & M (3)
9. YOU'RE THE ONE—VOGUES .....................CO & CE (30)
10. IT AIN'T ME BABE—TURTLES ................WHITE WHALE (5)
11. HELP!/I'M DOWN—BEATLES .......................CAPITOL (6)
12. HANG ON SLOOPY—McCOYS ...........................BANG (11)
13. IF YOU'VE GOT A HEART—B. GOLDSBORO UN. ARTISTS (18)
14. If I Didn't Love You—Chuck Jackson.................Wand (12)
15. Annie Fanny—Kingsmen ...................................Wand (13)
16. Action—Freddy Cannon ......................Warner Bros. (16)
17. Catch Us If You Can—Dave Clark Five..................Epic (23)
18. 3rd Man Theme/Taste Of Honey—Herb Alpert......A & M (28)
19. High Heel Sneakers—Stevie Wonder...................Tamla (24)
20. Ain't It True—Andy Williams ....................Columbia (27)
21. The Way Of Love—Kathy Kirby......................Parrot (31)
22. Some Enchanted Evening—Jay & Americans..United Artists (29)
23. I'm A Happy Man—Jive Five ...................United Artists (10)
24. Colours—Donovan ........................................Hickory (26)
25. My Town, My Guy & Me—Lesley Gore ............Mercury (KS)
26. Baby Don't Go—Sonny & Cher......................Reprise (—)
27. You've Got Your Troubles—Fortunes .................Press (—)
28. Heart Full Of Soul—Yardbirds ...........................Epic (—)
29. I'm Yours—Elvis Presley ..........................RCA Victor (—)
30. With These Hands—Tom Jones ......................Parrot (—)
31. Dreams Come True—Ronnie Dove .................Diamond (—)

## KEY SONG OF THE WEEK
**JUST A LITTLE BIT BETTER—HERMAN'S HERMITS**..................MGM
Figure in parentheses indicates last week's position.

# WKNR
**THE STATION THAT KNOWS DETROIT**

WKNR presents "Herman's Hermits." 1966. Lead singer Peter Noone in front. Behind are
J. Michael Wilson, Bob Green, Paul Cannon and a group member. *Courtesy Bob Green*

WXYZ personalities on a parade float with the "Wixie Whirlybird" traffic helicopter. 1966. Dave Prince, Danny Taylor, Pat Murphy, Jimmy Hampton, Lee Alan and Marc Avery. *Courtesy Jim Hampton*

CKLW's Joe Van, Bud Davies, Dave Shafer, Duke Windsor and Tommy Shannon with British rock group, The Mindbenders. 1966. *Courtesy Dave Shafer*

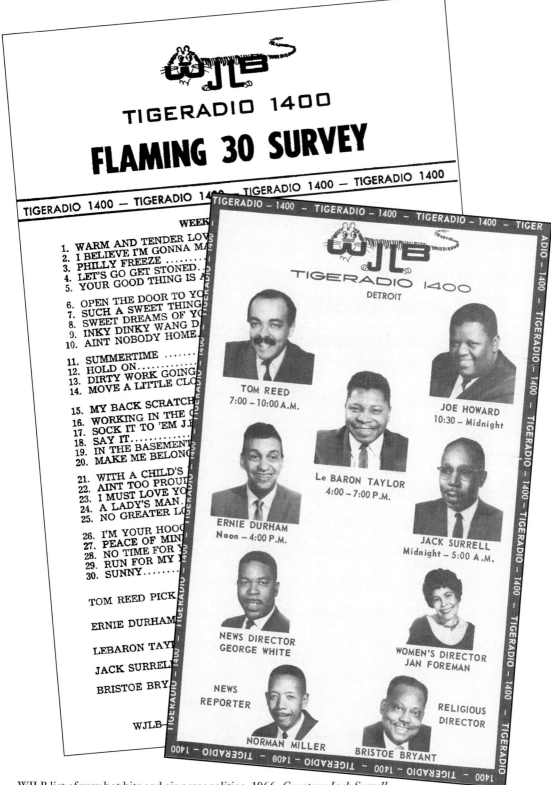

WJLB list of very hot hits and air personalities. 1966. *Courtesy Jack Surrell*

WXYZ personalites were featured on the back of the station's weekly "Detroit Sound Survey."

Newspaper promo for Lee Alan's new TV show. 1965. Politics at ABC prevented the show's national release.

WCHB's line up of air talent included the incendiary "Rockin' Robbie D," from 8 to midnight. 1967.

The line up at Detroit's number one radio station. January, 1967.

Front of WCHB's weekly record survey.

Before arriving at Detroit's WCHB in 1963, Martha Jean Steinberg was broadcasting on WDIA in Memphis, Tennessee. Here she interviews guests at a social function. Late 1950s. *Courtesy Martha Jean Steinberg*

Martha Jean "The Queen," on the air at WDIA, Memphis. 1962. *Courtesy Martha Jean Steinberg*

A remote broadcast with Martha Jean "The Queen" (second from right). WJLB, Detroit. 1968. *Courtesy Martha Jean Steinberg*

Dick Purtan greets the new day from the studios of WKNR. 1966. *Courtesy Dick Purtan*

WKNR personalities were featured on the cover of Keener's fourth volume of oldies. Tough guys included Dick "Mugsy" Purtan, second from right, next to Scott Regen. In back: Paul Cannon, J. Michael Wilson, Bob "Babyface" Green, and Dave Forester. In front: Jerry "Sly Sneer" Goodwin, Bob Harper, Steve Robbins and Ted Clark. *Courtesy Bob Green*

Robin Seymour shows the dancers how to "get down" on "Swingin' Time." 1967. The show ran Monday through Friday on Channel 9. *Courtesy Detroit News Archives*

CKLW introduces a tight, fast sound in April of 1967.

The very first of CKLW's new record surveys following the switch to the "Drake format." April 4, 1967.

CKLW's famous music director, Rosalie Trombley, surrounded by gold records. *Courtesy CKLW Collection*

After a bad sports prediction, WJR's J.P. McCarthy receives the award for "Loser of the Day." 1966. *Courtesy Judy McCarthy*

"Master of Suspense," meets master interviewer. Alfred Hitchcock with J.P. on WJR's "Focus." 1968. *Courtesy Judy McCarthy*

This is not the home of the "Good Guys." WABX air staff on a television fund-raiser, January, 1969. Left to right: Jim Hampton, Dave Dixon, John Sinclair, Jerry Lubin (wearing hat) and Larry Miller. *Courtesy Jim Hampton*

Dave Dixon, Captain of the WABX Air Aces, holds station banner. *Courtesy Dave Dixon*

MICKEY SAYS:
FEEL THE COSMIC VIBRATIONS OF MUSIC EMINATING FROM THE STEREO TAPE REALM. YOU WILL SAVE MANY RUPEES AND WILL RECEIVE OUR SPECIAL CELESTIAL BLESSINGS......OM
925 SOUTH WOODWARD AVE.
North of 10 Mile Road, Royal Oak
PHONE 398-7204

Mickey Shorr was off the radio but in tune with the times.

Official WABX T-shirt
logo designed by Gary
Grimshaw.
*Courtesy Dave Dixon*

Some left-of-center advertising for
Detroit's first "underground"
progressive rock station. 1968.
*Courtesy Dave Dixon*

# TRUTH
# JUSTICE
# HONOR
# BEAUTY
## and just a pinch of smut

## wabx 99.5 stereo

Dick Purtan visited by his daughters in the WXYZ studios. Left to right: Jill, Jackie, JoAnne and Jessica Purtan.
*Courtesy Dick Purtan*

Detroit's legendary "Frantic" Ernie Durham out on the town with wife Jacqueline. Also in attendance on the other side of the table, at far left, CKLW program director Alden Diehl (smiling) next to Kathy and Dave Shafer. 1971.
*Courtesy Dave Shafer*

Even a revamped Keener 13 couldn't slow down the powerful "Big 8" as it surged ahead into the '70s.

short time later he bailed out of the sinking WKNR and accepted a morning position at WBAL in Baltimore.

In Detroit, people hadn't been able to get enough of Purtan's irreverence; Baltimore would be a different story. Purtan was only on the air a couple of days when, telling a story, he used the word *guts,* as in "that guy has a lot of guts." Management quickly informed him that he had uttered a "non-WBAL word" and that language such as that would not be tolerated on Baltimore's stately fifty thousand-watt radio station, where he had already been advised not to refer on the air to a couple of nearby towns, Cockeyville and, just down the road, Dickeyville. Other nearby towns vulnerable to Purtan included Boring and Finksburg. Purtan: "One day a Texaco commercial ran and there was a tag at the end saying that there was a new location in this particular little town and I made a harmless comment, saying: 'I'm glad they finally got their first gas station.' Well, the boss comes in the studio all upset and sternly says: 'Dick, they have had a gas station in that town for quite some time!' Looking up, I said, 'It was a joke, I was telling a joke.' I called my wife, Gail, and said 'I think I've made a real mistake coming to this place.'"

Spiro Agnew was still the governor of the heavily taxed state of Maryland, and when Purtan referred to him on the air as "Spiral Tax" Agnew, people were offended. Agnew himself called WBAL's general manager, Al Burke, to complain. "Burke calls me in and says the governor wasn't pleased with what I said," recalls Purtan. "He tells me not to do that line again. Well, the next morning I got on the air and said it again and Burke blew his stack. A couple of weeks later, Burke, myself, and the program director, whose name was Don Kelly, went to Annapolis to smooth things over. We met Agnew and then went to a luncheon with a couple of his aids. As we are sipping our iced tea, out of nowhere, this guy starts pounding on the table and is practically yelling at me: 'Don't ever do that again!' Of course, now it was war and as soon as I got back on the air, I did the line again and they fired me. I lasted five weeks."

Dick says what really made the 'BAL experience so weird is that the station knew what they were getting when they hired him: "They had flown me in on two occasions and told me they wanted to take the station in a new direction but every time I would do anything slightly funny, the hammer would come down."

Baltimore was a weird experience for Purtan right till the end. "It was very strange, but no sooner was I off the air permanently, than the general manager asked me to lunch. As we're sitting there, he leans in and calmly says: 'Dick, what can I do to make WBAL a better station?' I replied, 'I really don't know as you just asked me to leave,'" Purtan chortles, still reeling from the absurdity of it all.

At home, Dick gazed at a wife and three daughters and, realizing his need for fast employment, got back in touch with Joe Bacarella at WXYZ about that $40,000 job in the afternoon. "I told Joe I was interested and he said, 'Let me talk to Fritz [general manager] and get back to you.' Three weeks later I get a phone call: 'Dick, I talked it over with Charlie and he wants you! Oh, by the way–the offer is $25,000,'" Purtan remembers, shaking his head.[8] After this lesson in the laws of supply and demand, Dick returned to Detroit, working afternoons at WXYZ while waiting for the eminent demise of the "Martin and Howard Show," where the duo was sweating rating-point bullets as Fritz gave them one last shot.

In a promotional move, WXYZ arranged for Dick to appear on their new morning television program hosted by Bob Hynes. It was obvious that Hynes knew nothing of who Dick Purtan was or his style of humor as he stumbled through an introduction: "Our guest is a funny disc jockey, Dick Purtan, who is going to be on WXYZ radio." He tried to get Dick to demonstrate how funny he was. Purtan sat uncomfortably on a couch across from him, delivering deadpan responses: "Yes, Bob," "No, Bob," and "That's right, Bob." Hynes: "Well, Dick, I understand that we have one of your loyal listeners on the phone and she wants to say hello." A goofy woman was suddenly on the air in a very excitable voice, gushing over Bob's guest: "Hello, Dickie P! It's so wonderful that you're back!" she exclaimed, as if in a state of rapture. Purtan squirmed, unsuccessfully attempting to slide down the couch and out of camera range. It was a great television moment.[9]

Back in his element on radio, Purtan was soon organizing a "White Socks Day" for Detroit office workers. Dave Prince had been sacrificed to make room. Soon, Purtan could be heard again in the morning as the plug was pulled on the "Martin and Howard Show." Here's a sampling of what kept people tuned in to WXYZ and laughing as they waited out traffic lights in the morning:

This is Dick Purtan, polished in the arts, proficient in the languages, pain in the neck.

Yesterday I had the *Playboy* Playmate of the Month here in the studio with me. We talked on the air, I got her autograph and everything. Well...I got her autograph.

This is Dick Purtan with the sweetest music this side of the Boblo boat.

I understand that Rita Bell has decided to publish her own magazine. She's calling it Rita's Digest.

This is Dick Purtan, all dressed up in my seersucker suit, my French cuff shirt, and my disc jockey shorts.

At WXYZ, Purtan also started to use the telephone as a humorous device, dialing up a donut shop to place a torturously detailed order for "fifteen glazed donuts, twenty-five jelly filled, six chocolate covered," and so forth, and then having the poor counter guy read it all back. Purtan: "No, I'm sorry...that should have been twenty-five glazed and sixteen chocolate covered," as the audience giggled, waiting to see how long Purtan could keep him hooked. Soon listeners were contacting Dick, begging that he call their boss, husband, girlfriend, and so forth, with similar nonsensical put-ons. In a 1968 newspaper interview, Purtan was somewhat of a hoot, revealing himself as a "Sinatra man," who decorated his den in a "mod manner."[10]

The WXYZ lineup in 1968 included: Dick Purtan, 6 A.M.–10 A.M.; Johnny Randall, 10 A.M.–2 P.M.; Mike Sherman, 2 P.M.–6 P.M.; Jack Hayes, 6 P.M.–10 P.M.; Dave Lockhart, 10 P.M.–2 A.M.; and Jim Davis, 2 A.M.–6 A.M.[11] The music was very contemporary middle of the road and the station had a certain show-bizzy sound that was hard to duplicate.

ASIDE FROM DICK PURTAN, dawn in Detroit was still dominated by J. P. McCarthy at WJR, the station where time seemed to stand still. J. P. had returned from San Francisco at the end of 1964, after the station's sale to Capitol Cities, and ascended to the number one position in Detroit's morning race for the ratings. In 1966, he added new duties, hosting the noon hour talk show called "Focus." The program had as much impact as any television talk show, becoming a must-stop for famous folks visiting the Motor City, and McCarthy developed a reputation as one of the best interviewers anywhere. "Joe was so good at interviewing because he was a really great listener," recalls his wife, Judy. "He was curious about everything. Joe would read about fifteen newspapers every morning. He had a great capacity for storing information."[12]

J. P.'s morning show, while still serving up lots of popular middle-of-the-road music, was also starting to encompass more news and current events, with J. P. opening a dialogue with Detroit listeners about anything that seemed interesting. It was also becoming a program of regulars, such as Fat Bob Taylor, the "singing plumber," discovered after placing a phone call to J. P. in 1967. Fat Bob turned out to have not only an impressive voice but also a wild sense of humor and would call J. P. regularly as himself and in the guise of other odd characters, such as "Mrs. Pennyfeather," who engaged McCarthy in some suggestive early morning banter.

Another regular was "Benny da Bookie," a character conjured up by a local advertising executive named Fred Yaffe. Yaffe had orchestrated much of J. P.'s 1968 mock run for the presidency, which included writing the official campaign theme and arranging for *Playboy* bunnies to pose with McCarthy in his campaign convertible. It was a major promotion for 'JR.

Fred and J. P. were friends and would occasionally talk on the phone during the show, while the records were on. "One morning I was talking with Joe while I was shaving," recalls Yaffe.[13] " I had my head tilted to hold the phone and I think I might have had a cigarette dangling from my lip. Anyhow, Joe asked me about the line on the upcoming Michigan–Ohio State game, and just to kid around, I answered him in sort of a low, rough voice, kind of a tough guy with a lot of 'deese' and 'dems.' Well, he jumped right on it and said, 'Hey, I want you to go on the air with me and do that voice.' So, we go on with me playing a bookie and I predict that Michigan will win by 3 points, 24 to 21. The next day, Michigan not only wins but it's a huge upset with a score of 24 to 12 and Benny looks like he really knows what he's talking about. And that is how the whole 'Benny da Bookie' thing started back in 1969."[13]

Pretty soon, McCarthy's producer was contacting Fred regularly to schedule calls. It was J. P., playing Nick Charles, the cool private eye from the *Thin Man* movies, who seemed to know and relate to all the strange characters around, including unsavory types like Benny.

> [*J. P.*] Now folks, live from Las Vegas, here's our pal, the guy with the inside scoop, "Benny da bookie." [*Benny*] Hey, Joe, what's goin' on back dere in Detroit? [*J. P.*] Well, Benny, I think we're all more interested in what's going on down in Kentucky, with the Derby just around the corner. [*Benny*] Yeah, I know what ya mean. Well, I gotta horse for ya!

So went another visit with McCarthy and his bookie. According to Fred, these conversations were always improvised with no preparation. Joe didn't share the put-on with his audience and many listeners assumed Benny was for real.

Yaffe went on to do other "sidekick" characters on Joe's show, including "Mr. Dow Jones." "If there was something big happening in financial news, Joe would put a call through to Dow Jones himself in New York," relates Fred. "I would come on in this thick Yiddish accent, with some astute financial observations. We did get complaints about this routine."

> [*J. P.*] Hello, is this Dow Jones? [*Dow Jones*] Yas, dis is he speaking. [*J. P.*] Well, sir, the market is awful shaky this week and people seem to be quite concerned, if not downright worried. Perhaps there is something you could share with our listeners that would explain what's happening? [*Dow Jones*] Well, Mr. McCarthy, ya' know, what goes up–goes down. You don't want to put all your eggs in one basket.

Other features WJR's morning audience came to expect included the listener nominations for "Winner and Loser" of the day as well as a visit with the "Answer Man," who just happened to be J. P.

"Joe was just himself on the air," says Judy McCarthy. "He was so creative and always coming up with ideas. I think the listeners could pick up his energy."

In a sixties interview, J. P. described his music selection at 'JR: "We play a lot of things on the Top 40 list but our appeal is broader. We play a lot of albums, especially the new ones."

In between records, McCarthy would mimic voices of people

such as Cary Grant and Charles Boyer. "I'm the man of a thousand voices," he would say. "Unfortunately, they all come out sounding like Bela Lugosi." J. P. was pretty much able to play what he wanted and say what he wanted. "A disc jockey can't really take credit for the music he plays. You can only take credit for what goes on between the records," he commented in the same interview. "I try to have fun on the air. I'm a sports nut and talk a lot about sports."[14]

In fact, for a "disc jockey," McCarthy probably reported on sports in more detail than sportscasters did on other stations. Detroit, having four professional teams, provided lots to talk about—and then there was golf, a sport McCarthy played with a passion. If that wasn't enough, college football filled in the gaps. As alluded to earlier, J. P. was a big University of Michigan fan and each November he devoted an entire show to previewing the Michigan-Ohio State game. Just ahead of playing the Michigan fight song, he would get real close to the mike and deliver his own low-key cheer: "Go get 'em...you great big beautiful Blue!"

After being named head coach at Michigan, Bo Schembechler became a regular on the McCarthy show, along with other popular sports figures.

What was it like in the "golden tower?" "For the most part, it was quite pleasant," recalls 'JR veteran Mike Whorf. "It was friendly but everyone sort of went their own way. I always had a good working relationship with J. P, but I know there were a few folks who seemed to hold a grudge after he started to gain so much power at the station. What could you do? He earned it. He really was the best at what he did and I think any of those kind of attitudes were just born out of jealousy."[15]

Bob Talbert of the *Detroit Free Press* arrived in town in 1968 and immediately connected with McCarthy. "It didn't take long to realize that being on the air with J. P. was the quickest way to get known. In the beginning, I would have more people respond to something I said on his show than anything I had in my column," says Talbert. "He was always doing something interesting and there were many times I would find myself sitting in a parking lot for ten minutes because I didn't want to turn off the radio."[16]

Although J. P. McCarthy was number one in listenership ages twenty-five to fifty-four, Dick Purtan held the top spot with listeners eighteen to forty-nine. "Joe liked Dick Purtan, but I think he felt their styles were miles apart," comments Judy McCarthy.[17] As for Purtan, when asked at the time what he thought of J. P., he responded, "The guy's great, what a voice! It's too good for everyday use. He could make a million doing nothing but commercials."[18]

McCarthy had, in fact, become one of the top commercial voices in the country and could be heard on national spots for clients, including Buick and Kelly Services. The rest of WJR's schedule included the last radio show in the country (except the Grand Old Opry) to feature live music: "Open House," starring singer Jack Harris along with Jimmy Clark and the WJR Orchestra. Middays featured Arthur Godfrey on CBS, plus "Adventures in Good Music" with Karl Haas, "Kaleidoscope" with Mike Whorf, and J. P.'s "Focus." Jimmy Launce was in the afternoon "Music Hall" from 3:15 to 6:00. There was usually sports in the evening, and Jay Roberts was still piloting his way through the night.

WWJ WAS TRYING TO PROJECT a more contemporary image, adding some jingles and a little hipper music selection and calling it "Audio 68." The result was that, despite the new trappings, the station still evoked a somewhat square and orderly sound. Morrie Carlson was new in the morning, followed by longtime 'J personality Bob Allison, who was having continued success with his "Ask Your Neighbor" gabfest from ten to noon. Detroit veteran Marty McNeely held down afternoons.

BILL DELZELL, RON ROSE, AND JIM DAVIS were part of the air staff at WCAR, a fifty-thousand-watt station that stuck to the standards and a fairly rigid format. W-car differed in operation from most of the other AM stations in town because of its private ownership by the somewhat quirky Hy Levenson. "One afternoon I was going along as usual and the private line rang," recalls Davis, who was doing afternoon drive in 1967. "It was Mrs. Levinson and she was all upset about a song I'm playing. It was nothing wild, something by the Association, I think. Well, I thought it wasn't right that the owner's wife should be calling me like this, so I ran down the list of choices she had if she didn't like what I was doing. I'm telling her that she can listen to Dave Prince on WXYZ or Jimmy Launce on WJR and so forth. The next day I was out of a job."[19]

AT THE OTHER END OF THE MUSIC SPECTRUM, CKLW continued its relentless blitzkrieg through the explosive year of 1968. The CK lineup now included Chuck (Browning) Morgan, 6 A.M.–9 A.M.; Mark Richards, 9 A.M.–noon; "Big" Jim Edwards, noon–3 P.M.; Mike Rivers, 3 P.M.–6 P.M.; Tom Shannon, 6 P.M.–9 P.M.; Scott Regen, 9 P.M.–midnight; and Frank Brodie, midnight–6 A.M. Shannon was ecstatic as his rating share hit a 36! The fast a cappella jingle said it all: "The Big 8, CKLW."

## CHAPTER 21

# Over Under Sideways Down

FM RADIO IN DETROIT was still pretty much on the back burner at the beginning of 1968, with penetration at less than 10 percent. WOMC and WLDM were about the only FM stations with any audience to speak of.[1] Both played uninterrupted, mainly instrumental background music, popular in elevators and dentist offices, with WOMC being the livelier of the two. WDTM had been sold to Texas broadcaster Gordon McClendon and the calls changed to WWWW. The station, which referred to itself as W4, was also playing "easy listening" music but presenting it with more promotion. Although restrictions had been imposed by the FCC four years earlier requiring separate programming for at least 50 percent of the day on FM stations that had previously been simulcasting their AM sisters, FM remained a seldom listened to and, in most cases, money-losing medium.

A year earlier, something had begun to happen in San Francisco that would now be impacting radio in Detroit: the emergence of FM as an outlet for rock music. The Bay Area's leading Top 40 disc jockey, "Big Daddy" Tom Donahue of KYA radio, tired of the musical limitations of AM Top 40 stations, had started broadcasting in the evening on KMPX, an FM station that normally survived by running foreign language programming. "I had all these great albums I played at home, but I couldn't put them on the air," said Donahue in a later interview with *Life* magazine. "Groups like Country Joe and the Fish could sell a hundred thousand albums by word of mouth but never get airplay. They were too long to squeeze between the commercials. A generation raised on overground radio graduated to albums no one would broadcast."

Donahue had persuaded station management to let him replace a four-hour block of Chinese music, news, and drama each evening with Donahue's format: "I played everything I wanted to hear—acid rock, protest, classical, jazz. There were mood segments, entire albums, all-Dylan nights, and oldies." As Donahue brought up the ratings, the whole station adapted the free-form approach. Thus, in April of 1967, "underground radio" was born.[2]

This account, as given in a 1968 issue of *Life* magazine, was nearly accurate except for its failure to mention that a guy named Larry Miller was already on the air with a free-form show from midnight to 6 A.M., at the same San Francisco station at the time of Donahue's arrival. According to Detroit broadcaster Dave Dixon, Miller should get more credit: "I don't believe Donahue had a 'moment of enlightenment' and decided to invent free-form radio. I believe he and his friends were sitting around at night smokin' dope and listening to Larry Miller, who had done that kind of program in Detroit and then went out to San Francisco."[3] Dixon recalls that Miller had done an eclectic program on one of Detroit's seldom listened to FM stations, most likely WDTM or WQRS, about 1966.

"Donahue was a big blowhard who pushed himself into a position of power and grabbed all the attention,"[3] Dixon claims. Although Dave Dixon's opinion is probably true to some extent, it often takes the type of person he describes to really get something off the ground. Donahue was a racehorse, nightclub, and record label owner as well as concert promoter and all-around hustler, and if he, in fact, was inspired by Larry Miller, he had the vision to take it to the next level. Besides slighting Larry Miller, Donahue also ignored the fact that WOR-FM in New York experimented with an "underground" format in 1966, although it only lasted a little less than a year.

After Donahue and his staff went on strike, he got wind that a manager of another station was floating the idea of hiring the entire KMPX staff and going free-form rock on their station, KSAN. Donahue flew to the station's corporate offices in New York, and when the meeting was over, not only was Metromedia hiring the KMPX staff, but they were also putting Tom Donahue in charge, and the guy in San Francisco who first had the idea went to work for him. That's just the way it was with Tom Donahue.

Back in Detroit, WABX was one of many struggling FM stations. Deejays played a mishmash of nondescript pop vocals during the day and in the evening a "Best of Broadway" show aired, followed by Jim Rockwell's jazz program. The station wasn't a contender to anything. They didn't even bother to sign on the air until nine in the morning[4] and a package of seven sixty-second commercials could be purchased for $9.[5]

In July, Mickey Shorr had roared back into town, having secured an agreement with WABX to install a very rudimentary all-girl format, such as he had done in Chicago during his years in exile.[6] It was quite a sexist affair, featuring purring voices with names such as "Lo-Cal," "Super Sport," and "Lady Kitten Galore." Shorr admitted that he was more interested in the looks of his female announcers than in their skills at elocution, as he was booking personal appearances for his "Collector's Items." After six months, this concept was dropped and things went back as they had been.

Toward the end of 1967, in the 7 P.M. to 8 P.M. period that formerly featured a "Sinatra at Seven" program alternating with Broadway show tunes, WABX introduced a program called "Troubadour," featuring some album rock, blues, and folk music.[7] The show, hosted by station manager John Small, got a good response. Small then picked up on what was happening in San Francisco and soon the smell of incense was wafting through the thirty-third floor of the David Stott Tower in downtown Detroit, where 'ABX maintained small studios and offices. "Troubadour" was the direct link to a free-form rock format that took to the air in February of 1968.

During this early period, the station really didn't know exactly what they were supposed to be doing. Although they were trying to be an "underground" station, they were airing overproduced, flashy station breaks much like the Top 40 stations. A newspaper ad promoted all-night deejay George Brown as the "Night

Tripper" but the photo showed Brown posing in a director's chair, looking more like the host of a travel show. "Troubadour" was being broadcast remote from Arthur's, a trendy downtown discotheque, hardly an underground environment. One can only imagine someone in a "Tommy Chong voice" dropping in to say: "Hey, man...you don't do stuff like that with this kind of radio station." The breaks were soon eliminated along with anything else that resembled establishment radio.[8] John Small departed in May and John Detz, who had been engineer and operations manager, became general manager, some say because he was the only one with the key to the front door.

Dave Dixon was a native of Birmingham, Michigan, and grew up with a strong attachment to radio. "Radio was a very big thing in my life and I would go and visit all the great deejays working in Detroit while I was growing up in the fifties," he recalls. "I went to Ferris State College in Big Rapids and worked on the college station, and Don Zee hired me to work weekends at the old WPON in Pontiac when I was around seventeen."[9] Other stops included WKMI in Kalamazoo and a programmer's position with WAUK AM and FM in Milwaukee. Outside of radio, Dixon put in time as a songwriter for Peter Paul and Mary, and along with high school friend Paul Stookey, cowrote their 1967 top-ten hit "I Dig Rock 'n' Roll Music."

After living in New York, where he was exposed to pioneer progressive station WOR-FM, he returned to Detroit and hounded John Small for a job at 'ABX to no avail. A tip from the soon-to-be retiring Jim Rockwell put him in touch with Detz. Dixon recalls showing up for the interview: "Even though John Small had left the station, his girlfriend was still working at 'ABX as office manager, which was kinda strange. I don't know what sort of impression I made on her, but when she was leading me into Detz's office, I noticed her making that little sign with the rotating index finger, indicating that she thought I was a little crazy." Detz went ahead and hired Dixon anyhow.

"When I arrived, there were a couple of guys on the air going by the names Jerry O'Neill and Terry King," says Dixon. "I said, 'Both you guys are from the local area, why don't you just use your real names and maybe some people listening will know who you are and call up and say hi.' That's how Jerry Lubin and Dan Carlisle suddenly appeared on 'ABX. Of course, I can't guarantee that they will back up that story," he warns. Along with Lubin and Carlisle, there were a few holdovers from the previous format, including George Brown and Dick Crockett. Jim Hampton, formerly of WXYZ, was heard in the afternoons. In September, Larry Miller returned to Detroit and joined 'ABX and things began to fall together.

As opposed to the high-speed delivery of the new AM announcers on CKLW, deejays on 'ABX spoke in a very laid-back fashion, which included occasional coughing on the air along with the sounds of squeaking chairs and rustling papers. They started to refer to the music as rock 'n' roll again. Album cuts by artists such as Jefferson Airplane, Cream, Jimi Hendrix, Vanilla Fudge, and the Chambers Brothers along with the Beatles and Stones, were woven into "sets" with Memphis soul, such as Otis Redding and Sam and Dave, and original rock oldies by Chuck Berry and Little Richard. Other '68 musical landmarks heard often on 99.5 were "Alice's Restaurant" by Arlo Guthrie and "Fixin' to Die Rag" by Country Joe and the Fish, as well as introspective songs by Leonard Cohen and Laura Nyro. The disc jockeys had complete control of the music and how it was presented.

"Everybody liked to play their personal favorites but no one went too overboard in just one thing," recalls Jerry Lubin. "I played a lot of r&b, blues, rock 'n' roll, and just a little jazz, Dixon threw in more folk."[10]

While the AM Top 40s were playing the hit singles by many of the same artists featured on 'ABX, they were also playing "Honey" by Bobby Goldsboro, "Love Is Blue" by Paul Mauriat, and "Simon Says" by the 1910 Fruitgum Company. That was the essence of Top 40 radio–you play the hits. None of the above records were going to fit into the "underground" sound.

Radio stations such as WABX tried to convey a "cool, hip" attitude on the air. Larry Miller believes that underground radio grew out of a "hip underground movement" that was going on in the early 1960s. In the book *Voices in the Purple Haze: Underground Radio in the Sixties*, Miller tells author Michael Keith: "People who listened to folk, jazz, blues, classical and foreign music and people who read Kerouac, Pynchon and Ginsburg, were in search of hip."[11]

Along with the hip, Larry Miller felt WABX programming "reflected the radical leftist liberal political point of view" and said the station's agenda included the "legalization of dope, racial equality and the termination of the Viet Nam conflict."

An honest appraisal of WABX's audience, however, would include, besides the "hip and politically enlightened," droves of young people just getting off on the long versions of "Light My Fire" and "Time Has Come Today," played in stereo. Miller eluded to this, telling author Keith that there was "an obvious need for stations that would play the music that people were listening to at home and the way they were listening to it."

In the same book, Dan Carlisle says that the deejays on the underground stations were a "totally self-indulgent lot and sounded like it to many outsiders." He blamed this on the excessive amount of freedom that was afforded the FM announcers. Carlisle went on to say that many of the people in underground radio had grown up listening to mid-fifties rock radio where the disc jockeys were performers who certainly played the hits but, more important, made the hits. "We sensed that they loved the same music we did and that the freewheeling style of the 1950s was more fun and better radio."[12]

Although it didn't seem so at the time, underground radio in 1968 had a lot in common with the passion and excitement in the presentation of rock music in the heydays of Mickey Shorr and Tom Clay. Besides these obvious icons, Dave Dixon remembers being influenced by an announcer on WJR: "There was a guy named Buck Matthews who took over 'JR's all-night show from Clark Reid in 1956. He called it the 'all-night show without a name' and he played a pretty wild mix of music, not rock 'n' roll but a lot of way-out stuff. I also remember that he spoke in a very unaffected, conversational style and it had a lot to do with my style on WABX."[13]

Dixon and Dan Carlisle started to get into some bizarre conversations during their shift change each evening. The two encouraged listeners to "show your support for WABX and go naked for a day." Zealous station manager John Detz was outraged: "I'll kill you guys if you name a real 'Go Naked Day,'" he warned, worrying of legal problems that might arise should a listener be arrested for indecent exposure.

Aware of the many strange phone calls that came from an assortment of weirdos, the two devised a "sickest listener contest," with the winner receiving a free hour of psychiatric help. This sort of subject matter made up their nightly "eleven o'clock raps."[14]

More than just a source of music, WABX became the center of a new rock culture that was already happening in Detroit with the counterculture newspaper the *Fifth Estate,* a Love-in on Belle Ilse, put on by John Sinclair and his TransLove Energies, soon to be the White Panthers, and clubs such as the Grande Ballroom. There was hippie-inspired clothing, and Plum Street, the neighborhood trying to cop the flavor of San Francisco's Haight-Ashbury district. 'ABX provided the sound track for all of this and was viewed as having entertainment and information the audience was looking for. "It didn't take long to realize that we were having an impact," recalls Jerry Lubin. "We were pioneering something new, we were the first in Detroit."[15]

WABX built on its communal image by putting on free monthly concerts, starting with the one at Rouge Park featuring the MC 5 and SRC. There were also kite fly-ins at Belle Isle and "free movie nights."

The station gave album exposure to the local bands that had struggled on the Top 40 charts and now rocked the stages of the Grande Ballroom and the Eastown theater. The Grande, in particular, had become the Fillmore of the Motor City, and its owner, Russ Gibb, saw himself as the local equivalent of Bill Graham. All the big acts came to play at the Grande, and Motor City bands such as the Up, Rationals, Underdogs, SRC, Iggy and the Stooges, and the MC 5 opened for many of them. These groups developed national reputations as "killer" Detroit bands. The MC 5, in particular, who opened for Jimi Hendrix, rocked so hard that many famous national acts did not wish to follow them on stage.[16]

In the summer of 1969, Dennis Frawley and Bob Rudnick arrived at 'ABX from New Jersey, with their eclectic late-night show, "Kocaine Karma." The program's name had originally been coined for a regular column the two had written for New York's *East Village Other*. Their radio program was a weird mix of live conversation, music, and spoken word. "We would just converse on the air in the same way two friends would if they were sitting around at home. Rudnick's rather acidic personality along with my laconic presence seemed to jell," recalls Frawley. "We played about everything–rock, blues, and jazz like Coltrane. I remember playing a recording of Marine boot camp training and some Arthur Godfrey Hawaiian music. We also would blend in some spoken word like Malcom X or Lenny Bruce."[17] After a few months, Rudnick was fired for, among other things, insulting the bathrooms at the Grande Ballroom.

While Rudnick left for Chicago, Frawley stayed on at 'ABX, eventually settling in the six to ten evening slot.


JOHN DETZ CAME TO DAVE DIXON one day and explained that he wanted him to come up with a logo, something else that the station would be remembered for, because, if a listener mentioned it to a rating service it would count as much as call letters and frequency. "The first thing I came up with was to call the station 'Killer Radio,'" recalls Dixon. "It was a little dark so we dropped it after three months and then Alice Cooper came out with his album called 'Killer.' Anyhow, we started calling ourselves the 'Air Aces,' and it stuck."[18]

Jerry Goodwin, who had become a refugee from top 40 radio, joined the 'ABX crew in the morning. Goodwin also was among the cast of "The Sunday Funnies." Larry Monroe produced this creative throwback to old-time radio that featured Goodwin as Prince Valiant, Leonard, the night watchman, as Dick Tracy, and Harvey Ovshinsky as Sluggo.

At the beginning of 1970, 'ABX decided they needed a news director and hired Harvey, who in 1965, at seventeen, had founded the *Fifth Estate,* Detroit's first underground newspaper. This was his second time around at 'ABX, having been on in 1968 with his own memorable Sunday night show called "Up against the Wall." "It's kind of a blur, but I think we played thematic music with some talk," Harvey recalls. "One show focused on the theme of death by drowning, just to show you where my head was back then."

No one was going to confuse news reports on 'ABX with anything they might hear on typical AM broadcasts. "We played music behind the news that would fit what was happening. If the story was about a demonstration, we would play something like 'War' by Country Joe and the Fish. Of course, a lot of the time I would be taking part in the demonstration," confides Ovshinsky. "We rewrote the news for people who didn't know what was really going on and we didn't touch those Vietnam statistics being fed to the American public by mainstream media. Rather than rely on standard wire service copy, we gathered some of the national stories from the Liberation News Service and we were at our best covering things like the big 'free John Sinclair' rally in Ann Arbor. That was quite an event, with Jerry Rubin and Abbie Hoffman coming in and the music from John Lennon."[19]

On another day, Harvey recalls the whole staff being assembled for a photo shoot: "We were all there to have our picture taken for a poster or some promotion. Somebody thought it would be great if we all crammed in the elevator with the old guy who ran the thing. Well, we're all in there and just as they are going to shoot, the elevator slips and I thought we were going down thirty-three floors and no one would know because we had put on one of those long, long album cuts. We jumped out real quick and that was the end of that adventure."

In the early days, kids would say: "Yeah, that 'ABX is cool man. They don't play all those commercials like AM stations." They didn't play commercials because no one wanted to advertise on a station without listeners. Century Broadcasting and its owners, Howard and Shelley Grafman, were definitely in the business to make money and if they could do so under the guise of being an underground station, so be it. As WABX started to build a reputation, local head shops, record stores, and other counterculture enterprises began to advertise. Once the station started pulling respectable ratings, they attracted the attention of advertising agencies who wanted to run national ads for soda pop, breath mints, and other assorted merchandise that did not fit the image of a "people's radio station." There were many instances where national commercials would be rewritten by the staff, so as not to be offensive to the audience. After a while, the agencies got smarter and started producing commercials specifically for so-called underground stations.

There was constant conflict between the staff and the owners regarding what sort of advertising the station should accept. Harvey Ovshinsky recalls a volatile staff meeting that took place after it was found out that station manager John Detz was planning on accepting some advertising from the defense department: "I guess the station wasn't really doing that well financially and Detz was looking at some quick money from the army and we were all just adamant that it wasn't going to happen. Those commercials did not belong on WABX, where we were outspokenly opposed to the war."

It seemed that John Detz was in a world of his own at 'ABX, serving in the military reserves and having no qualms about putting recruitment ads on the air. In the end, the staff prevailed and the United States Army was held at bay.

Because of the popularity of WABX, people started scrambling to purchase cheesy little FM converters for their cars, as manufacturers began to produce more AM/FM radios for automobiles as well as the home.

Impressed with what was happening at WABX, WKNR-FM, which had pretty much been simulcasting Keener AM, had adopted a similar format, or nonformat if you will, in June of 1968, hiring away John Small from 'ABX to be general manager. Small eventually brought Dan Carlisle to become their top deejay. Jim Dulzo, Dick Thyne, and "Uncle Russ" Gibb also worked there. The station became quite popular for a while, although it never had the emotional or "street" ambience of 'ABX.

Russ Gibb took a phone call the night of October 12, 1969, from a listener in Ann Arbor who identified himself only as "Tom." Gibb got so caught up in the wild story that Tom was telling about Paul McCartney that he put him on the air at WKNR-FM for two hours to discuss a series of clues that supposedly proved that the famous Beatle was dead and had been replaced by an imposter. Soon people were backing up Beatle records to hear "I buried Paul" and "Turn me on, dead man." It was a sensational story that spread rapidly. McCartney even put a call through to Gibb from Scotland to say it just wasn't so, he was alive and well. One thing that couldn't be denied was the windfall of publicity that was generated for "Uncle Russ" and 'KNR-FM.[20]


ON RECORD IN 1968, Bob Seger signed with Capitol Records as the Bob Seger System and had his first national top-twenty hit with "Ramblin' Gamblin' Man." It crested at number seventeen; locally it reached number two.

Ann Arbor's "Rationals," still recording for local A Square, went to number three in Detroit with "I Need You." Also from Ann Arbor were the Amboy Dukes, led by Ted Nugent. "Journey to the Center of Your Mind" pretty much described much of the mood of 1968. It was a national hit, peaking at number fourteen.

Ric-Tic Records poured on more soul, with the Detroit Emeralds' instrumental hit "Showtime" reaching number five and the Fantastic Four nudging the local top ten with "Love You Madly." Ric-Tic and Golden World Records were so successful that Berry Gordy bought the companies from owners Eddie Wingate and JoAnne Jackson.[21] Their roster of talent, including Edwin Starr, became Motown artists. The ever resourceful Harry Balk went on to become head of A&R at Motown, where he created a new label called Rare Earth. He brought along with him a popular local club band known as the Sunliners, who became the group Rare Earth and released a string of hits.

Another soul singer named Darrell Banks had a hit with "Open the Door to Your Heart" on Revilot.

IN FEBRUARY OF 1969, there was major excitement at CKLW's offices and studios on Riverside Drive in Windsor. A serious hockey fan who was more than upset that channel 9 was not carrying a play-off game because of a blackout clause hiked to the station and with his little ax chopped one of the guy wires that held the giant six hundred-foot, thirty-two-ton tower that was home to channel 9's antenna as well as those of CKLW AM and FM.

At about ten minutes before nine, Scott Regen came into the studio, where Tom Shannon was nearing the end of his shift. "I don't think you're going to be able and finish your show tonight," said Shannon. "Someone cut one of the tower wires and it doesn't look real stable."[22] Regen went on the air anyhow while Tom left the station and walked across the street where he could get a good look at CK's leaning tower of power. When Regen was finally ordered to leave the building he responded: "I can't leave right now, I've got a contestant waiting on the line!"[23] After this act of disc jockey heroism, Scottie threw on an album and quickly left the already evacuated building.

Meanwhile, morning man Charlie Van Dyke was en route to

CKLW's transmitter site some twenty-three miles away in Harrow, Ontario. Upon arriving, Charlie and his engineer surveyed the equipment: one microphone and one turntable that appeared not to have been used in years, if ever. Van Dyke started emergency broadcasting with the turntable that played at the wrong speed and because there was no 45 rpm adapter, the records were slipping off center. For a couple of hours, listeners heard a broken Big 8. Van Dyke did a great job explaining the situation and after a few hours the tower was secured and programming resumed from the main studios, and no one tuning in would have had any idea of how bad the station had sounded earlier.

IN MARCH, WJBK returned to rock with a hybrid "top 40" format put together by new program director Mike Scott, coming in from KGB in San Diego. Scott brought along West Coast hipsters Lee "Baby" Sims and K. O. Bailey to join Detroiters Tom Shannon (moving over from CKLW), Hank O'Neil, Tom Dean, and Jim Hampton.

Sims was one of the cockiest characters in radio. Usually a creature of the night, Scott wanted to be bold and put him on in the morning. Sims had a very hip and somewhat nasty way of speaking. One particular morning he was complaining on the air that his coffeepot was missing from the lounge: "I don't know who would take a thing like that, it's just a stainless steel coffeepot and makes really bad stuff. The coffee is purple and has little red specs that glow." After the next record, Lee came on the air all excited:

> You won't believe what just happened, I mean it is incredible! I was walking down the hall when I heard yelling coming from the ladies room: "Help, help!" Being that I am a gentleman from the South, I was hesitant about going in but the screams continued: "Help, help!" I opened the door and there was this woman being attacked by the stainless steel coffeepot! Her dress was ripped and tattered and her stocking was torn. She was bleeding all over. It was horrible. I grabbed her out of there and now the coffeepot has barricaded itself in the ladies' room. I know this is hard to believe, ladies and gentlemen, but announcers don't lie. It's against FCC regulations. Ladies and

gentlemen, as soon as she calms down, I am going to try and have an interview with the woman who was attacked. I want to ask her what it's like to be savagely mauled by a thirty-cup stainless steel industrial coffeepot.[24]

Warm, fuzzy memories of mornings with Marc Avery's little girl, reminding her dad about the coffee man in the hall, were fading fast.

IN MAY, Lee Alan returned to nighttime radio in Detroit with a show on WHFI-FM. He brought along all his old routines, including the "horn," but when "Zing! Went the Strings of My Heart" collided with "In-a-Godda-Da-Vida," the show just crashed and burned.[25]

THE FM DIAL CONTINUED TO EXPLODE as WXYZ-FM started carrying the prerecorded album rock programming of their parent company, ABC. The "Love" format with "Brother John" premiered in the spring of 1969 and was an attempt by the corporate world to move in on the latest trend.[26] Hal Neal, the savior of WXYZ in the fifties and now head of all the ABC-owned stations, gave his blessing to turning ABC's FM facilities progressive. It lasted about a year and then WXYZ-FM went their own way as a free-form rock station, with Dick Kernen as program director. Arthur Penhallow, who worked at WNRS in Ann Arbor, was the first disc jockey hired on the station that would soon change its call letters to WRIF.

By 1970, FM penetration in Detroit was nearing 30 percent. It seemed that the lines had been drawn: AM Top 40 on one side and FM progressive rock on the other.

WABX continued to be innovative on FM. Staff members, including Dave Dixon, Dennis Frawley, and Mark Parenteau, hosted a series of twelve two-hour TV shows called "Detroit Tubeworks," simulcast over 'ABX, with performances by Johnny Winter, Alice Cooper, Phil Ochs, and Melanie, interspersed with some far-out commercials, selling products like Stinkers Forever incense. Ann Christ became an early female voice on the station. WABX also had a great promotion, where close to nine thousand loyal listeners sent in for Day-Glo red and green plastic "secret identification and decoder rings."

CKLW STAYED THE COURSE as the mass-appeal station of choice: "Whole Lotta Love" by Lead Zeppelin being played right alongside "Close to You" by the Carpenters. Deejays such as Ed Mitchell, Walt "Baby Love," Pat Holiday, and Steve Hunter kept it cookin' with nonstop hits and contests as the Big 8 went on to become one of the three most listened to radio stations in North America and among the most influential to get a record played on.

CHAPTER **22**

# Dateline Detroit: The 1970s

KEN DRAPER, FORMER PROGRAM DIRECTOR OF WCFL IN CHICAGO, takes over at WCAR and revamps the sagging station with a heavy personality/middle-of-the-road format.[1] Dave Prince incorporates telephone talk into his mid-morning show. Ray Otis, Wayne "Huggy Bear" Phillips, Dan O'Shea, Warren Pierce, and Ed Busch are other voices. The verdict: heavy payroll, light ratings.

WJBK radio goes country, changing its call letters to WDEE. The industry joke is that the new calls stand for "we've done everything else."

Dick Purtan accepts an offer to do mornings at WNBC in New York. He unpacks when his bosses at ABC threaten to sue NBC.[2]

Bob Green returns to Keener as program director in March of 1970 and puts together a great-sounding station, with Jim Tate, Dan "Hugger" Henderson, and Scott Regen back on board. Again, CKLW has too much muscle. After one year, Green and company are out and WKNR begins its final descent to oblivion.[3]

CKLW runs into problems of its own when the Canadian government forces American-owned RKO General to sell the station to Canadian owners (Baton Broadcasting), and the Canadian Radio Television Commission (CRTC) takes action to protect "Canadian culture." Stations are required to play 30 percent

Canadian content in their music.[4] Running short on Paul Anka and Guess Who product, music director Rosalie Trombley swings into action and starts breaking hits by Canadian artists such as the Bells ("Stay Awhile"), the Stampeders ("Sweet City Woman"), and Gordon Lightfoot ("If You Could Read My Mind"). CKLW remains solid, despite the departure of the Drake-Chenault consultancy.

Mickey Shorr returns to the airwaves briefly, with his "Night Train" theme, playing country on WEXL.[5] The rest of the time he can be found taking care of business at Mickey Shorr's Tape Shack on Woodward Avenue in Royal Oak.

At WCBS-FM in New York, Tom Clay tells his audience: "Tonight, I'm going to have intercourse with your mind."[6] After rest and relaxation in L.A., Tom makes another run at Detroit listeners when W4 general manager Don Barrett contacts him about playing oldies in the evening. The next morning Clay hops in his car and drives almost straight to the Motor City. Listeners hear what sounds like a Sermon on the Mount each night from the station's Jefferson Avenue studios. Tom lasts a year, which is longer than usual, then heads back to California.[8]

In 1971, it's "Tom Clay with a bullet" as he records in music and spoken word a dramatic interpretation of "What the World Needs Now Is Love/Abraham, Martin and John." In what must be a favor returned from long ago in Detroit, the record is released on Motown's new Mowest label and becomes a national hit, reaching number eight on the *Billboard* charts.

In the fall of 1971, WRIF, suffering from anemic ratings, drops the free-form approach. Consultant Lee Abrams designs a new "album-oriented rock" format and calls the station "Rock 'n' Stereo 101." Deejays stay low key but now work from a playlist. Only the best cuts from the best albums are featured and the ratings rocket up. No more eclectic sounds from left field. It's Lead Zeppelin, Elton John, Moody Blues, and the Stones.[9] As the Vietnam war winds down, the attraction of counterculture politics fades from the airwaves. There is no need for underground radio. The sound that had awakened FM from its long sleep begins to drift away as WKNR-FM transforms itself into "Stereo Island." WABX remains an island of its own.

Tom Dean gets the town hot and heavy with the top-rated "Fem

Forum" show on country-formatted WDEE. Dean, relying on a combination of talk and music punctuators, takes calls from listeners, who share intimacies on the air in this forerunner of Ricki Lake–Jerry Springer–style talk shows. Deano Day is a big draw for the "Big D" in the morning.[10]

Martha Jean the Queen and the rest of the black air staff stage a strike against Booth Broadcasting to protest the fact that, aside from the on-air personalities, there are no blacks employed anywhere else at WJLB. As the issue is settled, Martha Jean is relegated to an early-morning gospel program.[11]

WXYZ continues a successful middle-of-the-road format, led by Dick Purtan in the morning. WWJ survives on AM by moving into an all-news format. WCAR goes Top 40, then progressive, then back to MOR and eventually country as WCXI. Keener 13 never recovers, changing into WNIC and then WMTG, playing Motown oldies.

A heartbreaker: Motown packs up and leaves Detroit for the sunshine of southern California. Many of the great artists are lost in the shuffle as Berry Gordy focuses more on the film career of Diana Ross.

WQTE plays its last easy-listening LP cut from Greenfield Village and starts cranking out oldies as "Honey Radio," WHND.

After six years at the top, CKLW suffers its first ratings decline in 1973. Bill Hennes, who as a kid assisted Mickey Shorr, before going on to a successful radio career of his own, is brought in as program director to "toughen up" the station. Bill Gable, Ted Richards, and "Super Max" Kinkel are among the current "Big 8 Jocks." CK's main competition comes from WDRQ, proving that Top 40 can be successful on FM. Joey Ryan and Al Casey play the hits in stereo.

WJR airs their final live music broadcast with the WJR Orchestra, when longtime music director/bandleader Jimmy Clark retires in March of 1974.[12] Marc Avery stays on as host of "Open House," but with records.

The departure of Michael Collins from WRIF's hip topical morning show ushers in the era of the supposedly zany, but carefully contrived, "morning zoos and wake-up crews."[13]

Steve Dahl passes through WABX and W4 on the way to Chicago and on W4's horizon is one Howard Stern.

By the mid-seventies, the "fly by the seat of your pants" days of radio are coming to a close as new "consultants" begin popping up behind every tower, brandishing the latest research techniques designed to fine-tune station formats to appeal to more specific audiences. As FM reaches parity with AM, the number of radio stations and formats proliferate and nothing is left to chance. Top 40 and MOR give way to AOR and CHR. Stations feature mellow rock, light favorites, urban contemporary, heavy metal, all oldies, all news, all talk, and young country as the medium continues to fragment. Technological advances turn radio programming into an exact science, harnessed by computers.

Yet, floating through the static, on airwaves somewhere in the time compendium, are the sounds of "Jack the Bellboy," spinning 78s from "Swoon Boulevard and Jive Alley," Gentile and Binge wildly singing the praises of "Conn's Clothes," Eddie Chase—hand cupped over ear—in the "Make Believe Ballroom," Fred Wolf percolatin' in the "Wandering Wigloo," Robin Seymour, bobbin' with malt shop favorites, Mickey Shorr checking in with his "Time Tellin' Mo-chine," and "Frantic Ernie D with r&b." There's a "guy by the name of Clay" and "Lee Alan, on the Horn." If you listen closely, you can tune in "The Keener Sound," J. P. in the "Music Hall," a "Queen Named Martha Jean," early Dick Purtan put-ons, the Big 8, and 'ABX. They're all out there, mile markers in the history of pop music radio in the Motor City. It was a simpler, less sophisticated time, but what a great, fun time it was.

# Radio Round-up

**Lee Alan:** In the seventies, Lee started his own advertising agency, producing commercials for various accounts including Mickey Shorr's Tape Shack, Honda, and Birmingham Chrysler-Plymouth, as well as other car dealers around the country. In 1993, Lee produced an oldies show heard on CKLW-FM called "Back in the '60s Again." He remains president of Lee Alan Media, a full-service, Bloomfield Hills–based ad agency.

**Marc Avery:** After a ten-year run at WJR, Marc worked for WCZY and CKLW in the eighties. Recently retired, he resides in Florida.

**Ralph Binge:** The creative genius of Ralph Binge was silenced prematurely when he died from a heart attack in 1963 at fifty-eight.

**Bristoe Bryant:** This pioneer of black radio in the Motor City suffered a stroke in the eighties. He has since passed away.

**Jay Butler:** He was a top disc jockey for WCHB and WJLB for many years. Today he serves as program director at WQBH.

**Dan Carlisle:** An original Air Ace at WABX, Dan left Detroit after working for WKNR-FM. Stops along the way included KLOS Los Angeles and WNEW-FM New York. He was last heard from in San Francisco.

**Dave Carr:** After broadcasting from car lots all over Detroit and serving as program director for WEXL, Dave built his own radio station

239

from the ground up. He still operates WKKM in Harrison, Michigan.

**Eddie Chase:** After the ill-fated "target 560" format at WQTE, Eddie moved to Washington state and worked in programming and sales for a music service for radio stations. In 1964, he returned to Chicago and became a sales and marketing executive for a television publication. He retired in 1985 and is living in southern California.

**Tom Clay:** After years of hopping back and forth from L.A. to Detroit, Tom finally settled down in Los Angeles and in the mid-seventies, opened his own business on Sunset Boulevard, called Lip Service. Later the name was changed to Tom Clay Productions. He taught voice-over techniques and was featured on many commercials himself. On the television show "Santa Barbara," he provided the voice for God. The day before Thanksgiving, 1995, "a guy by the name of Clay" passed away after a long, tough battle with cancer. Casey Kasem delivered the eulogy at his funeral. Tom never stopped looking at his style of radio as an art form. His three daughters remain his biggest fans.

**Michael Collins:** After WRIF, Collins did talk radio at WXYZ before moving into television news positions in Lansing and Cincinnati. He came back to Detroit in 1995 to work for WJBK-TV. Today he resides in southern California.

**Bob Cordell:** After living the life of a radio nomad, he retired to southern Florida, where he operates an Internet music service.

**Mort Crowley:** After his famous on-the-air tirade at WKNR in 1964, Mort blew out of Detroit, never to return. Eventually, he landed and stabilized at KXOK in St. Louis, where he held down mornings for many years. Most recently he was the conservative host of a talk show carried by a satellite network. Mort Crowley passed away in 1995.

**Toby David:** Good old Captain Jolly retired to Arizona in 1971, but got back into television work for a while and then public relations. He died of a heart attack at age eighty while performing for a group of senior citizens in Mesa, Arizona, in September of 1994.

**Bud Davies:** The guy with the cuff links and great smile relocated to Toronto, where he worked at stations, including CFRB. In the eighties he moved to Florida and ran an oldies station until retiring in the early nineties. He still resides in Florida.

**Dave Dixon:** After a seven-year run with WABX, Dixon spent the rest of the seventies hosting an all-night movie program on cable TV in Florida. He returned to Detroit in the eighties to host a highly acclaimed free-form show on WDET-FM. Before his death in 1999, he was hosting a weekly arts and entertainment program, "Dave Dixon Radio Magazine," on WXYT, where he was known as "Detroit's cultural czar." Although he liked to project the image of a grumpy curmudgeon, he was only polite, cooperative, and enthusiastic regarding the publication of this book. He will be missed.

**Larry Dixon:** Larry hung on through the seventies with radio shows at talk stations WTAK and WPON in Pontiac before leaving the business. He resides in Detroit and has been successful in the auto financing business.

**Bill Drake:** After severing ties with CKLW in 1971, the Drake/Chenault team programmed WJR-FM as an oldies station for a time. The company then went on to become involved with syndicated programming, delivered by satellite.

**Paul Drew:** The Detroit native left CKLW to program WIBG in Philadelphia, and then returned to CK' briefly in 1970 and later as a consultant. Drew stayed on the cutting edge of pop music radio, programming KFRC in San Francisco, and in the mid-seventies taking over KHJ in Los Angeles from the Drake organization. He has remained active as a programming consultant as well as being successful in nonbroadcast business ventures.

**Ernie Durham:** The one and only "Frantic Ernie" stayed on at WJLB and its successor, WQBH, for years, although he worked at WJR for a time. He came out of retirement in 1992 to host a Saturday night r&b oldies show on WDET-FM. At home on December 2 of that year, Ernie complained of chest pains and went to lie down while Jacqueline, his wife of thirty-two years, prepared some soup. When she went to their bedroom, he was gone. She said he was the "kindest, gentlest man she had known." People who knew him felt the same way.

**Bob Eggington:** The "night beat" guy from WJBK became a newsman for WXYZ and later worked for WHFI-FM in the 1970s. He has since passed away.

**Dennis Frawley:** He survived various purges and managed to stay on the air at WABX for eleven years. After a part-time position at WOMC in the early 1980s, Frawley returned to his home state of

Florida. He remarried, got a real estate license, and settled down to raise two daughters.

**Joe Gentile:** The first half of the legendary morning comedy team of Gentile and Binge returned to CKLW after the team's demise at WJBK in the mid-fifties. He could be heard on a nightly sports broadcast well into the sixties. He and Ralph did occasional commercials, including a Dodge campaign, until Ralph's death. During his final years, Joe resided at the St. Joseph Home for the Aged in Detroit. He was eighty-six when he died of complications from pneumonia in January of 1995.

**Russ Gibb:** The former owner of the Grande Ballroom and the man that buried Paul on WKNR-FM, Gibb went on to do cable television talk shows. Today he is still teaching media classes at Dearborn High School.

**Jerry Goodwin:** He left 'ABX to teach theology in the Irish Hills in the mid-seventies. At last sighting, he and his wife were operating an antiques store in Michigan.

**Bob Green:** Keener's "Greenie Bob" relocated to Houston, Texas, in the mid-seventies, where he started his own company. "Bob Green Productions" is still in business, producing commercials for advertising agencies and clients all over the country.

**Jim Hampton:** After WJBK, Jim worked for WCAR and then went on to WLS in Chicago in the mid-seventies. Today he is president of a media promotion company based in southern California.

**Bill Hennes:** Bill left CKLW in the late seventies to program WMAQ in Chicago, and made it the number one country station in the nation. In 1981, he founded Bill Hennes and Associates, a full-service broadcast consulting company that serves hundreds of clients. Hennes resides and works near Wilmington, North Carolina.

**Joe Howard:** "Joltin' Joe" became program director at WGPR after leaving WJLB in 1967. In the seventies he returned to his hometown of Houston, Texas, where he recently retired from a human resources position he held with the city.

**Specs Howard:** After the demise of "Martin and Howard" on WXYZ, the team briefly returned to Cleveland before breaking up. Specs came back to Detroit and still operates the Specs Howard School of Broadcasting.

**Dave Hull:** He was hardly in town long enough to unpack before being asked to "vacate the premises" of WQTE in 1961. Radio stops in

Ohio and Florida eventually led to a long run at KRLA in Los Angeles. He remained in L.A. for the rest of his career. Today he is semiretired and living in southern California.

**Casey Kasem:** In 1970, after close to seven years with KRLA in Los Angeles, Casey had an idea for a national countdown show. A company called Watermark thought it would fly and began syndicating "American Top 40." After a contract dispute in 1991, Casey started his own show. In 1998, he returned as host of AT 40. Kasem also found success as the voice of Robin on the "Superfriends" cartoon series and Shaggy on "Scooby Doo." His voice has also been heard on thousands of radio and TV commercials. He resides in the Los Angeles area and is active in many humanitarian causes, including animal rights and homeless rights.

**Terry Knight:** "Terry Knight and the Pack" sputtered out after a handful of regional hits. Terry went behind the scenes as the group metamorphosed into Grand Funk Railroad and he became a millionaire as their manager. Knight resides in Arizona.

**Ron Knowles:** R. K. has remained active in the broadcasting industry, although the "kid" who was laying down the rock 'n' roll sounds on the "Platter Express" moved to the world of "Just Beautiful Music" programming stations in Phoenix and Dallas before returning to Detroit at WJR-FM in 1975. He later went back to Dallas, then on to Seattle, and today resides in Colorado.

**Robert E. Lee:** The Rebel lost his cause when WJBK stopped rocking in 1964. He stayed on as an all-purpose announcer for WJBK radio and television until the late sixties when he moved to Denver and worked for KHOW and KLZ. He is retired and residing in the Mile High City.

**Jerry Lubin:** An original member of the 'ABX staff when they launched "underground" radio in 1968, Lubin moved over to WRIF and then on to San Francisco and Washington, D.C. Returning to Detroit, he worked at WLLZ and then went back to 'ABX before signing off and going to work for the post office.

**Byron MacGregor:** The best remembered voice of CKLW "20/20 News" died in January 1995 of complications of pneumonia. He had gone on to be news director at the Windsor based station. His dramatic recording of "The Americans" became a million-seller in the winter of 1974. He donated one hundred thousand dollars in profits from the record to the Red Cross. His real name was Gary Mack and

he was married to JoAnne Wright, who was better known as helicopter traffic reporter, Jo Jo Shutty on CKLW in the late seventies.

**Bob Maxwell:** "Luke the Spook" never rode again, but Bob had great
success at WCBS in New York. He did even better doing national
commercial voice-over work. He is now retired, dividing his time
between southern California and a cabin in British Columbia.

**J. P. McCarthy:** By the late seventies, records were heard more infre-
quently on WJR. J. P. made a smooth transition to talk and information on his morning program and held on to the number one
position in the ratings. His Christmas Carol Sings and St. Patrick's
Day parties became legendary. His contributions to charity were
many, but he is probably most associated with the PAL Golf
Tournament for the Police Athletic League. McCarthy was an icon.
*Advertising Age* magazine estimated that J. P. was responsible for
more than 40 percent of the $18.4 million in advertising revenue at
WJR. He was inducted into the Radio Hall of Fame in 1992 and
received the Marconi Award from the National Association of
Broadcasters in 1994. He had been named National Radio
Personality of the Year by *Billboard* magazine on four occasions.
On August 16, 1995, the Motor City was stunned when J. P.
McCarthy died from a rare blood ailment called myelodysplastic
syndrome. Two days later, twenty-eight Detroit radio stations
observed one minute of silence in his honor. His funeral was tele-
vised by two stations and carried by WJR.

**Don McLeod:** After the payola fiasco, McCleod never again worked for
a major Detroit station. In the sixties he did an afternoon show at
WPON in suburban Pontiac and later went into real estate. He is no
longer living.

**Larry Morrow:** Remembered by Detroit radio listeners as "Duke
Windsor," Larry has been one of Cleveland's top radio personalities for more than thirty years and is currently doing mornings in
that city on WQAL.

**Ross Mulholland:** After WQTE, Mulholland took ownership of WGPR.
He has since passed away.

**Harvey Ovshinsky:** Also remembered for cocreating "Open City,"
Detroit's original crisis center, the former radical news director of
WABX is an award-winning filmmaker and president of HO
Productions, a most successful capitalist enterprise.

**Conrad Patrick:** After working for WJBK and WHFI-FM, Connie fought a battle with cancer and won. He popped up in Florida in the eighties and in a strange pairing, cohosted a cable movie show with Dave Dixon. He is no longer living.

**Arthur Penhallow:** Approaching his thirtieth year with WRIF, Penhallow has surely set a record for stability, especially at a rock station. Fans continue to tune in the "Grand Poobah of Detroit Rock 'n' Roll," every afternoon to hear him growl: "Baby!"

**Dave Prince:** "Sangoo" left Detroit for the warm sun of southern California in the mid-seventies. In L.A. he was on the air at stations KKDJ and KISS and then went into business with another former Detroiter, Jim Hampton. Prince came back to Detroit and joined WCZY in 1981 and then worked for CKLW during their "Music of Your Life" period from about 1984 to 1991. He is retired and living in Michigan where he can be seen cruising around in his van listening to Vivaldi.

**Dick Purtan:** After ten years with WXYZ, Purtan moved to CKLW to work with general manager Herb McCord, a highly regarded broadcaster who had lead CK' through some very successful years. One year after Dick's arrival, McCord resigned and the station started to flounder. One creative programmer instituted a format called "rock and talk." According to Purtan, "the rockers hated the talk and the talkers hated the rock." By 1983, Dick was working under program director and veteran Detroit broadcaster Dave Shafer at WCZY and stayed on as that station became WKQI, of which he was also an investor. Dick Purtan can now be heard in the morning presiding over "Purtan's People" on WOMC, where he has taken on the mantle of senior broadcaster in Detroit. Dick was honored with the Marconi Radio Award in 1993. His annual "radiothons" have raised hundreds of thousands of dollars to help feed and clothe Detroit's needy each year.

**Bill Randle:** The host of the "Interracial Goodwill Hour" went on to own Cleveland radio in the fifties. Today he is practicing law as well as hosting a morning radio show in that city.

**Scott Regen:** Scottie went into record promotion and today resides in his hometown of New York City.

**Clark Reid:** Clark returned to Detroit in 1965 and began a very successful career with Ross Roy Advertising. He recently retired and is residing in the Detroit area.

**Joey Reynolds:** After leaving WXYZ in 1966, Joey was up and down the dial, including stints at WDRC in Hartford and WNBC in New York. He returned to Detroit in 1984 at WHYT-FM and then left again. Today he can be heard nationwide doing an all-night talk show on the WOR network, based in New York, that is carried on one hundred stations across the country. He has also created a world-famous cheesecake.

**Mike Rivers:** Michael Donahue left the Motor City in the fall of 1968 to become Ed Richards at WIBG in Philadelphia. He then held other on-air and programming positions at stations, including WKLO in Louisville and KVIL, Dallas. No longer in radio Mike resides in Nashville.

**Jim Rockwell:** In the seventies he gave away his incredible collection of jazz recordings and moved to the Southwest, where he took up photography.

**Joel Sebastian:** When he left Detroit for WINS in New York in April of 1965, it was a brief stop. After only four months that station went to an all-news format and Joel then joined KLAC in Los Angeles. A short time later, that station went all sports. At the start of 1966, Sebastian moved to Chicago, where he became a longtime favorite at WCFL and WLS. In the eighties, he moved to New York and successfully pursued a voice-over career while doing weekend air work at WNEW. He was heard in Detroit in the early eighties on the syndicated "Solid Gold Country" show carried by W4. Joel Sebastian died of bone cancer in 1986 at the age of fifty-three. He influenced countless future broadcasters growing up in Detroit during the early sixties.

**Robin Seymour:** "Bobbin' Robin" has had his share of ups and downs, but today he is operating a successful infomercial production company, based in the Los Angeles area.

**Dave Shafer:** He had an off-and-on career at CKLW, spanning some thirty years. During the off time, Dave also served as program director at WCAR, WOMC, and WCZY, and whenever possible, he was loyal to his Detroit radio brothers, giving them first consideration when there was a job opening. He is retired and living in Florida, where the only hits he focuses on are on the golf course.

**Tom Shannon:** Mrs. Shannon's boy swung in and out of Detroit several times and then spent four years hosting on cable TV's "Home Shopping Network." Today he is broadcasting on WHTT-FM in his hometown of Buffalo, New York.

**Mickey Shorr:** After surviving four heart attacks, Mickey died during a triple bypass operation in February of 1988. His epitaph was the words he lived by: "If it ain't fun, I don't do it." Shorr was an original. His name lives on through a chain of car stereo stores.

**Martha Jean Steinberg:** After the old WJLB-AM, which had switched call letters with its FM sister, WMZK, was purchased, Martha Jean helped found WQHB, where she served as vice president and general manager for some fifteen years. In 1997, with help from Michigan National Bank, she bought the station. Martha Jean serves as president and general manager and can still be heard on the air each day.

**Gary Stevens:** After almost four years at WMCA in New York, Gary Stevens moved into a management positions in Phoenix and Minneapolis before returning to Detroit as general manager of WLLZ in 1980. Today he is the president of Gary Stevens and Associates, a New York–based company that brokers the sale of radio stations.

**Jack Surrell:** The star of the "Top of the Town" started a whole new career with the Defense Department, working with computers after leaving radio in the late sixties. He is now retired and living in the Detroit area. He recently performed a piano concert to benefit the Detroit Public Library.

**Swingin' Sweeney:** After programming positions in Toledo and Wheeling, West Virginia, Frank Sweeney went to work for the Miss Universe Pageant. Today he has his own company in New York, which produces beauty contests.

**Rosalie Trombley:** Bob Seger wrote a song about CKLW's famous music director called "Rosalie" that appeared on his album "Back in '72." Rosalie stayed with the station until the Big 8 expired, on October 18, 1984. After working on an ill-fated radio project in Toronto, she returned to the Detroit area in 1987 and for a time was music director at an FM station being programmed by former CKLW disc jockey Pat Holiday. Today she resides in Windsor.

**Joe Van:** The "ole lover boy" from CKLW spent the rest of his career in Montreal. He died of cancer in the mid-eighties.

**Fred Weiss:** After his "blooper of bloopers" on WXYZ, Fred wound up working for WMAL-TV in Washington, D.C. He still resides in the D.C. area.

**J. Michael Wilson:** After departing Detroit, J. Michael and Rodney the

Wonder Rodent made stops in Toronto, Boston, Buffalo, and Cleveland where the two finally got out of the business.

**Paul Winter:** When WTAK dropped its talk format in 1970, Paul continued to work on and off in radio and TV, including stints at W4, WJR, and WTVS-TV before turning to teaching full-time. He retired in 1995 as professor emeritus in humanities from Wayne State University.

**Fred Wolf:** The "old percolator" was more than happy to leave the world of Top 40 radio behind in 1965. He became the proprietor of the Eastland Bowl until he retired. In 1978, Fred suffered a stroke that caused him to lose the ability to speak. Today he resides in an assisted living home.

**Don Zee:** "Daddy Zee," real name Don Zamenski, died from a gun accident at his home in Midland, Texas, in August of 1984. He was fifty-four.

MEANWHILE, THE ORIGINAL JACK THE BELLBOY, **Ed McKenzie,** is alive and well as of 1999. He has had a most interesting life, making dozens of trips to Europe, China, Japan, Indonesia, Africa, and other parts of the globe. At seventy-six, he traveled to Italy, climbed Mount Vesuvius, and learned to speak Italian. He was making plans to sell his home and move to Florence, Italy, when he met a woman from the past and they started a new life together in Michigan.

In the mid-eighties, Ed began making videos about his art collection, writing narratives, and adding background music. He expanded his work to include music and history as well as art. He has produced some of the finest jazz videos and many are available in libraries and archives from New York to New Orleans. He has donated much of his photo collection, which includes pictures of the greatest black jazz musicians, to the African American Museum in Detroit. At eighty-eight, Ed stays busy producing shows and documentaries. He can look back, for better or worse, at more than fifty years of Detroit radio and much of the programming he set the tone for.

# Notes

## 1. The Bellboy and the Bobby-soxers

1. Ed McKenzie biography tribute from the Tuesday Club of Flushing, Mich.
2. Interview with Ed McKenzie.
3. Ibid.
4. References to recording artists are from my interview with Ed McKenzie.
5. Interview with Ed McKenzie.
6. McKenzie, quoted in "Disc Jockey Review," *Variety,* Nov. 5, 1947.
7. Interview with Ed McKenzie.
8. Osgood, *Wyxie Wonderland,* 249.
9. Interview with Ed McKenzie.
10. "Disc Jockey Review," *Variety,* Nov. 5, 1947.
11. Kubrick, "Saga of Jack the Bellboy," in *International Jazz Record Collector's Journal,* Summer 1995.
12. Ibid.
13. Interview with Ed McKenzie.
14. The Paradise as described by Ed McKenzie in interview.
15. Interview with Bill Randle.
16. Interview with Jack Surrell.

17. Ibid.
18. "Dean of Discs," *Radio-TV Mirror,* Sept. 1953.
19. Interview with Eddie Chase.
20. Owens, "Chasin' Chase," *Band Leaders,* Jan. 1945.
21. Eddie Chase quoted by Ed McKenzie in interview.
22. "Alias Jack the Bellboy," *Radio-TV Mirror,* 1951.
23. Promotional pamphlet, *Celebrating Five Years of Public Service, WJBK-TV,* 1953.
24. Kubrick, "Saga."
25. "Early Morning Frolic," *Radio-TV Mirror,* 1951, p.26.
26. Promotional pamphlet, *Celebrating Five Years of Public Service, WJBK-TV,* 1953.
27. "The Prop Man and the Plumber," *Radio-TV Mirror,* 1953, p. 10.
28. *The Real Captain Jolly,* family memoir, 1980.
29. "Early Morning Frolic."
30. "Memoirs That Jingle," *Detroit Free Press,* Feb. 5, 1994, p. 3F.
31. Rememberance of listener Gary Carson.
32. "Radio's Zaniest Team," *Teens,* Jan. 1949.
33. "Script Tease," *Liberty,* Oct. 1, 1945.
34. "Early Morning Frolic."
35. "The Prop Man and the Plumber."
36. Quoted in Osgood, *Wyxie Wonderland,* 248.
37. "Spell It Mulholland, *Radio-TV Mirror,* Aug. 1947.
38. *The Real Captain Jolly.*
39. Dunning, *Tune In Yesterday,* 196–98.
40. Interview with Ed McKenzie.
41. Osgood, *Wyxie Wonderland,* 291.
42. Interview with Ed McKenzie.
43. "Disc Jockey Review," Nov. 5, 1947.
44. *Guest,* 7.
45. Interview with Ed Mckenzie.
46. "Prince of the Airwaves," *Radio-TV Mirror,* July 1955.

## 2. Sounds and Styles

1. "Wolf at the Door," *Radio-TV Mirror,* June 1956.
2. Osgood, *Wyxie Wonderland,* 277.
3. "Wolf at the Door."

4. Osgood, *Wyxie Wonderland,* 291.
5. Interview with Emily Wolf.
6. Ibid.
7. Ibid.
8. "Radio Log," *Detroit News,* 1951.
9. "A Winter's Tale," *Radio-TV Mirror,* Sept. 1956, p. 76
10. Interview with Paul Winter.
11. Ibid.
12. Audiotape recording, WXYZ, Nov. 5, 1956.
13. Interview with Paul Winter.
14. Interview with Jack Surrell.
15. Ibid.
16. Lee Cotten, *Shake, Rattle, and Roll: The Golden Age of American Rock 'n' Roll,* 77.
17. "Michigan Madman," *Radio-TV Mirror,* Mar. 1951.
18. Interview with Paul Winter.
19. "WJBK's McLeod Resigns," *Detroit Free Press,* Nov. 24, 1959.
20. Interview with Clark Reid.
21. Interview with Bob Maxwell.
22. "Your Boy Bud," *Radio-TV Mirror,* July 1954.
23. Interview with Bob Cordell.
24. Interview with Ron Knowles.
25. Whitburn, *Top Pop Records.*
26. Warner, *The Billboard Book of American Singing Groups.*
27. Merlis and Seay, *Heart and Soul: A Celebration of Black Music in America.*
28. Jackson, *Big Beat Heat,* 110.
29. Background information on LeRoy White is from the Burton Historical Library and from interviews with Jack Surrell and Bill Randle.
30. "Prince of the Airwaves," *Radio-TV Mirror,* Sept. 1955.

### 3. "You're Not Planning on Staying in This Business, Are You?"

1. Interview with Robin Seymour.
2. As quoted by Robin Seymour in interview.
3. Interview with Robin Seymour.
4. Liner notes, *Cruisin' 1956,* Increase Records.

5. Re-creation recorded in *Cruisin' 1956*.
6. Interview with Bill Randle.

## 4. "He's a Rockin' Mo-chine"

1. "Shorr Gets Big Send-off," *Billboard*, May 12, 1956.
2. 'Teeners Rally to Mickey," *Detroit News*, May 1956.
3. Evely, "Views 'n' Reviews...Radio," school newspaper column, 1957.
4. Interview with Joe Howard.
5. "DJ Mickey Shorr Proves Showbiz Real Friendly," *Detroit Times*, June 1957.
6. Philips, "Good Buddy Mickey Shorr Makes Hit with Music Fans," *Guardian*, 1958.
7. Shorr, "Mickey Tells How to Be a DJ," *Teen Life*, Sept. 21, 1956.
8. Quote by Mickey Shorr from story.
9. Taylor, "Mickey Shorr May Be Back," *Teen Life*, July 27, 1956.
10. Mattson, "Mickey Shorr: Still Riding the Airwaves," *Daily Tribune*, May 20, 1984.
11. Taylor, "Mickey Shorr May Be Back."
12. Talbert, "Notebook," *Detroit Free Press*, Aug. 12, 1982.
13. "DJ Mickey Shorr Proves Showbiz Real Friendly."
14. *Detroit Times*, Nov. 23, 1959.
15. "DJ Mickey Shorr Proves Showbiz Real Friendly."
16. "Mickey Shorr: Still Riding the Airwaves."
17. Shorr, "It's the Gimmicks," *Detroit Free Press*, Sept. 1, 1956.
18. *Teen Life*, July 27, 1956.
19. Interview with Robin Seymour.
20. "Detroit's Own Mickey Shorr," program notes for Fox theater Rock 'n' Rollorama, Jan. 1956.
21. "Rock 'n' Rollorama Breaks All House Records at Fox theatre, Detroit," *Billboard*, Jan. 1956.
22. Jackson, *Big Beat Heat*, 107–8.
23. Interview with May Shorr.
24. "Presley on Shorr Show," *Detroit Free Press*, Mar. 1956.
25. News item from *Cashbox*, 1956.
26. News item about WJBK's decision to drop Shorr.
27. Robin Seymour, quoted in newspaper column.

28. Mickey Shorr, quoted in "Farewell Salute," *Cashbox,* May 12, 1956.
29. Interview with May Shorr.
30. "Shorr on the Air Aug. 27," *Teen Life,* Aug. 24, 1956.
31. "Mickey Tells How to Be a DJ."
32. Interview with Bill Hennes.
33. Interview with Paul Winter.
34. Interview with Ed McKenzie.
35. Interview with May Shorr.
36. Interview with Bob Cordell.
37. Notes from program from "Record Stars of '57," Mar. 1957.
38. Notes from program from "Rock 'n' Rollorama Easter Edition," Apr. 1957.
39. "Presley on Shorr Show," *Billboard,* Mar. 1957.
40. Program from "Rock 'n' Rollorama, Easter Edition."
41. Hyde, "News of Radio," *Detroit News,* 1957.
42. Program, Aug. 1957.
43. Marshall Chess, quoted in PBS documentary, *Rock 'n' Roll,* 1993.
44. Osgood, *Wyxie Wonderland,* 356.
45. Ibid., 327.

## 5. "Frantically Yours"

1. Audiotape recording, Dec. 1958.
2. Ernie Durham, quoted in Alterman, "Ernie Durham, First Record Hop Man," *Detroit Free Press,* Apr. 9, 1967.
3. Commercials aired on Ernie Durham show, WJLB.
4. Ernie Durham, quoted in "Alterman Picks Our Ten Top Disc Jockeys," radio in Detroit special, *Detroit Free Press,* May 15, 1966.
5. Neely, "Radio Legend, Ernie Durham Dies at 73," *Detroit Free Press,* December 4, 1992.
6. Alterman, "Ernie Durham, First Record Hop Man."
7. Interview with Joe Howard.
8. Smokey Robinson, quoted, Robinson, Rizt, *Smokey: Inside My Life,* 77.
9. Smith, *Pied Pipers of Rock 'n' Roll,* 135–36
10. Interview with Joe Howard.

11. Gordy, *To Be Loved,* 86.
12. Interview with Larry Dixon.
13. Gordy, *To Be Loved,* 104.
14. Interview with Larry Dixon.
15. Interview with Joe Howard.
16. Bego, *Aretha Franklin, Queen of Soul,* 19.

## 6. The Beat of the Top 40

1. Interview with Clark Reid.
2. Interview with Casey Kasem.
3. Ibid.
4. Casey Kasem, quoted at radio seminar in Los Angeles, Nov. 1998.
5. Interview with Casey Kasem.
6. Interview with Clark Reid.
7. Interview with Dave Dixon.
8. Interview with Clark Reid.
9. WJBK Top Tunes Survey.
10. Interview with Ron Knowles.
11. Ibid.
12. Hyde, "News of Radio," *Detroit News,* Sept. 1956.
13. Brown, *The Real Captain Jolly*
14. Robinson, *Inside My Life.*
15. Interview with Ed McKenzie.
16. Chart positions from Whitburn *Top R&B Singles.*
17. RGordy, *To Be Loved,* 73.
18. Dannen, *Hit Men,* 106.
19. Interview with Marilyn Bond.
20. Whitburn, *Top Pop Records.*
21. Warner, *Billboard Book of American Singing Groups.*
22. Sklar, *Rocking America,* 77.
23. Osgood, *Wyxie Wonderland,* 370.
24. Univ. of Memphis broadcasting archives.
25. Duffy, *Stay Tuned: My Life and the Business of Running the ABC Television Network,* 75.
26. Interview with Paul Winter.
27. Osgood, *Wyxie Wonderland,* 349.
28. Sklar, *Rocking America,* 28.

29. Station slogan, quoted by Hal Neal in Osgood, *Wyxie Wonderland,* 356.
30. Interview with Jack Surrell.
31. Ibid.
32. Interview with Ed McKenzie.
33. Osgood, *Wyxie Wonderland,* 361.
34. Mickey Shorr on the air, WXYZ, 1959.
35. "Chase Resigns," *Detroit Free Press,* Mar. 16, 1959.
36. "Radio Log," *Detroit News,* 1959.

## 7. "Words and Music"

1. Interview with Casey Kasem.
2. Program listing from *Standard Rate and Data,* Cincinnati, Jan. 1957.
3. Interview with Herbert Clague.
4. Program listing from *Standard Rate and Data,* Buffalo, Oct., 1955.
5. Tom Clay, quoted off the air at WWOL in Deeb, "My Favorite Year," *Buffalo Radio in 1955.* Buffalo Broadcast Pioneers.
6. Interview with Al McCoy.
7. Interview with Herbert Clague.
8. Interview with Al McCoy.
9. Interview with Kim Clague Tally.
10. Interview with Casey Kasem.
11. Interview with Dave Dixon.
12. Interview with Lee Alan.
13. Interview with Dave Dixon.
14. Interview with Clark Reid.
15. Interview with Kim Clague Tally.
16. Ibid.
17. Gordy, *To Be Loved,* 140.
18. Interview with Casey Kasem.
19. Osgood, *Wyxie Wonderland,* 365.
20. Hyde, "News of Radio," *Detroit News,* 1958
21. Interview with Don Schmitzerle.
22. Audiotape recording, June 1959.

## 8. Put Another Nickel in the Jukebox

1. Interview with Ed McKenzie.
2. McKenzie, "A Deejay's Exposé, *Life,* Nov. 23, 1959, p. 46.
3. Eliot, Rockonomics, 70–71.
4. Jackson, *Big Beat Heat,* 243.
5. Fred Wolf, quoted in "McKenzie Puts Needle on Payola," *Detroit Free Press,* Nov. 18, 1959.
6. WKMH's Patterson, in "DJs Mum on Charges of Payola," *Detroit Free Press,* Nov. 19, 1959.
7. Interview with Ron Knowles.
8. "DJs Mum on Charges of Payola."
9. Jac LeGoff, quoted in "Jac LeGoff Fired for Payola Talk," *Detroit Free Press,* Nov. 20, 1959.
10. "Disc Jockey Tom Clay Fired by WJBK," *Detroit News,* Nov. 23, 1959; "Jockey Fired, Defending Payola," *New York Daily News,* Nov. 23, 1959.
11. "Disk Jockeys: Now Don't Cry–The Wages of Spin," *Time,* Dec. 7, 1959, p. 47.
12. "WJBK's McLeod Resigns," *Detroit Free Press,* Nov. 24, 1959.
13. Interview with Lee Alan.
14. "Detroit Radio Star Confesses Payola," *New York Times,* Nov. 24, 1959.
15. Testimony of Lorrie Marks.
16. Interview with Clark Reid.
17. Interview with Harry Nivins, *Detroit Times,* Nov. 23, 1959.
18. Interview with Robin Seymour.
19. "Block that Schlock," *Time,* Nov. 23, 1959.
20. Interview with Clark Reid.
21. Lipson, quoted in *Detroit Free Press,* Dec. 1959.
22. Neal, quoted in *Detroit News,* Nov. 18, 1959.
23. "I'm a Goat," *Detroit News,* Nov. 28, 1959.
24. Interview with May Shorr.
25. "I'm a Goat."
26. Mickey Shorr, quoted in "I'm a Goat."
27. "Shorr Loan to Agent Told in Court," *Detroit News,* Nov. 28, 1959.
28. Jackson, *Big Beat Heat,* 223.
29. Ibid., 282.

30. "I'm a Goat."
31. Interview with May Shorr.
32. Interview with Paul Winter.
33. Neal, quoted in "I'm a Goat."
34. Jackson, *Big Beat Heat,* 250.
35. Ibid.
36. Orville Lunsford, quoted in "Royola," *Time*, May 1960.
37. Clark, *Rock, Roll, and Remember.*
38. Eliot, *Rockonomics*, 84.
39. Clark, *Rock, Roll, and Remember,* 224.
40. Ibid., 225.


## 9. Radio Rebounds

1. Tom Clay on the air at WQTE.
2. Interview with Dave Hull.
3. Mattson, "Mickey Shorr: Still Riding the Airwaves."
4. Interview with Paul Winter.
5. Description of Robert E. Lee show is from an audiotape recording, 1963.
6. Interview with Joe Howard.
7. Interview with Lee Alan.
8. Joel Sebastian's background is from an interview with Frances Sebastian.
9. Ibid.
10. Audiotape recording, Mar. 1962.
11. Interview with Marc Avery.
12. Ibid.
13. Ibid.
14. Ibid.
15. Interview with Dave Hull
16. Ibid.
17. Tom Clay, quoted in Passman, *The Deejays,* 246.
18. Powlowski, "Brav-ed David," *Detroit Free Press,* June 6, 1971.
19. Frank Maruca, quoted in an interview with Dave Prince.
20. Ibid.
21. Interview with Dave Shafer.
22. Interview with Marc Avery.

23. Interview with Dave Shafer.
24. Interview with Clark Reid.
25. Dannen, *Hit Men,* 32.
26. Ibid.
27. Interview with Dave Shafer.
28. Ibid.
29. Ibid.
30. Audiotape recording, Oct. 1962.
31. Pulse rating service for Metro Detroit, Wayne-Oakland-Macomb Counties, Jan.–Feb. 1962.
32. Interview with Jamie Coe.
33. Ibid.
34. Interview with Marc Avery.
35. Gilette, *Sound of the City,* 148.
36. Interview with Jamie Coe.

### 10. "The Cream of the Crop until Twelve O'Clock"

1. Osgood, *Wyxie Wonderland,* 392.
2. Interview with Lee Alan.
3. Audiotape recording of Lee Alan at WXYZ, 1962.
4. Audiotape recording, 1963.
5. Interview with Lee Alan.
6. Audiotape recording.
7. Interview with Lee Alan.
8. Ibid.
9. Interview with Dick Kernen.
10. Ibid.
11. Interview with Dave Prince.
12. Audiotape recording.
13. Interview with Dave Prince.

### 11. Winners and Losers

1. Interview with Robin Seymour.
2. "Motor City Mourns WJR's J. P. McCarthy," *Radio and Records,* Aug. 28, 1995.

3. Interview with Don Schmitzerle.
4. 1962 radio logs, *Detroit News.*
5. Interview with Lee Alan.
6. Weiss, quoted in interview with Lee Alan.
7. Audiotape recording.
8. Interview with Dave Prince.
9. Interview with Ed McKenzie.
10. Interview with Casey Kasem.
11. Interview with Sheldon Brown.

## 12. The Return of "a Guy by the Name of Clay"

1. Tom Clay, quoted on air, in Barrett, *Los Angeles Radio People.*
2. Summers, *Goddess* (*The Secret Lives of Marilyn Monroe*).
3. Interview with Kim Clague Tally.
4. Audiotape recording.
5. Audiotape recording.
6. Audiotape recording.
7. Reel Radio Web site, www.reelradio.com.
8. Sebastian at State Fair: my recollection.
9. Cantor, *Wheelin' on Beale.*
10. Interview with Paul Winter.
11. Audiotape recording.

## 13. The Keener Sound

1. Interview with Robin Seymour.
2. Shovan, "Radio's Pioneer Programmers," *Radio Ink.*
3. Interview with Robin Seymour.
4. Hyde, "News of Radio," *Detroit News,* Oct. 31, 1963.
5. "He Dreamed a Dream of Radio," *TV-Radio Mirror,* Sept. 1964.
6. Interview with Bob Green.
7. Frank Maruca, quoted in "The Keener Sound of Success," *Detroit News,* Mar. 30, 1967.
8. Gary Stevens on the air at WKNR; audiotape recording, 1964.
9. Interview with Bob Green.
10. Nye, "The Keener Sound of Success," *Detroit News,* Mar. 30, 1967.

## 14. Beatle Boosters, Morning Madness, and Other Weird Tales

1. Interview with Bob Green.
2. Interview with Tom Gelardi.
3. Interview with Bob Green.
4. Interview with Dave Shafer.
5. Interview with Ron Knowles.
6. Interview with Dave Shafer.
7. Interview with Ron Knowles.
8. Interview with Dave Shafer.
9. Clay, quoted in interview with Dave Shafer.
10. Interview with Bob Green.
11. Crowley on air; audiotape recording.
12. Goodwin on air; audiotape recording.
13. Interview with Paul Winter.
14. Osgood, *Wyxie Wonderland,* 418.
15. Interview with Dave Prince.
16. Osgood, *Wyxie Wonderland,* 419.
17. Terry Knight on audiotape recording.
18. Interview with Bob Green.

## 15. Cruisin' the Sixties

1. Interview with Clark Reid.
2. Audiotape recording.
3. Osgood, *Wyxie Wonderland,* 426.
4. Interview with Jim Hampton.
5. Osgood, *Wyxie Wonderland*, 427.
6. Wolfert, "Magic of PAMS web site.
7. Audiotape recording of Bruce Miller.
8. Mattson, "Mickey Shorr."
9. Calhoun, "A Mystique at the Mike," *Chicago Sun-Times,* 1966.
10. Interview with Robin Seymour.
11. Interview with Larry Dixon
12. Terry Knight on audiotape recording.
13. Interview with Gino Washington.
14. Otfinski, *Golden Age of Rock Instrumentals.*
15. Interview with Tom Shannon.

16. Tom Shannon, audiotape recording Aug. 1965.
17. Interview with Larry Morrow.
18. Audiotape recording of Fred Wolf show, Dec. 10, 1964.
19. Osgood, *Wyxie Wonderland*, 431.
20. Interview with Marc Avery.

## 16. The Purtan Principle

1. Audiotape recording.
2. Dick Purtan, audio recordings.
3. Interview with Dick Purtan.
4. Frank Maruca, quoted in interview with Dick Purtan.
5. Dick Purtan, quoted in Beasley, "Dick Purtan: Outlandish Promises at 6 A.M.," *Detroit News,* August 31, 1967.
6. Dick Purtan, quoted in Alterman, "Ten Top Disc Jockeys."
7. Dick Purtan audio recording.
8. Interview with Bob Green.
9. Interview with Dick Purtan.
10. Beasley, "Dick Purtan: Outlandish Promises at 6 A.M."
11. Ibid.
12. Judge, "Impertinent Purtan," *Detroit News*, Dec. 1, 1968.
13. Ibid.
14. Dick Purtan, quoted in interview with Tom Gelardi.
15. Interview with Dick Purtan.
16. Audio recording of J. Michael Wilson.

## 17. "Detroit Swings While Joey Stings"

1. Interview with Lee Alan.
2. Interview with Robin Seymour.
3. Robin Seymour on the air at channel 9.
4. Interview with Robin Seymour.
5. Interview with Dave Prince.
6. Audio recording.
7. Interview with Dick Purtan.
8. "Fill these": Joey Reynolds, quoted in *On The Air: Forty Years That Shaped the Sound of America,* 48.

9.   Audiotape recording, 1966.
10.   Joey Reynolds on the air.
11.   Interview with Bob Green.
12.   Audiotape recording, 1966.
13.   Fred Wolf, quoted in Osgood, *Wyxie Wonderland,* 441.
14.   Interview with Marty Greenburg.
15.   Interview with Lee Alan.
16.   Dick Purtan on the air.
17.   WKNR station pamphlet; audiotape recording.
18.   Audiotape recording.
19.   Interview with Dusty Rhodes.
20.   Dave Shafer, quoted in Alterman, "Ten Top Disc Jockeys."
21.   Interview with Dusty Rhodes.
22.   Interview with Marc Avery.
23.   Osgood, *Wyxie Wonderland,* 454.
24.   Ibid, 475.
25.   Robbie D, quoted off air. "The Decibelters," *Time,* Oct. 27, 1967.

## 18. "You're Gonna Like It...I Bet-cha"

1.   Hyde, "News of Radio," *Detroit News,* Nov. 1963; Smith, *Pied Pipers of Rock 'n' Roll,* 128.
2.   Interview with Martha Jean "The Queen."
3.   Cantor, *Wheelin' on Beale,* 91-92.
4.   Interview with Martha Jean "The Queen."
5.   Ibid.
6.   Martha Jean on the air, quoted in Smith, *Pied Pipers of Rock 'n' Roll,* 129.
7.   Interview with Martha Jean "The Queen."
8.   Ibid.
9.   Ibid.
10.   Licks, *Standing in the Shadows of Motown,* 46;
11.   "Radio in Detroit," *Detroit Free Press,* May 15, 1966.

## 19. Ladies and Gentlemen: The "Big 8"

1.   "The Executioner," *Time,* Aug. 23, 1968.

2. Interview with Dusty Rhodes.
3. Interview with Tom Shannon.
4. Interview with Dave Shafer.
5. Interview with Tom Shannon.
6. Audiotape recording.
7. Mike Rivers, quoted in "A Few Memories," Classic CKLW Web page, www.cklw.org.
8. Interview with Dave Shafer.
9. Interview with Dusty Rhodes.
10. Interview with Marc Avery.
11. Interview with Rosalie Trombley.
12. Interview with Tom Gelardi.

## 20. "Busted in Baltimore—Dawn in Detroit"

1. Interview with Dick Purtan.
2. Interview with Bob Green.
3. Interview with Dick Purtan.
4. Tom Clay on the air at WTAK.
5. Interview with Robin Seymour.
6. Audiotape recording.
7. As told at Radio and Records Reunion, Apr. 1998.
8. Interview with Dick Purtan.
9. My recollection.
10. Judge, "Impertinent Purtan."
11. "Radio Log," *Detroit News.*
12. Interview with Judy McCarthy.
13. "Interview with Fred Yaffe.
14. McCarthy, quoted in "Ten Top Disc Jockeys."
15. Interview with Mike Whorf.
16. Interview with Bob Talbert.
17. Interview with Judy McCarthy
18. Dick Purtan, quoted in Judge, "Impertinent Purtan."
19. Interview with Jim Davis.

## 21. Over Under Sideways Down

1. ARB ratings for Metro Detroit, spring 1968.

2.  Rapoport, "The Underground Radio Turn-On," *Life,* 1968.
3.  Interview with Dave Dixon.
4.  WABX program log, Dec. 1967.
5.  WABX rate card, Sept. 1967.
6.  "Judging It," *Detroit News,* Aug. 7, 1967.
7.  I was present.
8.  Audiotape recording.
9.  Interview with Dave Dixon.
10. Interview with Jerry Lubin.
11. Larry Miller, quoted in Keith, *Voices in the Purple Haze: Underground Radio in the Sixties,* 70.
12. Dan Carlisle, quoted in Keith, *Voices in the Purple Haze,* 32.
13. Interview with Dave Dixon.
14. Described in WABX Fifth Anniversary brochure.
15. Interview with Jerry Lubin.
16. MC5 article, *Goldmine,* 1995.
17. Interview with Dennis Frawley.
18. Interview with Dave Dixon.
19. Interview with Harvey Ovshinsky.
20. Patterson, *The Walrus Was Paul,* 77.
21. Gordy, *To Be Loved,* 160
22. Interview with Tom Shannon.
23. Scott Regen, quoted in history of CKLW part of Classic CKLW Web site.
24. Audiotape recording of Lee Sims at WJBK, 1969.
25. Audiotape recording.
26. Described by Alan Shaw in Keith, *Voices in the Purple Haze.*

## 22. Dateline Detroit: The 1970s

1.  "Bravid-David," *Detroit Free Press,* 1971.
2.  Interview with Dick Purtan.
3.  My remembrance.
4.  O'Brian, "Laying the Giant to Rest," Classic CKLW Web site.
5.  My remembrance.
6.  Passman, *The DeeJays,* 265.
7.  Interview with Don Barrett.
8.  Whitburn, *Billboard Book of Top 40 Hits.*

9.  Keith, *Voices in the Purple Haze*, 174, 193.
10.  Interview with Tom Dean.
11.  Interview with Martha Jean Steinberg.
12.  *Detroit News,* Mar. 1974.
13.  Interview with Michael Collins.

# References

## Books

Amburn, Ellis. *Buddy Holly, a Biography*. New York: St. Martin's Press, 1995.

Barrett, Don. *Los Angeles Radio People*. Valencia, Calif.: DB Marketing, 1997.

Bego, Mark. *Aretha Franklin, Queen of Soul*. New York: St. Martin's Press, 1989.

Cantor, Louis. *Wheelin' on Beale*. New York: Pharos Books, 1992.

Clark, Dick. *Rock, Roll, and Remember*. New York: Popular Library, 1978.

Clarke, Donald, ed. *Penguin Encyclopedia of Popular Music*. Penguin Books, 1989.

Cotton, Lee. *Shake, Rattle, and Roll: The Golden Age of American Rock 'n' Roll*. Vol. 1, 1952–55. Ann Arbor, Mich.: Pierian Press, 1987.

Dannen, Fredric. *Hit Men*. New York: Times Books (Random House), 1990.

Duffy, James. *Stay Tuned: My Life and the Business of Running the ABC Television Network*. New York: Dunhill Publishing Co., 1997.

Dunning, John. *The Encyclopedia of Old-Time Radio*. New York: Oxford Univ. Press, 1998.

——*Tune in Yesterday*. Englewood Cliffs, N.J.: Prentice-Hall, 1976.

Eliot, Marc. *Rockonomics: The Money Behind the Music*. New York: Franklin Watts, 1989.

Erlewine, Bogdanou, Woodstrap. *All Music Guide to Rock*. San Francisco: Miller Freeman Books, 1995.

Gillett, Charlie. *The Sound of the City*. London: Souvenir Press, 1983.

Gordy, Berry. *To Be Loved*. New York: Warner Books, 1994.

Herman, Gary. *Rock 'n' Roll Babylon*. London: Plexus, 1994.

Holland, Dave. *From out of the Past: A Pictorial History of the Lone Ranger*. Granada Hills, Calif.: Holland House, 1988.

Jackson, John A. *Big Beat Heat: Alan Freed and the Early Days of Rock 'n' Roll*. New York: Schirmer Books, 1991.

Janick, Wayne. *One Hit Wonders*. New York: Billboard Books, 1998.

Keith, Michael C. *Voices in the Purple Haze: Underground Radio and the Sixties*. Westport, Conn.: Praeger Books, 1997.

Larkin, Colin. *Guinness Who's Who of 50s and 60s Music*. England: 1992.

Licks, Dr. *Standing in the Shadows of Motown: The Life and Music of Legendary Bassist James Jamerson*. Wynnewood, Pa.: Dr. Licks Publishing, 1989.

Merlis, Bob, and Davin Seay. *Heart and Soul: A Celebration of Black Music Styles in America 1930–1975*. New York: Stewart, Tabori and Chang, 1997.

Osgood, Dick. *Wyxie Wonderland*. Bowling Green, Ohio: Bowling Green Univ. Popular Press, 1981.

Otfinoski, Steve. *Golden Age of Rock Instrumentals*. New York: Billboard Books, 1997.

Passman, Arnold. *The Deejays*. New York: Macmillan, 1971.

Patterson, R. Gary. *The Walrus Was Paul*. Nashville, Tenn.: Dowling Press, 1996.

Reese, Della, with Franklin Lett and Mim Eichler. *Angels along the Way: My Life with Help from Above*. New York: Berkley Boulevard, 1997.

Reeves, Martha, and Mark Bego. *Dancin' in the Street: Confessions of a Motown Diva*. New York: Hyperion, 1994.

Selvin, Joel. *Summer of Love*. New York: Dutton, 1994.

Singleton, Raynoma Gordy, with Bryan Brown and M. Eichler. *Berry, Me, and Motown*. Chicago: Contemporary Books, 1990.

Sklar, Rick. *Rocking America*. New York: St. Martin's Press, 1984.

Smith, Wes. *Pied Pipers of Rock 'n' Roll*. Marietta, Ga.: Longstreet Press, 1987.

Summers, Anthony. *Goddess (The Secret Lives of Marilyn Monroe)*. New York: Onyx, 1985.

Szatmary, David P. *Rockin' in Time*. Englewood Cliffs, N.J.: Prentice-Hall, 1987.

Warner, Jay. *The Billboard Book of American Singing Groups.* New York: Billboard Books, 1992.

Whitburn, Joel. *Top Pop Records.* New York: Billboard Books, 1991.

——. *Top R&B Singles, 1942–1995.* Menominee Falls, Wis.: Record Research, 1996.


## Articles and Documents

"ABC Says Clark Takes No Payola." *Detroit Free Press,* Nov. 19, 1959.

"Alias Jack the Bellboy." *Radio-TV Mirror,* 1951.

Alterman, Loraine. "Ernie Durham, First Record Hop Man." *Detroit Free Press,* Apr. 9, 1967.

——. "Take a Chance Tom Shannon." *Detroit Free Press,* Jan. 1967.

Beasley, Alice. "Dick Purtan: Outlandish Promises at 6 A.M." *Tempo Magazine, Detroit News,* Aug. 31, 1967.

"Black Radio History...Just the Tip of the Legacy." In "Radio's 75th Celebration." *Radio Ink,* July 10, 1995.

"Block That Schlock." *Time*, Nov. 23, 1959.

Burkhart, Kent. "Top 40: The Omaha Story." In "Radio's 75th Celebration." *Radio Ink,* July 10, 1995.

Calhoun, Lillian. "A Mystique at the Mike." *Chicago Sun-Times,* 1966.

"Celebrating Five Years of Public Service and Entertainment." WJBK-TV, 1953.

Copeland, Robert. "Script Tease." *Liberty,* Dec. 1, 1945.

David, Toby, and Don Brown. "The Real Captain Jolly." Memoir, 1983.

"The Decibelters." *Time,* Oct. 27, 1967.

Deeb, Gary. "Buffalo Radio in 1955, My Favorite Year." *Buffalo Broadcast Pioneers.*

Dell, Charlie. "Popular Disc Jock McKenzie." *Guest*, 1953.

D'Hondt, Frances. "Shorr Clicks Quickly." *Detroit Times,* 1955.

"Detroit Radio Legend Falls Silent." *Detroit Free Press,* Aug. 17, 1995.

"Detroit Radio Star Confesses Payola." *New York Times,* Nov. 23, 1959.

Disc jockey review: "Jack the Bellboy Show." *Variety,* Nov. 5, 1947.

"Disc Jockey Tom Clay Fired by WJBK." *Detroit News,* Nov. 23, 1959

"Disc Jockeys Curbed." *New York Times,* Dec. 1, 1959.

"Disc Jockeys: Now Don't Cry–The Wages of Spin." *Time,* Dec. 7, 1959.

"The DJ Is King of 'Background' Radio.' *Detroit Free Press*, Nov. 24, 1959.

"DJs Mum on Charges of Payola." *Detroit Free Press,* Nov. 19, 1959.

Downs, Rosemary. "Radio's Zaniest Team." *Teens*, Jan. 1949.

"Early Morning Frolic." *Radio-TV Mirror*, July 1953.

"The Executioner." *Time*, Aug. 23, 1968.

"Farewell Salute." *Cash Box*, May 12, 1956.

"Fox Show Really Rocks 'em." *Detroit News*, Jan. 1956.

Gormley, Mike. "WABX Is David, Knocking 'em Dead with Rock." *Detroit Free Press*, Aug. 9, 1970.

Hart, James. "1 Fired; 2 Quit in Payola Furor." *Detroit Times*, Nov. 23, 1959.

Haswell, James. "DJs Here Face Quiz on Payola." *Detroit Free Press*, Nov. 20, 1959.

"He Dreamed a Dream of Radio and It Came True." *Radio-TV Mirror*, Sept. 1964.

"Hit Parade Omits Words of Song Banned by WWJ." *New York Times*, Nov. 26, 1951.

Hushen, John W. "I'm Goat in Firing." *Detroit News*, Nov. 28, 1959.

Hyde, Betty. News of Radio. *Detroit News*. Various columns, 1956–65.

"Jac LeGoff Fired for Payola Talk." *Detroit Free Press*, Nov. 20, 1959.

"Jockeys on a Rough Ride." *Newsweek*, Dec. 1, 1959.

Judge, Frank. "The Keener Sound of Success." *Detroit News*, March 30, 1967.

——. "Impertinent Purtan." *Detroit News*, Dec. 1, 1968.

Kubrick, Stan. "The Saga of Jack the Bellboy." *International Association of Jazz Record Collectors Journal*, Summer 1995.

Latshaw, Bob. "It's 1927, and the Voice Is Familiar." *Detroit Free Press Sunday Magazine*, May 15, 1966.

"Look Who's Talking." *Radio-TV Mirror*, Dec. 1958.

Mattson, Eileen. "Mickey Shorr: Still Riding the Airwaves." *Daily Tribune*, May 28, 1984.

McKenzie, Ed. "A Deejay's Exposé," *Life*, Nov. 23, 1959.

"McKenzie Puts Needle on Payola." *Detroit Free Press*, Nov. 18, 1959.

"Michigan Madman." *Radio-TV Mirror*, Mar. 1951.

"Mickey Shorr May Be Back." *Teen Life*, July 27, 1956.

"Motor City Mourns WJR's Legendary J. P. McCarthy." *Radio and Records*, Aug. 28, 1995

Nelson, Ralph. "Chase Is Quitting CKLW." *Detroit Free Press*, Mar. 16, 1959.

Orlean, Susan. "Casey at the Mike." *New York Times Magazine*, May 6, 1990.

Owens, Kenneth J. "Chasin' with Chase." *Band Leaders*, Jan. 1945.

Pawlowski, Diane. "Brav-ed David." *Detroit Free Press Sunday Magazine*, June 6, 1971.

"Payola Blues." *Newsweek*, Nov. 30, 1959.

Peterson, Bettylou. "How a Station Picks Its Records." *Detroit Free Press Sunday Magazine,* May 15, 1966.

"Prince of the Airwaves." *Radio-TV Mirror,* July 1955.

"The Prop Man and the Plumber." *Radio-TV Mirror,* 1951.

"Radio in Detroit." Special section, *Detroit Free Press,* May 1966.

Rapoport, Roger. "The Underground Radio Turn-On." *Life,* 1968.

Reynolds, Joey. "Show Biz in Buffalo." *On the Air,* special magazine produced by the *Gavin Report,* 1998.

Rivers, Mike. "A Few Memories." Classic CKLW Web Site, www.cklw.org.

"Royola." *Time,* May 9, 1960.

Serafin, Raymond. "Detroit's WJR Mourns McCarthy." *Advertising Age,* Aug. 28, 1995.

"Shorr Fired by WXYZ; Denies He Took Payola." *Detroit Free Press,* Nov. 28, 1959.

"Shorr Gets Big Send-off." *Billboard,* May 12, 1956.

Shorr, Mickey. "It's the Gimmicks." *Detroit Free Press,* Sept. 1, 1956.

——. "Showbiz Real Friendly." *Detroit Times,* 1956.

"Shorr on Air." *Teen Life,* Aug. 24, 1956.

Shoven, Tom. "Radio's Pioneer Programmers." In "Radio's 75th Celebration." *Radio Ink,* July 10, 1995.

"Spell It Mulholland." *Radio-TV Mirror,* Aug. 1947.

Talbert, Bob. "Dick Purtan Gears Up for Fund Raiser." *Detroit Free Press,* Feb. 23, 1999.

——. "Notebook Column." *Detroit Free Press,* Aug. 12, 1982.

Tausig, Ellen. "He's One in a Million." *Radio-TV Mirror,* Jan. 1956.

"Teeners Rally to Mickey," *Detroit News,* May 1956.

Tucker, Neely. "Radio Legend Ernie Durham Dies at 73." *Detroit Free Press,* Dec. 4, 1992.

Van Lopik, Carter. "WJBK Fires Disc Jockey." *Detroit Free Press,* Nov. 23, 1959.

"WABX Air Ace 5th Anniversary." Station brochure, 1973.

"A Winter's Tale." *Radio-TV Mirror,* Sept. 1956.

"WJBK's McLeod Resigns." *Detroit Free Press,* Nov. 24, 1959.

"Wolf at the Door." *Radio-TV Mirror,* June 1956.

Wolfert, Johnathan. "The Magic of PAMS." PAMS Web site, www.pams.com.

"WWJ, WWJ-TV (Detroit) Bans Lyrics of 2 Songs." *New York Times,* Oct. 27, 1951.

"Your Boy Bud." *Radio-TV Mirror,* July 1954.

# Interviews

All interviews were conducted by David Carson on the indicated dates.

| | |
|---|---|
| Lee Alan | Jan. 26, 1999 |
| Marc Avery | Mar. 5, 1998 and Jan. 26, 1999 |
| Marilyn Bond | Dec. 28, 1998 |
| Sheldon Brown | Jan. 19, 1999 |
| Eddie Chase | Aug. 12, 1998 |
| Herbert Clague | Jan. 10, 1999 |
| Jamie Coe | Jan. 21, 1999 |
| Bob Cordell | Apr. 17, 1998 |
| Tom Dean | Nov. 24, 1998 |
| Dave Dixon | Oct. 3, 1998 |
| Larry Dixon | Oct. 7, 1999 |
| Dennis Frawley | June 5, 1999 |
| Tom Gelardi | May 7, 1998 |
| Bob Green | Feb. 9, 1998 and Nov. 5, 1999 |
| Jim Hampton | June 25, 1998 |
| Bill Hennes | Jan. 24, 1999 |
| Joe Howard | Feb. 17, 1998 |
| Dave Hull | Feb. 19, 1998 |
| Casey Kasem | Feb. 20, 1998 |
| Dick Kernen | Feb. 10, 1998 |
| Ron Knowles | May 5, 1998 |
| Jerry Lubin | June 9, 1999 |
| Bob Maxwell | Oct. 20, 1998 |
| Judy McCarthy | Jan. 23, 1999 |
| Al McCoy | Jan. 10, 1999 |
| Ed McKenzie | Feb. 1, 1998 |
| Larry Morrow | Nov. 25, 1998 |
| Harvey Ovshinsky | Nov. 2, 1998 |
| Dave Prince | Mar. 11, 1998 and Jan. 18, 1999 |
| Dick Purtan | Apr. 7 and May 11, 1998 |
| Bill Randle | Apr. 20, 1998 and Feb. 15, 1999 |
| Clark Reid | Feb. 25, 1998 and Nov. 6, 1998 |
| Dusty Rhodes | June 15, 1998 |
| Don Schmitzerle | Mar. 9, 1998 |
| Robin Seymour | Mar. 13, 1998 |

| | |
|---|---|
| Dave Shafer | Feb. 23, 1998 |
| Tom Shannon | Feb. 18, 1998 |
| May Shorr | Mar. 16, 1998 |
| Martha Jean Steinberg | May 12, 1998 |
| Jack Surrell | Jan. 4, 1999 |
| Bob Talbert | Feb. 25, 1999 |
| Kim Clague Tally | Jan. 10, 1999 |
| Gino Washington | Feb. 3, 1999 |
| Emily Wolf | Jan. 21, 1999 |
| Mike Whorf | Feb. 24, 1999 |
| Fred Yaffe | Mar. 3, 1999 |

## Miscellaneous

Burton Historical Library, Detroit.
"Cruisin' 1956." Robin Seymour at WKMH. Increase Records, Mar. 1970.
Decker, Joe. Classic CKLW Web site, www.cklw.org.
Library of American Broadcasting. Univ. of Maryland at College Park.
Promotional station pamphlets from WXYZ and WKNR, Detroit.
Radio-TV Dial Pages. Web site by Michael Lewis, http://metronet.lib.mi.us.
Rock Radio Retrospective Web Site http://home.istar.ca~rockroll/rocksite.html.
Stage show program booklets from the Fox, Broadway-Capitol, Michigan, and
    Shubert theaters, 1956, 1957.
Standard Rate and Data Services: Spot Radio, Des Plaines, Ill. Various editions,
    1950–1960.
Univ. of Memphis Broadcasting Archives.

## Local Chart Positions

"CKLW Big 30"
"CKLW CK' Survey"
"WJBK Formula Forty-five"
"WJBK Radio 15 Record Review"
"WKNR Music Guide"
"WXYZ Detroit Sound Survey"

## Airchecks

In the radio industry, these are generally demo tapes; as such, they generally don't contain any music and few jingles.

Lee Alan, WXYZ, 1962, 1963.

Marc Avery, WJBK, 1963.

Tom Clay, CKLW, 1963, 1964.

Mort Crowley, WKNR, 1964.

Toby David, CKLW, 1960.

Dave Dixon, WABX, 1969.

Ernie Durham, WJLB, 1964.

Jerry Goodwin, WKNR, Aug. 1966.

Bob Green, WKNR, 1964, 1967.

Terry Knight, CKLW, 1964.

Robert E. Lee, WJBK, 1964.

Dave Prince, WKMH, 1961 and WXYZ, 1962, 1963.

Dick Purtan, WKNR, 1965.

Clark Reid, WJBK, 1962.

Joey Reynolds, WXYZ, 1966.

Mike Rivers, CKLW, 1967.

Joel Sebastian, WXYZ, 1962.

Robin Seymour, WKNR, 1964.

Dave Shafer, WJBK, 1962, 1963.

Tom Shannon, CKLW, 1965, 1967, 1968.

Mickey Shorr, WABX, 1967.

Lee "Baby" Sims, WJBK, 1969.

Martha Jean the Queen Steinberg, WJLB, 1967.

Gary Stevens, WKNR, 1964.

J. Michael Wilson, WKNR, 1966 and 1967.

Paul Winter, WXYZ, Nov. 5, 1956, and Mar. 1962.

Fred Wolf, WXYZ, Dec. 10, 1964.

Don Zee, WXYZ, 1963.

# Index

# About the Author

DAVID CARSON WAS BORN AND RAISED in the Detroit area and grew up tuned in to "Frantic Ernie," Tom Clay, Lee Alan and other popular disc jockeys of the late '50s and '60s. A graduate of Royal Oak's Dondero High School, he was on the air at age fifteen at the city's public station, WOAK-FM. He also hosted a program that featured interviews he had recorded at the legendary Baker's Keyboard Lounge of jazz greats such as Kenny Burrell, Joe Williams and Cannonball Adderly.

In 1967 Carson worked the all-night DJ spot on WEXL, Detroit's first country music station. At the same time he emceed country music stage shows with big stars such as Conway Twitty, Merle Haggard and Buck Owens, and rising stars such as Tammy Wynette and Dolly Parton.

After working for a number of midwest stations, Carson left broadcasting and moved to Houston, Texas, where he earned a degree in Journalism. Since 1985 he has pursued a career as an advertising/publishing executive in Los Angeles, Atlanta, and Nashville where he currently resides with his wife and daughter.

It was while working for a broadcast company that Carson was flooded with memories of his early radio days. He decided to do a magazine article on the subject and contacted radio veterans Ed McKenzie, Paul Winter and Dave Shafer. The article soon blossomed into this definitive book on pop music radio in the Motor City from the 1940s to the mid 1970s.